THE CUSTODY EVALUATION HANDBOOK

Research-Based Solutions and Applications

THE CUSTODY EVALUATION HANDBOOK

Research-Based Solutions and Applications

Barry Bricklin, Ph.D.

With contributions by

Gail Elliot, Ph.D.

and

Michael H. Halbert

BRUNNER/MAZEL *Publishers* • New York

Library of Congress Cataloging-in-Publication Data

Bricklin, Barry.
  The custody evaluation handbook : research-based solutions and
applications / by Barry Bricklin ; contributions by Gail Elliot and
Michael H. Halbert.
      p.   cm.
  Includes bibliographical references and indexes.
  ISBN 0-87630-775-6 (hc)
  1. Custody of children—United States—Evaluation.   I. Elliot,
Gail.   II. Halbert, Michael H.   III. Title.
KF547.B75   1995
346.7301'7—dc20   95-32936
[347.30617]   CIP

Published by
BRUNNER/MAZEL, INC.
19 Union Square West
New York, New York 10003

Manufactured in the United States of America

10 9 8 7 6 5 4 3 2 1

Contents

ABOUT THE AUTHOR

Barry Bricklin, Ph.D., President of Bricklin Associates, oversees a large clinical practice focusing on custody assessment issues. Dr. Bricklin is an Adjunct Associate Professor at Widener University, Institute for Graduate Clinical Psychology and has served on the faculties of Jefferson Medical College and Hahnemann University. He is past president of the Philadelphia Society for Clinical Psychologists and the Philadelphia Society for Projective Assessment. Dr. Bricklin, with world famous psychologist Zygmunt A. Piotrowski, created the first scoring system for the *Hand Test* and has written several papers on the prognosis of schizophrenia. He is the author of several books and many articles.

Dr. Bricklin is the Executive Chair of the Professional Academy of Custody Evaluators, creator of the first data-based research-derived custody instruments, and Editor of the *Custody Newsletter*.

THE CONTRIBUTORS

Gail Elliot, Ph.D. is Head, Child Development and Family Processes Research, Bricklin Associates, Vice Chair of the Professional Academy of Custody Evaluators, and a psychologist in private practice. She is coauthor of the *Parent Perception of Child Profile* (PPCP), a widely used custody evaluation instrument, and is responsible for much of the research behind Bricklin custody instruments. Dr. Elliot is coauthor with Barry Bricklin of ACCESS (A Comprehensive Custody Evaluation Standard System).

Michael H. Halbert is a management consultant who specializes in the application of philosophical and scientific approaches to complex, real problems and renders them more tractable to the people who have to solve them. His expertise has been utilized by General Mills, the World Bank, and the United States Secret Service. Mike Halbert has taught operations research, statistics, and marketing at several graduate schools, including Case Western Reserve, Harvard Business School, and the Wharton School (University of Pennsylvania).

Foundations: Leaps, Halos, and Bitterness

Three of the most challenging problems in the custody evaluation field follow from: (1) the difficulties involved in adapting data derived from group studies and/or traditional psychological tests into forms that can be used in individual cases; (2) the absence of clear and compelling guidelines to aggregate the mountains of information collected in the course of a comprehensive evaluation; and (3) the bitter adversarial attitudes among custody disputants, which disincline them to cooperate in forging and maintaining *any* custody plan.

Whether one seeks help in deciding what to measure in a custody evaluation from written legal criteria (e.g., the Uniform Marriage and Divorce Act; see Sales, Manber, & Rohman, 1992) or from the world of clinical experience, the above challenges remain.

Simple solutions have not been found. The hope that one particular custody disposition, such as joint custody, same-sex custody, etc., would prove universally superior to competing arrangements has not been realized. As one very knowledgeable researcher put it, ". . . there is no single best arrangement for all children . . ." (Bray, 1991, p. 420).

In the pages to follow, we will address these challenges. In so doing, we will describe some concepts our research teams have found to be very helpful in understanding parent-child interactions (symbol systems and information processing strategies). The issue of getting untainted data from children who, in the midst of custody disputes, are being coached, threatened, bribed, and subjected to loyalty conflicts, will be addressed. We will spell out what our various teams have come to see as the essential targets of a truly comprehensive evaluation. As editor of the *Custody Newsletter*, I hear about specific custody dilemmas (e.g., allegations of abuse) from evaluators all over the country. Suggestions will be offered.

I am frequently asked how I use the tools we have developed interactively *as a set*. Chapter Ten addresses this issue.

Finally, the evaluator must learn to feel comfortable in court, where he or she will often have to present evaluation information to an audience that, in part, will be composed of a nasty inquisitor, possibly a bored, hostile, or intimidating person in a black robe, and at least one person who *used to* like the evaluator and now considers him or her a total betrayer.

DIFFICULTIES WITH TRADITIONAL TESTS AND TOOLS

This group of challenges for the evaluator follows from the fact that the typical tools and tests in the mental health professional's armamentarium—procedures that are so good at measuring cognitive capacities and identifying sources of conflict and underlying personality variables—are not data-based to yield information that is maximally helpful in custody cases.

In the approach spelled out in this book, a good bit of emphasis is placed on obtaining measurements from the involved children. This follows from the fact that we are far more interested in attempting to determine the actual impact a parent is having on a child than we are in what a parent may or may not be doing. It is certainly not that we have *no* interest in what parents do; this body of information comprises a very important part of a comprehensive custody evaluation. But without knowing the *effects* of these behaviors on a child, the aforementioned data have little informational value to a custody decision-maker. In fact, it may be correct to say that just as in the subatomic world of quantum mechanics in which there is nothing "really out there" independent of the design of some particular experiment or observational mechanism, there is no "parental behavior" independent of its impact on a given child at a particular time.

We were heavily influenced in coming to this approach by observations we made during research carried out in the early 1960's, while developing the *Perception-of-Relationships Test* or PORT. One observation was how frequently what a child was taking as the "meaning" of a given parent's communications seemed to all observers pretty much unrelated to what the parent was intending to communicate.

Over the years, we have been influenced by similar conceptual approaches. One is the "utilization" model of Milton Erickson. Translated into our purposes, this model suggests that a *child's ability to utilize parental behavior is a more salient piece of information to a custody evaluator than is the meaning or label the evaluator might assign to the parental behavior.*

These ideas are also similar to those proposed by Thomas, Chess, and Birch (1968) with their goodness-of-fit assessment of parent-child interactions.

We have also been influenced by the important statement by Bandler and Grinder (1979) that the meaning of a communication is the response it elicits, regardless of the intentions of the sender (see also Dilts, 1983, p. 14).

Likewise, these ideas have been shaped by the importance of utilizing feedback information in fashioning truly effective and congruent communications, as spelled out by McMaster and Grinder (1980).

The approach has much in common, overall, with the justly famous analysis of legal competencies proposed by Grisso (1986). Our tools, collectively, reflect a "function" (what a given parent knows, believes, and can do), a "context" (the setting in which this function is relevant, e.g., offering homework advice, modeling the skills of competency, etc.), a "causal" implication (the tools used to assess parents can help to explain what is found in those which reflect the impact of parental behavior on a child), an "interactive" component (the tests measure the utilizability of that which is offered by a parent), and *can* offer a judgmental and/or dispositional element (e.g., a recommendation for primary custodial or caretaking parent, abbreviated PCP). But beware regarding the latter item. This is an "ultimate issue" piece of information (a recommendation for PCP) and must be addressed quite carefully. More on this in Chapter One.

There is another, as yet unmentioned advantage to utilizing a test-based approach for custody decision-making. It is my contention that the tool most widely used around the country and probably the world in custody decision-making is the interview. Someone once told Winston Churchill that a person he did not hold in high regard at least had the redeeming virtue of being "modest." Replied Winston: "Indeed, he has much to be modest about."

I feel similarly toward the interview.

I believe the interview, important as it is, serves as an iatrogenic force in the custody evaluation procedure. Yes, we must interview people, we must learn their wants, worries, and concerns, and what they think. Indeed, all of their worries and concerns must be carefully and individually addressed in the final report. However, in dutifully paying heed to and writing down all of the horror stories that each parent has to tell about the other, we are also showing, by the attention we pay to them, that yes indeed, this is the way to "win" a custody battle. For this is exactly what the typical custody disputant thinks: The way to prevail in a custody battle is to have lots of bad stories to tell about the hated opponent. By dutifully responding to and writing down all of these things, we are simply encouraging each disputant to go out and find (create?) more of the same.

This is what I call the "negative incident model" in custody decision-making. It is a model that leads each parent to believe safety resides in compiling a long list of terrible things to say about the other parent.

It is my thesis that the negative incident model not only encourages, but in many ways, by virtue of the self-fulfilling prophecy, co-creates the so-called parent alienation syndrome, a scenario (covered in later chapters) in which one parent deliberately sets out to alienate a child from the other parent. I am indeed mindful of the fact that most parents caught up in custody disputes may have hated each other before the custody battles began. It is also obvious that the legal system itself, in spite of any "procedural fairness" perceived by the participants, co-creates a "fault model" in a custody dispute by allowing (and hence encouraging) one participant to prevail over the other by means of proving "unfitness," e.g., adultery, drug abuse, mental illness, etc. (Rohman, Sales, & Lou, 1987, p. 86). Nevertheless, any *clinical* process that contributes heavily to a parent's believing that the way to predominate in a custody situation is to collect negative incidents is not really helpful.

With a test-based approach, the evaluator sends a different message. Essentially, the custody evaluator within this approach is saying to an involved parent that although I will listen to your concerns and worries, and indeed will address them, I am far more interested in measuring how successful you are at being a parent than I am in hearing negative stories about your opponent. The subtle message is this: If you want to prevail in a custody dispute, spend a lot more time thinking about how to be a better parent and a lot less time creating bad things to say about your opposition.

How this orientation is actually implemented will be covered in many of the following chapters, since I am certainly aware that one cannot conduct a comprehensive custody evaluation *without* using the interview.

AGGREGATING INFORMATION IN THE ABSENCE OF WEIGHTING CRITERIA

While some states spell out what a custody evaluator should take into consideration in attempting to determine which disposition and/or which of two competing parties can better serve in a child's best interests—as does the Uniform Marriage and Divorce Act (1979)—none offer clear guidelines on how to aggregate the resulting information to yield one message—that the mother/father is the better of the two candidates for PCP (primary custodial or caretaking parent). Some states do make the a priori assumption that joint custody is the best custody disposition unless there exists important information to the contrary.

The Uniform Marriage and Divorce Act directs the court to consider "all relevant factors," including: the wishes of the child's parent or parents as to proper custody; the wishes of the child; the interactions and interrelationships between the child with the parents and other significant persons; the child's adjustment at home, school, and in the community; and the mental and physical health of all the individuals concerned. It also mandates that the court should not consider parental behaviors that do not have any effects on the child.

The document does not, however, tell the evaluator or decision-maker *how to prioritize* the information it directs to be gathered.

It is the rule, not the exception, for the custody evaluator to end up, in the wake of a comprehensive evaluation, with a file six inches thick, consisting of the originals and/or copies of documents, the results of tests and observations, questionnaire responses, and transcripts of interviews with a literal parade of people, including each of the competing party's friends, relatives, and baby-sitters, each having stepped forward to champion his or her choice.

And now the custody evaluator stares at this horrendously high pile of papers and wonders not only if he or she has gotten credible measurements of all of the variables involved, but also how in the world to assign some kind of "importance" rating to each of the findings. How does one assign differential "weightings," in terms of "meaningfulness to the child," to such things as: parental physical health; the neighborhood a child would live in under competing arrangements; parental time availability; parental ability to furnish appropriate babysitters; parental financial status; etc.

With no firm criteria, Rashomon.

There is the creepy feeling that 10 different people could look at the information and come up with 10 different time-sharing plans, each person finding something different to label "really important."

I have traveled the country offering workshops in comprehensive custody evaluations where I had extended opportunities to talk to savvy participants. As editor of the *Custody Newsletter*, I speak via telephone daily to custody evaluators around the country and the world. I have spoken formally and informally with fellow evaluators both in their professional offices and, with each of us nervously catching "breathers," in the corridors of courthouses during breaks in trials.

What I hear *sometimes* makes me feel terrific, even if my companion evaluator is on a different side of the fence than I: articulate, thoughtful, well reasoned assertions.

But often—alas, too frequently—I am not so thrilled.

Lacking ways to meaningfully aggregate data, the evaluator moves all too easily in the direction of subjective biases. Here are some reasons given to me as the controlling aspects in certain cases, the items seen by the involved evaluators as the most important pieces of information gathered.

"She smoked a lot of dope during the seventies."

"He's so rich, he's a real snob. I believe he thinks he can buy whatever he wants."

" You should have seen all the oral themes in her *Rorschach!*" (The conclusion was that the mother would be "smothering.")

Some of these evaluators had the—shall we call it—"courage" to actually say these things out loud in courtrooms as the controlling reasons for their recommending a certain parent for primary custodial parent.

A bigger fear of mine centers on cases where the evaluators do *not* spell out how they have assigned importance to the various assessed elements. The great majority of subjective biases operate subtly. It is likely that many evaluators do not even consciously realize how they have assigned significance to the items they have selected to assess. And the much vaunted, supposedly remedial, cry by some organizations that only neutral "bilateral" evaluators be utilized in conducting evaluations does nothing whatsoever to protect against the operation of such biases.

Part of the problem here is the same as that which underlies the importance of an expert witness's *not* giving ultimate issue testimony. That is, there is no way within our legal system that science alone can decide what is a "best" outcome. For example, one judge may consider a miserably unhappy, highly achieving child to represent an outcome vastly superior to one exemplified by a contented underachiever; the judge in the next courtroom may find the reverse. (This dilemma will be covered in greater detail in Chapter One.)

The solution we will suggest for dealing with mountains of disparate data involves the use of models by means of which one can aggregate the information collected during the course of a comprehensive evaluation. One data-based decision-tree model will be offered, one informal model, and two formal ones.

One advantage of such models is that each allows the custody evaluator (and anyone who would review his or her decision-making) to explicitly review the decision-making process.

Each further allows the custody evaluator to take an explicit look at how he or she has assigned credibility and relevance (or probative value) estimates to each piece of evidence gathered.

The formal models dampen any unwanted halo effect.

The models contribute toward confining errors in the decision-making strategy to that part of the process the typical mental health clinician does best: the eliciting of information. The process of "putting the pieces together" is done formally. While some experienced evaluators believe human beings are particularly gifted in doing this "intuitively," available evidence is not wildly supportive of this belief (see e.g., Schum & Martin, 1982, pp. 104–151).

Perhaps most important, and this is an advantage that will be seen more clearly after a reading of Chapter One, the use of a model helps to create a subtle mind-set shift in the evaluator that I believe is beneficial for anyone who would serve as an expert witness.

Without realizing it, too many expert witnesses approach their tasks with the mind-set of a judge rather than of a scientist. Stated more precisely, the use of a formal model shifts the mental health professional's mind-set away from asking this kind of question: "Given the evidence before me, what is the probability that a certain hypothesis is true?" e.g., "Given this evidence, what is the probability that the mother/father is the better bet for PCP?" Instead, the professional with a scientist's mind-set approaches each piece of evidence by asking: "Assuming a hypothesis is true, what is the probability that I would find this particular piece of evidence?"

Suppose, in the course of conducting a comprehensive evaluation, it is ascertained that when it comes to school conferences, the mother attends 70 percent of the time and the father 50 percent. In too many instances, the evaluator decides how much value or how many "goodie points" to assign each state of affairs (each attendance record). He or she might think that a person who attends 70 percent of the school conferences deserves to be the primary custodial parent more than a person who comes 50 percent of the time. This kind of thinking involves putting oneself in a judge's role, literally saying what *should* or *ought* to be true.

A more scientific approach would be for the evaluator to frame two important questions. The first one would be: "In similar custody cases of which I have knowledge where the *mothers* were the better choice for primary custodial parent, what is the probability that I would find this particular piece of evidence (the mother attends 70 percent of the time, the father 50 percent of the time)?"

The second one would be: "In similar custody cases of which I have knowledge where the *fathers* were the better choice for primary custodial parent, what is the probability that I would find *this same piece* of evidence (the mother comes 70 percent of the time, the father 50 percent of time)?"

By framing it this way, the custody evaluator is far more likely to either seek a published database or go into his or her internal storehouse of memories and experiences, in an attempt to ascertain the probabilities of finding such evidence under the two sets of conditions. Hence, the approach may remind the evaluator that the probability of a father attending school conferences less often than the mother occurs with equal frequency in *both* sets of conditions (where the mothers have been the better PCPs *and* where fathers have been the better PCPs within "traditional" marriages where mothers were homemakers and fathers often worked a significant distance away from home) and hence has no real ability to discriminate between these two conditions (i.e., is not really a piece of information with probative value). The critical question for the evaluator is in a comparison of the probabilities with which the evidence would occur under two competing hypotheses—i.e., the degree to which the evidence (the 70/50 mother versus father attendance records within traditional marriages where the fathers work far away from home) truly differentiates suitable from non-suitable custodial parents. More about this in Chapter Ten.

ADVERSARIAL BITTERNESS

There are three sources of the adversarial anger and bitterness many custody disputants experience. (Remember that we are dealing with a highly selective part of the population when we speak of the need for evaluations. The estimated number of divorcing parents who end up in a custody dispute in which testimony may be required from an expert witness range from about two percent of all divorcing parents (Hoppe, 1993) to about 10 percent (Melton, Petrila, Poythress, & Slobogin, 1987, p. 329). The thrusts and counterthrusts that result from this adversarial anger and bitterness impede resolution of the disputes. In Chapter Eleven, we will offer information the custody evaluator can use to make a contribution in this area, without blurring any critical professional role boundaries.

One source of angry, adversarial attitudes would best be explained by individual characteristics of the involved disputants. Hoppe (1993) studied a group of custody/visitation litigants and identified personality traits he believes predispose them to suffer "relationship disorders" (see Chapter Thirteen).

Another source of adversarial bitterness is best explained by qualities of a specific dyadic relationship. Within concepts developed in Chapter Three, we see such parents—those who seem to go on arguing into eternity—as having incompatible symbol systems and information-processing strategies.

A third source of adversarial bitterness stems from aspects of the legal/evaluative process itself.

In subsequent chapters, we will present evidence that while *some procedural aspects* of the legal system (those that provide a disciplined forum in which each participant can put his or her best foot forward in front of what is perceived as a "fair" judge) are actually helpful, other aspects are decidedly not helpful, e.g., unrealistic standards and/or whimsical, unscientific rulings. In one case in which I participated, a father was denied unsupervised visitation with a child because he was labeled by the mother and her friends as suffering from "alcoholism," an idea bought by the judge. No real definition of "alcoholism" was given. He was an "alcoholic" because, although he rarely had more than one drink a day, *"he needed"* that drink. Never mind that no operational procedure was advanced by means of which one could tell the difference between a person "needing" to do some particular thing as opposed to "choosing" to do this same thing. More importantly, no evidence was offered that this "alcoholic condition" was having any negative effect whatsoever on the involved child.

Standards or rulings that result in arbitrarily limiting a parent's access to a child will, of course, raise the level of adversarial bitterness.

Other qualities of the legal/evaluative system that contribute to the bitterness harbored by the parents would include: exorbitant attorney fees; the long waits (continuances) between hearings (eating away at people who already feel desperate); overly aggressive attorney attitudes both in and out of the courtroom, along with totally blind client-loyalty; the know-it-all demeanors of some judges; the coercive threat of further lawsuits as a bargaining chip; and, as mentioned, an overreliance on the interview by mental health professionals. This last attitude perpetuates and fuels the negative incident model, which in turn co-creates the need for each parent to "discover" situations in which the other parent is "wrong."

We are going to propose a specific system (in Chapter Eleven) of nonadversary communication strategies that can be used and modeled in all interchanges with the evaluation participants, and in the wording of all written reports.

Further, I almost always recommend the direct teaching of this approach to battling custody disputants. Negotiation, the flowing back and forth of information and energy fields, is a necessary and probably sufficient condition of health. This would apply regardless of the entity or entities in question—an individual within himself or herself, a dyad, a family, an organization, or a single cell and its environment. It is no accident that the first comprehensive system of thinking that the Western World has known (Plato, 427–347 B.C.) was presented in the form of a back and forth dialogue, adversarial on the surface, yet characterized at a deeper level by the principles proposed later.

Please note well that the teaching of nonadversarial skills to highly argumentative, cantankerous, hostile parents is *not* a substitute for the offering of highly detailed recommendations. The more that remains open for hostile parents to argue about, the more the potential damage to the children.

AN APOLOGY TO MARK TWAIN

An editor once asked me why I use the terms "we" and "us" when I write, as in "*We* found such and such to be true" or "*We* believe it best to do such and such."

She said: "Don't you really mean that you, personally, found such and such to be true? Shouldn't you use the word 'I' in these sentences?"

Mark Twain once said the only people who may legitimately use the term "we" instead of "I" are members of a royal family and people with tapeworms.

Well, I am not a member of a royal family (a *great* family, but not a royal one) and so far as I know, harbor no intestinal visitors.

What I *do harbor*, however, is a profound sense of all the people in the various research teams of which I have been a member. And it is these people I have in mind when I write. They worked directly in forging the materials in this book.

Although I am not a psychoanalyst, Dr. Robert Waelder has had a profound effect on my approach to intellectual endeavors. He and I had frequent conversations while our data-based tests were being fine-tuned.

When I joined the faculty at Jefferson Medical College to work under Zygmunt A. Piotrowski, I had, on my first day, an encounter with what I call a classic or "continental" lunch (i.e., how one went about gaining an education on the "Continent," in pre World War II Europe). Dr. Piotrowski, over the course of a three hour meal, spoke of the naval history of World War II in the Pacific Theater, the psychology behind the techniques of various Renaissance artists and sculptors, problems in the developmental history of Franklin Delano Roosevelt, a good bit about Poland's relationships with the USSR (not terrific), Freud's theories of psychosexuality, Jacob Burckhardt's approach to art and history, and the correct way to drink tea.

I realized I would have to go back to school and study world history from the Sumerian peoples on, just to be able to survive lunch times. Needless to say, over the course of working together on many mutual research projects, I learned vastly more from Dr. Piotrowski than I had in earning all three of my degrees.

Mike Halbert, my coauthor of Chapter Ten, by encouraging me in the 1950's and 60's to become involved in the newly developing field of Operations Research (of which he was a pioneer), expanded enormously the mind-set tools I had acquired up to that time. He has remained my greatest mentor, although since there is not sufficient time to run all of my ideas past him, I accept responsibility for what is less than adequate about them.

Dr. Gail Elliot, head of Child Development and Family Systems research for Bricklin Associates, coauthored Chapter Three in this book, as well as the *Parent-Perception-of-Child-Profile*. She contributed to the development of all Bricklin Associates tests and tools.

A dictionary definition of the word "seminal" goes something like this: Having the character of an originative power or source; making a powerful contribution to the seeds of later development. This entry, in my personal dictionary, would simply read: Bruce D. Sales, J.D., Ph.D. A pioneer in law-psychology education, the holder of 67 honors and awards and author or coauthor of 11 books and 129 articles on law-psychology issues, Bruce Sales has not only contributed greatly to the field of custody decision-making directly, but has been personally supportive of our teams' endeavors in this field.

Dr. S. Richard Sauber was one of the first custody evaluators to fully grasp the importance of a utilization model in custody decision-making.

My daughter, Carol Bricklin, assisted tremendously in the preparation of this work.

A WORD ON THE STATISTICS EMPLOYED

I deliberately employ simple statistics whenever possible, e.g., percent of agreement. I have a practical reason for this, as well as a conceptual reason.

The practical reason is that these statistics must be readily understandable to parents, attorneys, and judges. This "ability to understand" is required in situations that are typically very tense and, too often, adversarial in nature. Keep in mind that at least one purpose in developing these tests and tools was to get the individuals caught up in custody disputes on to an approach that measures a parent's usefulness to a child and away from an approach that depends on counting up negative incidents. To do this, to get the involved parents on the track of seeking to be good parents and away from spying on the opposition, one must enable them to understand what the involved tests actually seek to do. This approach, the use of tests and tools that aim to explore how a parent can be maximally helpful to a child, must be explained to these parents at the earliest possible point of contact in a dispute process.

The second reason for choosing simple statistics is conceptual. I have some distrust for complicated statistical strategies (i.e., procedures that have complex assumptive structures). To use Piotrowski's words: "If you need complicated statistics to demonstrate relationships, you probably could have done a much better job of choosing and defining your concepts in the first place" (personal communication).

I am sure there are those who would disagree with this thought (as well as with other thoughts expressed in this book). I would like to quote Arthur S. Reber (1985) who, in the course of preparing a remarkably thoughtful and useful *Dictionary of Psychology*, had the following to say after struggling (successfully) to define an elusive concept: "(G)entle criticisms concerning specific failures . . . should be sent to the publisher or the author" (p. 181).

I ask the same: Please keep them gentle.

THE CUSTODY EVALUATION HANDBOOK

Research-Based Solutions and Applications

Chapter One

Loving the Courtroom

Forensic psychologist Reid Meloy (1993) believes people either love the excitement of court or hate it. My observations are similar. This chapter is about how the custody evaluator, who often winds up there, can make certain he or she will end up in the former category.

Although books and articles on custody evaluations typically put their "going to court" sections at the end of their works, I have chosen to put it first.

Anyone who does forensic work should have the court in mind from the very first instant of contact with a particular case. I'm talking about a topic not frequently mentioned: the controlled paranoia anyone who would serve in a forensic area must learn to adopt—and shed! The custody evaluator must learn at all points during the comprehensive evaluation to inwardly ask: "How would whatever I am currently doing or concluding appear if an aggressive and brilliant attorney were asking me about this in a courtroom?" (And nowadays, "What must I do to decrease the probability of an ethics complaint?")

There is no other endeavor quite the same as a forensic one for encouraging the inward asking of why one is choosing to do, or not do, some specific thing.

No one comes into our clinical offices and asks us to explain why and how we chose to use a certain test or psychotherapeutic strategy, or how and why we came to each and every conclusion.

But this is exactly what can happen in a forensic context.

It is best to keep such a scenario in mind from the very moment one enters a case.

Just as in a chess game where the opening few moves can prove decisive, so too with a court-related procedure. How one positions oneself in relation to the task at hand is crucial. Legal, ethical, and psychological issues must be ascertained accurately. The tools and tests chosen for use must be relevant to these issues. One must decide who among potential participants needs to be evaluated extensively, as well as identify those whose evaluations can be more limited in scope. One must especially be aware that any eventual testimony will need to be justified by what is done during the evaluation. Hence, if there is a particular area one wishes to address via testimony, one must make sure that information that is both credible *and* relevant is gathered.

This chapter is laid out in three major sections. The first considers science, as a whole, in court; the second, the mental health professional in court; and the third, the custody evaluator in court.

The comfort and excitement promised in the title of this chapter will in large part depend on how well you can feel psychologically aligned with, and excited by, many of the concepts to follow. There is also an "access code state-of-arousal" exercise offered in Chapter Thirteen (in the section on testifying in court) that is not only useful for dealing with cross-examinations, but also to get into, and out of, the ultracautious attitude often necessary during forensic evaluations and/or courtroom testimony.

SCIENCE IN COURT

The "law," while in actuality constantly evolving and striving to satisfy diverse and often conflicting goals (e.g., establish blame and assign guilt, punish, rehabilitate, protect society, be an agent for explicit and implicit moralities, seek social fairness, etc.), at any given moment is philosophically a closed system assumed to require no further input and operates with an absolutistic (moral) authority.

Science, essentially the notion that there are optimal ways to ask the world questions such that the answers lend themselves to proof and systematization, does not claim that any specific answer or outcome is morally "best" or necessarily lasting. Science is characterized by an open-ended, never-ceasing asking of such questions, followed by answers, followed by new questions.

This was essentially the message the Delphic Oracle gave to Socrates and his companion, Chaerephon, when it identified the "wisest person" as the one who realizes there will always be new questions to ask. The epistemologically minded members of a field strive to delineate what constitutes legitimate questions, and which forms valid answers to such questions might take. Every few years, there is a so-called "paradigm shift," which changes the rules of the game, so to speak, as to what constitutes legitimate questions and answers.

From a very practical perspective, a mental health professional who would aid the court should be familiar with critical philosophical differences between science and the law. These differences are particularly important in regard to how "truth" is discovered in each field. For example, mental health professionals are often upset at the adversarial nature of the legal process. But the pursuit of scientific truth is *also* an adversarial process. The manner in which the members of a given science present data, opinions, and information to other members and the manner in which these persons respond are strikingly similar to what happens in a court of law, i.e., people challenging and responding to each other. (In fact, as any random reading of the "comments" section of the *American Psychologist* would show, the pursuit of scientific truth is often more adversarial and filled with name-calling than is the pursuit of justice.)

Other important considerations here are the time constraints of a legal process (science has no such thing), the hearsay evidence restriction in a courtroom (science can seek data wherever it wishes), and the court's jaundiced eye regarding statistics (Tribe, 1971; Stromberg et al., 1988).

Melton, Petrila, Poythress, & Slobogin (1987, pp. 3–13), among others, call the following differences to our attention: the supposedly ultraconservative view of attorneys as opposed to the more liberal view of mental health professionals (which they dispute); difficulties that arise when a deterministic model of the world is pitted against a free-will model (since the law seeks to punish people, it needs a "blame' concept, hence people "choose" their actions); the law's fear of group statistics in individual cases; and law's penchant to ask the mental health professional unanswerable questions (e.g., one of the authors was asked to contrast the effects of a child's spending one week per year with his mother as against two weeks).

A mental health professional's effectiveness in court is greatly enhanced if he or she has some concise, but complete, notion of the scientific process. This affords a much-needed "mental structure" for the offering of information in court.

Science may be thought of as a set of propositions about the real world formulated in the belief that they are probably true. Any given science ends up being a collection of potentially true generalizations, which are constantly being improved or enlarged or simplified or proven. Science is generally "ordered knowledge about reality" (Piotrowski, 1957, p. 12). It is important that the knowledge be ordered because if this were not the case, it could not be mentally assimilated and very small amounts of it would be remembered. This need for order and logic constitutes utilitarian goals; they are the result of human intellectual limitations.

Piotrowski divides the scientific process into activities that take place within four separate categories. The first has to do with concepts. The second

deals with the formation of principles. A principle defines the logical relationships that exist between various concepts. A third category refers to "empirical referents," the "real life" exemplifications of concepts that are considered to exist in the real world and to be accessible through the human senses.
The fourth category has to do with validation, the process of ascertaining the
degree of correspondence between principles and the relations that exist
among relevant empirical referents. "Propositions about reality are 'true' if
the observed relations among the empirical referents of concepts correspond
closely to the relations among concepts as stated in the principles" (p. 13).

When psychiatrists and/or psychologists and/or clinical social workers
argue over whether or not an individual is "depressed," it is usually because
each subscribes to a different set of "empirical referents" in terms of which
depression is to be recognized in the sensory world, and this in turn is based
upon conflicting values and goals in what is sought from the concept and/or
"definition" of depression. (A fuller discussion of these issues can be found in
C. W. Churchman's important book, *Prediction and Optimal Decision,* 1961.)

The point here is that the difficulty of predicting, say, "dangerousness"
or "insane behavior" has to do not only with the huge array of variables that
interact in creating such behaviors, but also with differences in the goals society seeks regarding each type of individual and the resulting differential markers one looks for to identify examples of each. For example, to the degree that
one's concept of dangerousness places a high premium on the protection of
others, the easier it becomes to predict "dangerousness" (high levels of false
positives would be acceptable).

Summarizing, the manner in which science and the law approach the
discovery of "truth" are in many instances very similar. Further, many of the
so-called "limitations" of the behavioral sciences, especially in the legal system, have less to do with nonremediable aspects of these sciences, and more
to do with conflicting goals in the concepts used to study the materials in
these fields, leading to subtle disagreements in what constitutes the "empirical referents" or "evidence in the real world" of these concepts. Another way
of saying this is that what *we seek* in the concepts we employ to look at the
world, will, in very large part, determine how we draw boundary lines around
the world. This, in terms, will influence not only what we call a "fact," but also
the degree of certainty we demand to prove any given proposition about these
"facts." Further, just as it is very difficult to predict what a single individual
will "do," it is also very difficult—impossible, according to quantum mechanics—to predict what a single electron will do. Hence, in the psychological sciences as in the physical world, it is easier to make accurate statements about
the prospects of large collections of things ("group statistics") than about individual things. My conclusion? The criticism that psychology is a "soft science" is misleading.

THE MENTAL HEALTH PROFESSIONAL IN COURT

This section of Chapter One will deal with general issues surrounding the mental health professional in a courtroom setting. The next section will deal with the same kinds of issues that are more specific to the mental health professional serving as a custody evaluator.

If one frames the theoretical issues in a debate via broad concepts, one will easily find "facts" in the real world to represent them.

It is into this "sweeping generalizations" category that I would place the aura created by the assertions of critics such as David Faust and Jay Ziskin who are interpreted as saying that mental health professionals do not belong in court. The resulting controversy has become a "Yes, mental health professionals belong in court" versus a "No, they don't" kind of argument. It is important to note that in any event the key question, if one subscribes even in part to an operational philosophy, is not really whether their assertions are "true," but whether they are useful. I believe they are, and that this is the intention of the Faust-Ziskin works (Ziskin, 1993).

Perhaps the most cogent remarks on this issue have come from Heilbrun (1992, p. 257). He summarizes the position of members of the Faust-Ziskin camp—the camp critical of the usefulness of psychological assessment procedures in court—as follows: "Critics have described such (psychological) assessment procedures as 'controversial' and 'of doubtful validity and applicability in relation to forensic issues' " (Ziskin, 1981, p. 225; see also Faust & Ziskin, 1988, 1989; Ziskin & Faust, 1988).

Heilbrun goes on to make the very important point that amidst all this controversy, supposedly made on research bases, there exists "...virtually...(no) normative data on the uses and abuses of psychological testing in the forensic context" (1992, p. 258).

Let us now look at some of the issues surrounding the appearance of a mental health professional appearing as an expert witness in a courtroom.

Stromberg et al. (1988) remind us of the basics that all mental health professionals who practice in a forensic area should know: "Federal Rule of Evidence 702 (1984) states the basic rule on the admissibility of expert testimony: (I)f scientific, technical, or other specific knowledge will assist the trier of fact (the judge or jury) to understand the evidence or to determine a fact in issue, a witness qualified as an expert by knowledge, skill, experience, training or education, may testify thereto in the form of an opinion or otherwise" (p. 647). In order that testimony from an expert be admitted, it is necessary that the judge or jury should need assistance concerning the issues at hand, the scientific foundations permitting the testimony should be sufficiently reliable to permit generalizations to be made on their bases, and the specific witness must be qualified as an appropriate expert on the subject.

(The Federal Rules of Evidence have been adopted in many states. It is important to know what your own jurisdiction considers admissible evidence.)

Regarding the question of what is a "legitimate" contribution, Federal Rule of Evidence 403 warns that the value to a decision maker of "opinion testimony" must be greater than its "prejudicial value." This suggests that critical decision makers may be predisposed to believe what experts say. Rule 403 cautions that the basis upon which an expert offers information should be stronger than this predisposition.

Stromberg et al. go on to note that under Federal Rule of Evidence 703, in order for testimony to be admissible, the expert's opinion must be based on any of the following: direct observation; facts acquired by hearing (or reading) the testimony offered at a given trial; materials that are gotten through books, literature, or "...experience to which the expert has access" (p. 647). Further, an expert may rely on hearsay or evidence ordinarily not permissible in a courtroom, "if it is of the type ordinarily relied on by persons in his profession" (p. 647).

A key issue, on which participants in the legal process still do not agree, has to do with the area of the so-called "ultimate issue." In a custody context, this would mean that while an evaluator who served as an expert witness could offer lots of facts and information about a given case, he or she could not address the "ultimate" legal issue, that is, who should serve as the primary caretaking or custodial parent. (An "ultimate issue" is essentially the legal matter that must finally be answered or resolved in a given case.) "However, this distinction was gradually seen as artificial and unworkable since the judge or jury easily inferred the ultimate conclusion from the expert's testimony anyway" (Stromberg et al., 1988, p. 648).

Federal Rule of Evidence 704 was engendered to deal with this issue and provided that testimony that in fact is given in the form of an opinion or inference would be legitimate even if it embraced an ultimate issue that was to be eventually decided by the trier of fact. Stromberg and associates note their own objections or, at least, caveats to this, while I would argue that the expert should *never* address the ultimate issue. We will make the argument that to refrain from doing so obviates many of the controversial issues surrounding the feasibility of a mental health professional's appearing in a court. (However, one *can* address this issue if what is presented is offered as information. See the remarks that follow a bit later.)

For many years, the question of just what kind of facts a scientist or expert could testify about in court was controlled by the so called Frye standard (*Frye v. United States,* 293F, 1013, 1014 D.C. Cir. 1923). It essentially stated that anything "scientific" the scientist testified about had to have general acceptance within the field of which he or she was a member.

This rule has been subject to much debate. The essential argument against the Frye standard is that it is overly restrictive. So long as one follows acceptable scientific practice, one should be able to offer materials and data that have not yet had an opportunity to gather acceptance in an entire field, whatever "entire field" may mean. Science often moves slowly; it can take many, many years for enough data to accumulate for members of a field to even know that some new test or some new information exists. Further, as Stromberg et al. (1988) note: "...testimony about technique should be admitted if a qualified expert would testify to it, even if the technique...(is) not yet widely accepted. The theory is that cross examination will reveal any flaws in the basis for the testimony and the judge or jury can take them into account. Many states by statute, and others by court decisions, have moved gradually to this view, and the federal system has adopted this more flexible rule" (p. 649).

In the opinions of all the attorneys I have consulted on the so-called "Daubert" ruling of the United States Supreme Court (*Daubert v. Merrell Dow Pharmaceuticals, Inc.* [92-103] 727 F. Supp. 570 [1981]), the ruling will move courts around the country even more toward expanded admissibility of expert testimony. (However, for a divergent point of view, see Underwager and Wakefield, 1993, who argue that by bringing in the criteria, legally called 'dicta,' of falsifiability, refutability, or testability as criteria by means of which evidence is judged for "legitimacy," i.e., can be admitted in testimony, we are in for "a revolutionary change that shifts the entire enterprise into new and untried ground" [p. 165]. The authors conclude: "The process of working out the implication of this decision will... take many years, countless cases, and [involve] a multitude of confused attorneys and irate judges" [p. 165]).

Perhaps the key issue as to whether a psychologist has a meaningful contribution to make in a courtroom is the *relevance* of what he or she brings to the decision process. Heilbrun (1992, p. 260) makes some useful distinctions. He points out that relevancy can take two major forms. "An assessment instrument might directly measure the legal construct underlying a given forensic issue." He goes on to list a number of instruments developed over the past 20 years that are representative of this particular category, e.g., tools to measure competency to stand trial. "A second kind of relevancy is seen when a psychological construct (such as intelligence) that is presumed to underlie part of a legal standard (such as 'understanding of charges') is measured using a standard psychological test of intelligence, and the nature of that relationship is clarified in the report or through testimony" (p. 260). Heilbrun goes on to make the very important point, a point to which I will return in the next section, that courts go out of their way to be inclusive in what is invited to be brought to the decision process in regards to forensic instruments or psychological tests "...so long as their relevance to the legal standard can be demonstrated. Such a demonstration could be made in the report itself or during direct testimony" (p. 260).

Another major variable of that which the psychologist brings to court involves the accuracy of tests and/or observations relied upon. This important area will be covered in Chapter Twelve.

We will further argue that the only legitimate thing an expert should bring to a court is information. The best way for any piece of information to be offered is in terms of conditional probabilities or likelihood ratios, that is, the probability of discovering a certain piece of evidence given that some hypothesis is assumed to be true. This may seem a difficult concept to grasp at the moment, but it will be explained in much greater detail presently. It makes the judgment of relevance a more operationally clear process.

A point that comes up repeatedly is whether or not a mental health professional can (or should) come into court with just one piece of evidence, for example, the results of a single test.

Heilbrun (1992) makes the point in the following way: "Because of... (the) premium on the accuracy of information provided to the factfinder, the results of psychological tests should not be used in isolation from history, medical findings, and observations of behavior made by others" (p. 263). He reminds us that this point has been made by others, including Matarazzo (1990) as well as Melton et al. (1987, p. 342) plus several others. Heilbrun (1992) concludes that: "...impressions from psychological testing in the forensic context should most appropriately be treated as hypotheses subject to verification through history, medical tests, and third party observations" (p. 263).

While I agree with the *intentions* behind all of these assertions (with the exception of the implication that data from history, medical tests, and third party observations are more "accurate" than psychological test data), I believe they create a tension between what a mental health professional may bring to court and the intentions behind due process. Said another way, I do not believe that each participant in a legal process must present what we can call in layperson terms, the "big picture." It is certainly important that *someone* in the process provide this, but this does not mean each participant must bring wide-ranging data in order to make a legitimate contribution. The conditions under which more limited contributions are feasible are spelled out in the next section.

Many of the controversial issues surrounding the appearance of a mental health professional as an expert witness in court are addressed by Wagenaar (1988) in an article of exceptional brilliance. Wagenaar believes that most of the controversies in these issues stem from a misunderstanding of the expert witness's task. He distinguishes between opinions formed in the minds of members of a court, and the information on which such opinions are based. His solution asks us to accept the idea that expert witnesses should do no more than offer information that can be used to aid in the formation of opinions. This is a controversial issue; currently many courts *will accept* an expert having an opinion that addresses an ultimate issue. (In fact, some family law court judges become irate if the expert witness will *not* do this.) Wagenaar believes this muddies the waters and makes it more difficult for the mental health professional to make a noncontroversial contribution to the legal decision process. He believes an expert *can* offer a conclusion or opinion, but in such situations it is up to the ultimate decision-maker *to consider these opinions as part of the information offered.*

Within this orientation, opinions are expressed in terms of prior and posterior odds. Prior odds stand for the probabilities that two mutual hypotheses, H_1 and H_2 are true, prior to the consideration of evidence, $p(H_1)$ and $p(H_2)$. Posterior odds are to be understood in terms of a ratio of two conditional probabilities, $p(H_1/E)$ and $p(H_2/E)$. These two quantities stand for the probabilities that H_1 and H_2 are true after a consideration of the evidence. Information is seen as a ratio between two different likelihoods, $p(E/H_1)$ and $p(E/H_2)$. They represent the conditional probabilities of obtaining the evidence, given that Hypothesis 1 or Hypothesis 2 is true.

Let us try to express these ideas in several different ways. First of all, as mentioned, if one does not wish to think about these notions in terms of Bayesian decision theory, odds and likelihood ratios can be understood as subjective degrees of belief. "(A)n opinion is related to the probability that a hypothesis is true; the informational value of evidence is related to the probability of finding evidence only when a hypothesis is true" (Wagenaar, 1988, p. 500).

The task of the ultimate decision-maker is quite different. It is up to this individual to decide if an hypothesis is in fact true, given the evidence.

Here is yet another way to think about Wagenaar's ideas. This is in the form of a small vignette furnished by Michael Halbert, coauthor of Chapter Ten.

Imagine two people approaching a lake, about to go fishing. One of the fisherman proposes a hypothesis about the amount of fish in the lake. He says: "There are a lot of fish in this lake." This would be Hypothesis 1, H_1. (Hypothesis 2, H_2, would be that there are *not* a lot of fish in the lake.) The two people fish for two hours, without catching a single fish. This may be thought of as the evidence.

An expert witness, testifying on the matter of whether there are many or few fish in this lake, would have to confine his or her statement to one like the following: "If it is true there are a lot of fish in this lake, this particular piece of evidence would be highly improbable."

The expert witness could not make a statement in the following form: "Given this evidence, I conclude that there are very few fish in this lake." A statement such as the latter would be the province of the ultimate decision-maker, as there might be many other things the ultimate decision-maker might want to take into consideration before coming to this conclusion. These factors may include such things as whether there could have been a lot of bait-like substances poured into one end of the lake, drawing all of the fish to a particular location, or other environmental factors that may have made for biased data, as well as considerations of definition and purpose such as what does the phrase "a lot of fish" actually mean and even to what uses a conclusion will be put. In Chapter Ten, we will offer ways to give "conclusion evidence," but they are based on approaching each piece of evidence in the manner suggested by Wagenaar.

The ultimate issue dilemma is argued from yet another perspective by Grisso and Saks (1991). In their article, they consider the types of amicus briefs it is feasible for organized psychology to file with the Supreme Court. They make specific mention of a brief in which the *American Psychological Association* sought to advance one of its policy issues and hence argued for a particular outcome in a case. The thrust of their article is that the goal of achieving specific case outcomes is improper, and that to pursue such goals threatens to undermine other important objectives. In their words: "Psychology's expertise is not in constitutional analysis; it is in the study of human behavior" (1991, p. 205). They go on to make the point that to attempt to do the former weakens organized psychology's effectiveness in achieving the latter. Their summary: "In public interest cases, when acting as a true friend of the court, APA's obligation is to share with the court what empirical research and theory tell us about human behavior, and not to argue for any particular outcome of the case before the court" (p. 205).

The last sentence says it all. Whether a mental health professional or a mental health professional organization is acting as an expert witness or filing an amicus brief, it is not feasible within the conceptual framework that seems to work best within our legal system to argue for any particular outcome. It may seem like nitpicking, but there is a big difference between a situation in which an individual's data obviously point to a certain outcome and one in which the individual is personally arguing for that outcome. (For an important discussion of positioning testimony as about an "ultimate factual issue," as opposed to an "ultimate legal issue," see Myers, 1992, pp. 115–116.)

Interestingly, from a purely practical perspective, it may make an expert witness more convincing in regard to reported information to *avoid* giving ultimate conclusions. Rogers, Bagby, Crouch, and Cutler (1990, p. 231), in an informative piece of research, concluded that expert witnesses may very well *lose credibility* when ultimate conclusions are tacked on to proffered information.

Regarding other expert witness issues, Garb (1992a) (in addition to providing a carefully reasoned and balanced response to members of the Faust-Ziskin camp) makes some very important (and positive) points about the role of *training* in relation to the effective expert witness. He offers the following wisdom: "(T)here is general agreement that, depending on the type of judgment that is to be made by a judge or jury, expert witnesses should be allowed to (a) describe a person's history and mental status, (b) make diagnoses, (c) evaluate whether a person is malingering, (d) make predictions of behavior (or at least describe difficulties in predicting behavior), and (e) evaluate psychological processes related to competence (e.g., competency to stand trial)" (p. 453).

If ever a writer could be said to "feel" the complexities of hammering out an acceptable role for the mental health professional as expert witness, it is Michael J. Saks. His article, "Expert Witnesses, Nonexpert Witnesses, and Nonwitness Experts" (1990), must be read in its entirety for he brings not only a learned perspective but a very human touch. His subtleties (and angst) do not lend themselves to paraphrase.

He casts his task as an attempt "...to understand the role of 'fact' people in an essentially normative system" (1990, p. 291).

He goes on: "We are unlikely to find clear answers. The more layers I have managed to peel away from this topic, the more confused I have become" (p. 292).

Here is just a brief sampling of some of the issues covered by Saks: the confusion resulting when opinions are offered; the role of personal value systems both among judges and mental health professionals in shaping what is seen as "legitimate;" the extreme importance of an expert witness's being familiar with all relevant literature; whether or not there are conditions under which it is "okay" to withhold information even if this is misleading; a discussion of possible roles of an expert witness (or a nonwitness expert) before a trial even begins.

THE MENTAL HEALTH PROFESSIONAL
IN CUSTODY EVALUATIONS

As we look at what has been written on this issue and inspect what actually seems to be practiced around the country, we can discern the various ways in which a mental health professional can make a useful contribution to the custody decision-making process within a legal context. It will also be necessary to spell out the conditions under which each of these manners of participating is feasible. Further, as the various participations are covered, the complexities—and caveats—associated with each will be considered.

The ways of participating, as they are written about, fit generally into three separate categories.

The first can be labeled the "All Critical Participants Evaluation." We will abbreviate this ALL-CPE. An evaluator conducting activities within this category would be referred to by Stromberg et al. (1988, p. 646) as acting in the role of an "expert witness." An ALL-CPE seeks to evaluate all of the critical participants in a child's familial milieu as well as possible others deemed appropriate by the evaluator. The ALL-CPE is frequently conducted by a single evaluator who is agreed upon by a child's parents and their attorneys and/or may be court-appointed.

The second category can be referred to as a "Limited Critical Participants Evaluation" (LIM-CPE). Stromberg et al. would describe the professional's activities in this role as a blend of that of the expert witness with that of a fact witness. In one particular situation this blend may lean toward "expert" participation, and in another lean toward "fact" participation. Respondents to a *Custody Newsletter* poll estimate that in up to 42 percent of cases with which they have contact it is not possible to secure the cooperation of all critical participants. In these instances, following especially careful suggestions, the mental health professional can play an important but more limited part than is possible within the prior category. Limited participation may also involve the task of assessing the merits of another evaluator's assumptions and methodologies, or assisting an attorney to develop rebuttal questions.

Warren adds a third activity for the mental health professional, which he calls "researcher." He says: "Psychologists in particular are trained as scientists, and research conducted within a subject realm can provide extremely valuable information to parties in litigation.... (My) research has ranged from investigations about a specific topic such as the effect of anorexia/bulimia on parenting, to presentations of scientific data which would seem to contradict 'common sense,' ideas such as the notion that the healthiest parent stays in the marriage no matter what" (*The Custody Newsletter*, 1991, p. 3).

Warren cautions that the activities of the researcher may blend with those utilized within an ALL-CPE and a LIM-CPE, but activities within the latter two must be mutually exclusive. I believe he makes this distinction because the LIM-CPE often comes about when the evaluator has been retained by one side in a disputed case. Hence, Warren's caveat has to do with the fact that the individual conducting a LIM-CPE could be viewed as an "advocate." My position is that "advocacy" is *never* justified by an individual who is serving, *even in part*, as an "expert," and further, that advocacy is not to be defined in terms of who is paying the bills.

Before we spell out the assets and possible liabilities of activities within these three categories, it might be important to recognize that perhaps the very best participation for the custody evaluator is to be part of a nonadversarial conciliation or mediation process. This follows from the fact that a "good" custody arrangement must do more than match available parental strengths to the involved children's needs; it must also motivate parents to follow it. One could actually argue that the "best" arrangement is an arrangement the parents wholeheartedly support, regardless of its time-sharing attributes.

However, a cautionary note is warranted. First of all, it would be unwise in most instances to blend the role of impartial custody evaluator with that of mediator. If one is to serve as a mediator, this should be clear to all involved participants at the outset. It is also of great importance to remember that the typical mental health professional does not have the broad base of knowledge required to mediate the huge variety of issues that require solutions in a custody context.

Melton et al. (1987, pp. 332–333) also sound a cautionary note. They are unconvinced that the research data paint a rosy picture of mediation as the universal answer to custody disputes. A complete discussion of this issue would take us too far afield at this point, but it is covered more thoroughly in Chapter Thirteen.

The ALL-CPE is by far the most comfortable role in which the mental health professional can appear. However, as I will spell out later, *the benefits of the ALL-CPE do not flow from the (misguided) notion that it has greater scientific or legal legitimacy than do activities within the other categories.* The optimality of the ALL-CPE flows from a practical advantage—that it is *seen* as more "neutral"—and from the fact that it can legitimately address a wider range of issues.

Let us now look at the assets and liabilities of activities carried out within each of the three categories: the All Critical Participants Evaluation (ALL-CPE), the Limited Critical Participants Evaluation (LIM-CPE), and the "researcher."

The ALL-CPE: Assets and Liabilities

One asset of the ALL-CPE is that it is usually seen as "evenhanded" by the participants. However, there are many exceptions to this assumed perception. I would estimate from the cited *Custody Newsletter* poll that in more than 20 percent of cases at least one of the main participants in an ALL-CPE comes to believe the evaluation is biased, and goes on to seek further consultation.

The assumption is often made in certain ALL-CPEs that because the evaluator is retained and paid by both sides there is a guarantee of "fairness" and "objectivity" on the part of the evaluator. While there is certainly some commonsense merit to this assumption, I will show presently that the dangers of using for custody decisions tools and techniques that are not data-based and especially the insidious workings of subjective biases compromise—often greatly—the advantage gained by this neutrality.

The ALL-CPE has an undeniable advantage in that the evaluator has access, at least theoretically, to a very wide range of data, including medical records, school records, documents, interviews with neighbors, etc. from both sides of the dispute. The problem with the resulting mountain of data is that the meaning of most of it is usually quite unclear regarding its importance to a given child. It is frequently impossible to assess the impact of any particular piece of data on a given child, and also—perhaps especially—impossible to *prioritize* the information. Is mild depression in a parent "worse" than obsessiveness? Is being unemployed "worse" than being an angry arguer? Is a parent who screams good advice "worse" than a parent who lovingly states stupid advice? Is a parent who grew up in the 60's and still occasionally smokes marijuana inherently "bad"?

Again, the problem with having copious amounts of data is not that it's copious; it's the illusion that the evaluator *knows how to interpret* these data in terms of their meaning to, and utility for, a given child. (More on this later; an attempt to develop tests and tools that measure the actual impact parental behavior has on a given child is at the heart of this book. Further, data-based test results frequently yield information critical in helping the evaluator understand and prioritize clinical and life history information.) The models in Chapter Ten directly address the issue of copious data.

There are at least two other factors the mental health professional should think about when operating within the ALL-CPE category. One is theoretical; the other is practical.

The theoretical issue is documented by Stromberg et al. (1988) in the *Psychologist's Legal Handbook* (pp. 592–593). It has basically to do with the fact that an "adversarial" way of arriving at the "truth" is indeed not a very bad way of arriving at the truth. In other words, in the absence of actual research data, *it is merely a presumption that it is better to have one "neutral" evaluator hired by both sides rather than one (or several) hired by each side.* (Further, there is an intriguing study by Wolman and Taylor (1991), suggesting that children in families in which the parents go through lengthy disputes may fare better psychologically than children whose parents reach nondisputed out-of-court settlements.)

One immediately sees a dilemma here, because this presumption *is* justified in the sense that adversarial professionals could very well add to the adversarial attitudes between the parents, as well as creating a bad image for the mental-health field.

In fact, most of the disputes between those who favor expanded involvement of the mental health professional, even in quite limited roles, and those who would limit participation to the ALL-CPE follow from any given disputant's position on a continuum. At one end of this continuum are those who have heightened faith in our adversarial legal system as a method of arriving at the truth. At the other end, are those of little faith. Those in the former category favor expanded involvement, since due process extends to any party in a legal dispute the right to make his or her strongest case by virtue of being allowed to bring forth *any* fact that contributes to this goal.

These remarks notwithstanding, the ALL-CPE is certainly the role in which the mental health professional should try to operate. Dr. Michael Hahn (1990), with the assistance of attorney William Hilton, offers some helpful information as to what the evaluator may do when a parent will not cooperate (and a court has not ordered his or her participation). This strategy would be especially useful in connection with the LIM-CPE, since it details what was done, what was not done, and what remains to be done to bring the evaluation to the level of the ALL-CPE as regards the scope of issues that may be addressed. It is offered here because it frequently applies subtle pressure on evaluation "hold-outs," making them more likely to consent to be included in the evaluation process. (Before deciding whether to use the following procedure or one similar to it, it would be wise to check out its usefulness in one's own jurisdiction.)

Dr. Hahn writes as follows: "The Declaration under Penalty of Perjury is a good remedy for dealing with a parent who will not cooperate with a neutral bilateral evaluation process. I always try to have both parents and both attorneys agree to the evaluation request because the data are more credible with the court, and a fuller picture regarding the family in question can be obtained. However, if one parent for whatever reason refuses this evaluation then I make it clear to all the parties concerned that I am prepared to provide a Declaration under Penalty of Perjury regarding partial observations of the child or children in question.

"The language of this statement is as follows: 'I Declare under Penalty of Perjury under the laws of the state of California that the foregoing is true and correct.' Executed on (date) at (place), followed by my signature. My Declaration is viewed by the court as evidence that is equivalent to sworn testimony provided by me in person in a courtroom.

"I make it quite clear to the parents, the attorneys and the court that this Declaration is limited and constrained by the fact that one parent did not provide input into the process. The Declaration has explicit statements in it that make it clear as to what was done, what was not done, and what still needs to be ascertained with regards to the questions at hand. The Declaration includes a careful description of the process that was attempted before it was decided to do a Declaration rather than (an ALL-CPE). The Declaration has specific language in it that explains that it is limited in comparison with a full evaluation because one parent did not provide information or because the child was not observed with both parents." (p. 3)

The LIM-CPE: Assets and Liabilities

The second category in which a mental health professional may operate is within the "Limited Critical Participants Evaluation" or LIM-CPE. When a sample of readers of the *Custody Newsletter* was polled (39 respondents), estimates ranged from 10 percent to 42 percent as regards situations where it was not possible to secure the cooperation of both parents and hence a wider range of critical participants in a given custody evaluation.

The advantage of the LIM-CPE is that it could provide to the court or any person in a position of making an ultimate decision information that would otherwise be absent.

This immediately brings up the thorny and controversial issue of whether a mental health professional should ever go into court having interviewed only one parent (or one parent and the involved children)—that is, with data that come from only one side of a debated matter, for the LIM-CPE is seen as especially "suspect" if it is initiated (and paid for) by one side in a disputed issue. The assumption is that such monies are buying a "hired gun," or, as this is referred to in more polite circles, "advocacy."

The LIM-CPE initiated by one side is also seen as suspect because the so-called "facts" in the case—obtained via interview—will have been presented to the evaluator in a biased and selective manner.

Before spelling out some steps that can be taken to eliminate—or at least greatly reduce—the shortcomings of the LIM-CPE, let us dispose of the last-mentioned caveat rather quickly. The danger of hearing only one side of a story is simply not a hugely compelling issue for those of us who have limited faith in the interview at the outset. I rarely worry that I am hearing "one side of a story only," since I do not put too much faith in *either* side of the "story." (There is, however, a reason to hear—in the very special way spelled out later—both sides of the "story." No participant will have faith in the evaluation if he or she does not feel "listened to." Further, the evaluator must come to understand all of the many factors each critical participant believes to be important in any disputed matter, whether or not the evaluator eventually agrees that these matters are indeed important.)

There is one further "danger" to mention here. It is a danger not only possible in relation to the LIM-CPE, but more importantly, one not protected against (or even mitigated by) an ALL-CPE. These are especially important dangers—those that occur within contexts that supposedly eliminate or at least reduce dangers. This is the danger of certain types of subjective bias. This danger is insidious because a custody evaluator whose judgment is swayed or even dominated by such a bias will be savvy enough not to mention it as critical or controlling in any report or testimony. He or she will rather use it by declaring the biased-against parent as the parent of non-choice by finding something in the interview or observational data to support this bias—a choice actually arrived at by the workings of the bias. Since interview and observational materials are not data-based, it is relatively easy to justify *anything* with something said or observed. There is a huge smorgasbord of "facts" out there in life, and if one is using interviews or observations one is pretty much free to select from this smorgasbord as one wishes.

Following are statements I have paraphrased that were heard in the corridors of courthouses and in informal discussions of custody evaluations. They were offered to me in all cited examples as the controlling factor in a given case, the factor that more than any other influenced the custody evaluator to come to the conclusion he or she in fact came to. Keep in mind that all of the custody evaluators who made these statements had sufficient credentials to be able to testify as an expert in a courtroom.

Here is a sampling of what I believe is a tremendous danger in the conducting of custody evaluations—one that can only be protected against by the use of data-based instruments.

She smoked marijuana.

He hits too much.

You should have seen her *Rorschach!* It was full of oral themes!

He has so much money that he's spoiled rotten. He thinks he can buy whatever he wants. That's how he controls people.

She's the more loving one [spoken of the mother of a child with a decided learning impairment who needed clear limits and information far more than she needed "loving"; further, and far more important, the love referred to was offered to the child in a way that she, the child, did not perceive as such].

She runs around.

He has to work, he's not really at home much of the time and I don't like it when a baby-sitter, even if it's a good baby-sitter, has to stay with the children.

I am not claiming there is no informational value in some of these statements; in the absence of a data base, they should hardly be considered controlling data. (For a discussion of subjective bias from the perspective of evaluator countertransference, see Freedman, Rosenberg, Gettman-Felzien, and Van Scoyk, 1993.)

Prior to suggesting solutions to the shortcomings of the LIM-CPE, there are some philosophical/practical thoughts to consider about why limiting a mental health professional's participation in a custody decision-making process to "ideal" situations only (the ALL-CPE with the evaluator obtained by both sides) is not a good idea: restricting the discovery of possibly important information; restriction of due process; setting up conditions inimical to a participant's cooperating with the ultimate decision; denying the well-accepted concept of the "second opinion"; unintended effects, such as exclusion of worthy seekers of help; false equation of ideal circumstances with attainable circumstances; probably would not be enforceable in the real judicial world; unintended effect of introducing unequal standards for those who would offer testimony in a courtroom situation. (See Saunders, 1993a for some further thoughts on these issues.)

A logical extension of the considerations around the LIM-CPE arises when the question comes up as to whether a mental health professional should ever offer testimony on the data from a single test. In responding to such a query, it is important here to make the distinction between what a given mental health professional offers as testimony (which I will claim may involve information from one test), on the one hand, and the warning issued by Matarazzo (1990) and seconded by Heilbrun, who wrote (1992): "Because of this premium on the accuracy of information provided to the factfinder, the results of psychological tests should not be used in isolation from history, medical findings, and observations of behavior made by others" (p. 263). This point has also been well documented by Garb in the work (1992a) already cited as well as in his important article (1992b) on the use of computer-based test reports.

Hence, although I believe it is psychologically and legally defensible to offer data from one test it is important that the ultimate decision-maker have access to all of the types of information mentioned above. The argument that the ultimate decision-maker is not in any position to interpret or understand the full significance of limited pieces of information, even if this information is offered in accordance with Wagenaar's (1988) previously mentioned notions, can be offset by following Sak's (1990) suggestion—compare below—concerning the ability of the ultimate decision-maker to appoint his or her own expert witness to assist in such matters.

Some of the complexity surrounding this issue has to do with what is seen as the scientific "weakness" of a test finding by a mental health professional as compared to, say, a finding by a radiologist.

Let us take a closer look at this very comparison. I do not think many people would claim a radiologist must perform and report on an entire "all-phases" medical evaluation in order to testify as to his or her radiological findings. Such an endeavor might involve what ordinarily would be the activities of a neurologist, a neurosurgeon, an internist, an endocrinologist, countless pathologists, and so on.

"Well," one might say, "a radiologic picture is much more 'scientific' than a psychological test finding." This is, I submit, a misleading argument. While people might more readily agree about what a radiological evaluation directly manifests (what is "revealed" by the procedure) than about what is revealed by, say, a *Rorschach* test, *the meaning or implication* of this manifestation depends on explicit or implicit data bases, either known or suspected, plus notions of probability—the exact same conditions as would apply for psychological test findings. That is, even if one can more readily identify some anomaly on a radiologic film than depressive moods on a *Rorschach*, the *meaning* of the anomaly as it plays itself out over a person's life, or the impact of it, is by no means apparent from what is on the radiologic film. Hence, in many instances what might be most useful to a court depends more on a data base than on a direct test manifestation.

Keep in mind that we are here discussing behavior in a courtroom where an individual other than the evaluator is assigned the role of "ultimate decision-maker" or trier of fact. It is this person's job to put together the elements that comprise the "big picture." Hence we should be careful not to confuse the use of one test in a courtroom with the use of one test in our clinical practices. In our clinical practices, *we* are often the ultimate decision-makers. This is not the case in a courtroom. Hence, it is a lot safer (and defensible) to bring one piece of evidence to a courtroom than it is to base a decision on one piece of evidence in a clinical setting, because in that setting it is *the clinician* who has the job of looking at the big picture and deciding where the single piece fits in and what relevance and accuracy-rating to accord it. Remember, too, that in a courtroom, if the ultimate decision-maker is not certain of the relevance or accuracy of some piece of the big picture, he can use what Saks (1990) calls "law's secret weapon," the ability to appoint its own expert. Saks says: "...and the law has a secret weapon for keeping expert witnesses honest; the court's power to appoint its own expert witnesses" (p. 299).

The Researcher

The third category in which a mental health professional may participate in a custody case is in the context labeled "researcher" by John Warren in the *Custody Newsletter* (1991).

When I first began thinking about a mental health professional in this role, things seemed simple enough; the professional is hired to help one side present its strongest case. However, the more I thought about this type of participation, the muddier things got, especially as regards the roles of discovery procedures. This refers to: "The pre-trial devices that can be used by one party to obtain facts and information about the case from the other party in order to assist the party's preparation for trial.... (Such tools would include): depositions upon oral and written questions, written interrogatories, production of documents or things...physical and mental examinations..."(*Black's Law Dictionary*, 1990, p. 466).

Before turning to the perils and pitfalls of the "researcher" (what Saks, 1990, calls the "nonwitness expert") in the discovery process, note that there are *many* services a mental health professional may provide in this category: bibliography, research conclusions, playing a "devil's advocate role," and so on.

Saks provides a very extensive look at what he calls the "nonwitness expert" (1990, pp. 305–330). Just to give some idea of the multiplicity of roles a mental health professional may find himself or herself in, here are just some of the categories mentioned by Saks: "(C)ourts and commentators have wrestled with distinctions among multiple status experts, twice-retained experts, second-tier experts, in-house experts, and non-witness experts (prior to versus after retention). When is an expert informally consulted versus retained? Complex mixtures of considerations are taken into account by courts called upon to decide what category an expert is to be placed in" (p. 306). Each category is surrounded by its own activities and caveats.

Things are much clearer concerning expert witnesses who will testify: If a mental health professional is hired to perform an evaluation and offer testimony, he or she may be required to reveal the subject matter on which testimony is to be given and to summarize the facts and opinions to be offered, as well as providing justification for proffered opinions.

Anyone who would serve in the role of researcher would be well advised to read Saks' 1990 article to discover the subtleties concerning which researcher roles are particularly susceptible to discovery and which less so.

SUGGESTED SOLUTIONS FOR CUSTODY EVALUATION PRACTICE DILEMMAS

These suggestions about practices to follow in conducting custody evaluations are offered in the hope they will solve some of the dilemmas most frequently mentioned in the literature on the conducting of such evaluations and in the various versions of "custody evaluation guidelines" mailed to me in my capacity as editor of the *Custody Newsletter*.

1. The evaluator should attempt to secure the cooperation of all major participants, and seek to be court-appointed to serve in a neutral, bilateral role. Confidentiality and consent issues should be openly discussed and signed release forms obtained. Consent is sought to perform the evaluation, seek and share information and make the results of the evaluation known. Note that in some instances you will be seeking not only to obtain information but also to reveal it, as when you want a participant's reaction to another participant's allegations. The evaluator should be absolutely certain the legal as well as psychological issues at stake are understood. Make certain all critical participants are advised as to the nature of what is entailed in the mental health professional's role.

Consent issues can be much more complicated than would appear to be the case. First of all, in some instances the term "consent" is used by itself, and at other times you will encounter the term "informed consent." The latter is usually used in connection with a surgeon and patient, wherein the surgeon must provide the patient with enough data on the benefits and risks of the prospective procedure so that the patient can make an "informed" decision. However, all "consent" agreements *imply* that the person giving consent knows what he or she is consenting to. (For some further complexities of consent issues, see Saunders, 1993a, p. 53.)

Have the attorneys clarify whether the change-of-circumstances issue must be addressed.

Obtain permission to visit the places a child may reside under competing arrangements.

Clarify whether there will be a written report and who will receive copies.

2. In the event a LIM-CPE is to be done, the first step is to try to move it to an ALL-CPE. If such efforts fail, try to get a court order for your involvement in a case, *whatever* the nature of this involvement, and/or docu-

ment your efforts to secure an ALL-CPE. Make certain (from your state licensing board and the pertinent divorce and/or preexisting custody order) that the person seeking your services has a legal right to do so, and whether or not you need the consent of the *other* parent to proceed. Remember that the role of an expert is to present information to the trier-of-fact, *not* to advocate. This does not mean an expert witness cannot present information that is clearly favorable to one particular side in a dispute. It is the expert witness's attitude or perspective that is neutral, not his or her information. To me, "advocacy" does not imply neutrality of stance. The best way for the evaluator to send this message to the potential client is to make sure all payments for the evaluation are made in advance, and there is nothing hanging over the head of the evaluator to push him or her in any particular direction insofar as a report and testimony are concerned.

It should be made clear that a LIM-CPE cannot *comprehensively* address the issue of who should serve as a PCP. Any report or testimony based on a LIM-CPE should specify what remains to be done to make the evaluation optimal. (For a dissenting point of view regarding fee collection, as well as some additional comments, see Saunders, 1993b, p. 250.) The oft-voiced warning that an expert witness may never venture an opinion about somebody not directly seen represents a more complex issue than is generally realized, because of the possible use of hypothetical questions.

3. The evaluator should make every attempt to have the heart of the evaluation consist of tools and tests data-based for custody decision-making. Should other materials be utilized, their data must be interpreted from a "What will it mean to the child" point of view.

4. The evaluator should be very wary of interview data and observational data for reasons that will be detailed in Chapter Three.

5. We are going to detail several forms of bias of which the evaluator should be aware. The most dangerous sources of bias are the deeply subjective forms previously mentioned. *These forms of bias more easily enter the picture when an evaluator relies on nondata-based sources of information.* In the absence of data that have a scientific story to tell about the match-ups for given children with each parent, the evaluator will tend to rely on interview and observational data—data that can more readily be used to support any given subjective bias. I have already listed examples of such biases in which certain statements (e.g., he buys everything he wants, the *Rorschach* was full of oral themes, etc.) were used as controlling themes.

6. Steven Bisbing and David Faust (1992) mention a host of conditions an evaluator should follow that not only make good scientific sense, but also lead to more effective testimony. These would include items all mental health professionals are probably taught, but then become careless about. We refer to being aware of validity and reliability figures whenever possible, being aware that some tests can be consciously manipulated, the need to *always* follow

standard procedures as outlined in test manuals when giving the tests, and the need to be aware of the degree to which any given examinee conforms to the population on whom the test or tool was data-based.

7. Arthur D. Williams (1992) does a fine job of summarizing other major forms of bias. He reaffirms the importance of *confirmatory* bias, a form of bias also mentioned by Wedding and Faust (1989). This is the tendency to overvalue evidence that supports one's hypotheses and a tendency to look away from nonconfirmatory evidence. This bias is particularly characteristic of experienced clinicians.

Anchoring is a subtype of confirmatory bias and occurs when excessive importance is assigned to initial information. It is important to remember that all people, and this would include clinicians, are uncomfortable when they deal with huge quantities of data and unsure of the categories into which to put these data. This is particularly true in the ALL-CPE, which tends to gather unto itself mountains of information. The custody evaluator, in a rush to decrease anxiety, attempts to provide structure to the data, often coming to conclusions too quickly. Once this is done, he or she will tend to see other pieces of data as confirming these initial diagnostic impressions. There is also a tendency for deeply held subjective biases to work here, since already held biases form all-too-available categories into which incoming data can be put.

Availability refers to the ease with which a person can recall prior data. People are more likely to remember vivid and dramatic events than things that are ordinary.

Illusory correlation is the habit of assuming there is a relationship between events or characteristics in the absence of supporting evidence. I see this all the time in custody evaluations, where an evaluator assumes he or she knows the "meaning" of a given piece of parental behavior, say, mild depressions, or anxiety, or mild obsessiveness.

A practice that can reduce all forms of bias is the use of explicit decision rules; this would go along with the use of known databases whenever possible, and the approaches spelled out in our later chapter on aggregating data.

8. Finally, the custody evaluator should limit what is offered to information. Further, one should specify to the best of one's ability the database in terms of which this information is offered. It is particularly important with the LIM-CPE to remember that one can only (directly) offer information on people who were examined. (This sometimes becomes a confusing issue when the tests described later in the book are utilized, since they yield information on a child's perceptions of his or her parents. It is important to remember that this kind of information is information about the *child, not the parents,* even though the information may sound like it is about the parents.)

The use of a forensic "mind-set" described in the beginning of this chapter can help the evaluator to deal with biases. For mental health professionals who are new to the game, or who are contemplating entering the "arena" of custody evaluations, some works are "must readings."

First and foremost, our team would recommend *Solomon's Sword: A Practical Guide to Conducting Child Custody Evaluations* (1989) by Schutz, Dixon, Lindenberger, and Ruther. This book, useful for the experienced evaluator as well as for the novice, will be particularly helpful for the novice who is also a busy practitioner. With an enormous ability to separate the essential from the nonessential, the authors manage to cover, with true economy, every important aspect of conducting a comprehensive evaluation.

I also very much like an article by Halon (1990) entitled *The Comprehensive Child Custody Evaluation.* While our approaches are different (especially in regard to the attention paid to a parent's "complaints"), I believe this work, more than any other, manages to convey the true flavor of what the evaluator's *unfolding relationships* will be like with the attorneys involved in a given case.

For a source that best considers the relationship between a given child's developmental status and the specific features of a particular time-sharing plan, see Bray's (1991) article (plus any other works by this productive researcher). However, note well that a custody plan based *solely* on a child's developmental status presumes each parent is a good match for the child and that a high degree of cooperation exists between these parents (see e.g., Stahl, 1994, pp. 31–44).

For those involved in any mental health forensic field, I would highly recommend the work by Melton, Petrila, Poythress, and Slobogin (1987) entitled *Psychological Evaluations for the Courts.* Written from what I would call a "conservative" position, it contains a wealth of important information.

In the article "Expert Opinions: 'Not for Cosmic Understanding,'" Melton (1994) presents a consideration of what constitutes legitimate expert opinion and evidence by analyzing the various legal standards set forth to define them. (He also presents an interesting argument that good forensic practices may be inimical to good clinical practices.)

Finally, for reasons already cited, I believe anyone who would serve as an expert witness should read the—what shall we call them?—thoughts? musing? worries? commiserations? of Michael Saks (1990). Whatever one calls them, they should be part of the mind-set of the forensic mental health professional.

Before we discuss some of the tests and tools our teams have developed to assist the custody evaluator, it is important to survey the research literature on postdivorce issues as we will do in Chapter Two. I am continuously impressed with the amount of information that *is* known, granting that it is not easy to adapt this information for use in individual cases. Even though I try to stay up on all of the research data in the custody field, I found many interesting surprises in our latest survey.

Chapter Two

Postdivorce Issues: Relevant Research

Gail Elliot and Barry Bricklin

There are some tantalizing surprises (e.g., the commonsense assertion that the more contact a child has with both of his or her divorced parents, the better for the child, is not always true), as well as much practical information in the research literature dealing with postdivorce issues.

The challenge for the custody evaluator is to translate statistical data into a form that can be used in an individual evaluation. One immediate problem is that there is virtually no finding that has not been refuted in some subsequent study, and there are other findings that emerge from a particular project that cannot be replicated in others.

Much of this has to do with methodological and conceptual issues. One must not let the term "research" serve to intimidate common sense. There are many instances in which a basically good concept had to wait a long time for an adequate empirical referent (the concept of "intelligence" persisted an awfully long time before the IQ test came along) and there are many measurement techniques that have lasted without an adequate or fully accepted conceptual basis (e.g., the *Rorschach* test). Such examples mirror the faith professionals have that some concept or measure is "onto something" useful and important, even though no one has as yet been able to either design and/or implement a compelling research project. Still, there are useful pieces of information in the literature for the custody evaluator, in spite of the fact that many of these items have not been proven conclusively.

So far as we can see, there are no sweeping generalizations or valid principles in the literature that a custody evaluator can apply universally. Even the few findings that *do* seem (at least "almost") universally valid (e.g., the healthier the parents were to begin with and the less the predivorce hostility between the parents, the better the children do following divorce; boys typically have a rougher time than girls in maternal custody homes) are difficult to apply meaningfully in an individual evaluation. *There are, however, many pieces of information* that can be exceedingly helpful in individual cases (especially in regard to the fallout from remarriage). *Because there are so many details in the research to be described, one's mind-set in reading this chapter should be to gather a strong impression of what data do in fact exist, so that one can later find specific pieces of information when they would be relevant.*

If one were to approach custody decision-making in an ideal empirical world, one would seek to find research data with which to address each of the legal criteria set forth to inform such decision-making. The Uniform Marriage and Divorce Act (UMDA) (1979) adopted by about 10 states (Leonard & Elias, 1990, p. 171) represents the most frequently mentioned legal attempt to define the factors that should be considered when one is determining an arrangement in a child's best interests.

Among other things (defined as "all relevant factors," whatever such may constitute), the UMDA instructs the evaluator to consider: the wishes of the parents; the wishes of the child; the child's relationships with virtually all of the people with whom he or she would interact under competing arrangements; the child's adjustment in home, school, and community; and the physical and mental health of "all" individuals involved.

Leaving aside the first mentioned category, the wishes of the parents (which presumably can be ascertained by asking them), there is at least *some* social science research relevant to all of the other categories (Sales, Manber, & Rohman, 1992).

However, aside from PORT- and BPS-type data, which at least at some level are relevant to the issues of a child's wishes, the nature of his or her relationship with each disputant, and the mental health of the latter (insofar as how such "health" manifests itself in a given parent-child dyad), it is awfully difficult to adapt the existing research to help out in *any* area deemed critical by the UMDA *in an individual case.*

Here are some suggestions regarding things to be alert for in a custody evaluation.

A custody evaluator must be particularly sensitive to the specific forms of stress to which people in a postdivorce situation are susceptible. A related issue has to do with when mandatory psychotherapy or counseling should be part of one's recommendations. In the case of a child, the vulnerability to stress may be a product of several interactive variables. Hence, it would be wise to pay attention to the age, the gender, and the gender-age combinations associated with heightened stress in children. The above often interact with the overall "quality" of newly formed families, the presence or absence of stepparents (whose presence, under certain circumstances, often creates heightened levels of tension), the predivorce adjustment of the parents, and the particular nature of any parental conflict in codetermining stress levels.

Preschoolers are particularly vulnerable to stress; both boys and girls of all ages are as well, but under different circumstances. Girls often show a "sleeper" effect, whereby problems do not emerge until many years have passed.

It is particularly important to pay attention to the *details* of the research to be described, since no single custody disposition (e.g., sole versus joint) shows any consistent superiority in all cases. Hence, in situations where all other things are equal (i.e., the mother and father are fairly evenly matched in their resourceful utility to the children), it would be helpful to know when stepparents help and when they hurt, who seems to do better with paternal versus maternal custody, and which factors seem most highly correlated with a child's resilience.

The research is organized as follows. First, a sampling of the most important studies on the effects of divorce on children will be reviewed in some depth in more or less chronological order. This will provide a sense of the evolution of ideas over the past two decades and the theoretical orientations representative of the body of research as a whole.

Following this, there is a series of summaries of research findings concerning the most studied variables or issues believed to mediate the effects of divorce on children's adjustment. These include age and developmental issues, gender, parental conflict, parent adjustment, custody dispositions, resilience (favorable outcomes), and preexisting conditions (prospective studies). We close with a general discussion of the complexities of the research to date.

EFFECTS OF DIVORCE ON CHILDREN

One of the pioneer works on the effects of divorce on children is the California Children of Divorce Study. Begun in 1970, this longitudinal study assessed long-term effects of divorce on children (Kelly & Wallerstein, 1976; Wallerstein, 1984; Wallerstein, 1991; Wallerstein & Corbin, 1989; Wallerstein & Kelly, 1976, 1980). The sample consisted of white, middle-class children who were three to 18 years of age at the time of parental separation. Clinical interviews of the children and their parents, teachers, and siblings were supplemented by assessment of the children in the sample by means of play, art, and fantasy. Follow-up data were gathered at 18 months, 5 years, 10 years, and 15 years.

Children who were preschoolers (ages two and a half to almost six) at the time of parental separation intitially seemed the most disturbed of any age groups under study (Wallerstein, 1984). At the 18-month follow-up, nearly half of the preschoolers were more disturbed than they had been initially, with boys significantly more disturbed than girls. However, by the 10-year follow-up, children who were preschoolers at the time of the divorce were functioning adequately (Wallerstein, 1984, 1991).

Children in early latency (five and a half through seven years old) initially responded to parental separation with extreme pain and sadness, and experienced great difficulty finding relief for their distress (Kelly & Wallerstein, 1976). Later-latency-age children (eight to 10 years old) initially seemed more poised than younger children (Wallerstein & Kelly, 1976). They were energetically intent on the mastery of their fears and emotions (through play and fantasy) in order to achieve a sense of coherence. However, they experienced intense anger and a shaken sense of identity. By the one-year follow-up, responses to parental separation had become less intense, with anger the most enduring response. Half of the children were more disturbed than they had been initially.

At five years postdivorce, a follow-up of all the children revealed a strong relationship between the psychological adjustment of the child and the quality of life within the family (Wallerstein, 1991). A nurturant postdivorce or remarried family environment and positive family relationships were significant, while age at the time of separation and gender were not. At the 10-year follow-up, the children who had been older during the initial assessment were plagued by adjustment problems (Wallerstein, 1984, 1991). At 15 years postdivorce, Wallerstein (1991) was finding her subjects involved in resolving the issues surrounding heterosexual relationships. A sleeper effect was noted in young women who had been untroubled in early adolescence, but whose interpersonal relationships were now conflicted, characterized by their concerns about rejection and betrayal (Wallerstein & Corbin, 1989). Therefore, while boys suffered more adjustment problems throughout the early years following divorce, problems surfaced for girls as they approached adulthood.

Wallerstein concluded that "complexly interlocking factors...must be taken into account when delineating the divorce experience over time" (1984, p. 445), that divorce is "a psychological progression taking place over time and many developmental milestones" (1991, p. 354), and that "the child of divorce faces many additional psychological burdens in addition to the normative tasks of growing up" (1991, p. 354).

The Virginia Longitudinal Study of Divorce and Remarriage (Hetherington, Cox, & Cox, 1982; Hetherington, 1989) is another landmark longitudinal study. Employing a variety of standardized objective measures along with interview and observational data, the study assessed both the more immediate and the long-term effects of divorce on children. The subjects were middle-class, white preschoolers and their parents. Half were from divorced, maternal custody families and half were from intact families.

It was found that emotional and behavioral problems were greater for the children of divorce than for those in intact families. The problems included acting out, noncompliant, and aggressive behaviors both at home and at school, antisocial behaviors, dependent behaviors, depression, and anxiety. These disturbances, found at the two year follow-up, were more enduring for boys, who also had problems in their relationships with their mothers. That is, social and emotional problems for girls from divorced families had disappeared at the two-year follow-up.

In a cluster analysis of the adjustment measures, children from divorced or remarried families were found to be overrepresented in three of the five clusters generated. One maladaptive cluster, representing insecure and aggressive children, was found to contain children (three times more boys than girls) from homes with high levels of conflict, negative affect, and ineffective parenting styles.

Hetherington concluded that children's adjustment to divorce and remarriage is determined by the interaction of many factors, including children's temperament, gender, age, and familial and extrafamilial relationships, which in combination can operate either to buffer and protect a child or to render the child more vulnerable to problems in adjustment.

The clinical interview and observational techniques employed in the earlier studies generated hypotheses for later investigators to subject to more rigorous analyses. The nature and correlates of children's long-term divorce adjustment and personal adjustment were assessed by means of correlational and multivariate techniques in a study with a two-year follow-up (Kurdek, Blisk, & Siesky, 1981). Based on the relationship between age and personal adjustment found in earlier studies of divorce adjustment, the researchers hypothesized that developmental changes would affect social-cognitive ability (defined here as an "understanding" of the divorce) as well as emotional acceptance of divorce (referred to as "feelings" about divorce).

The social-cognitive abilities considered by the researchers to be important for positive divorce adjustment include "the child's taking the parents' view of reasons for ending the marriage, comprehending the nature of reciprocal relations, separating oneself from the divorce, and experiencing cordial relations with both parents and friends" (p. 566). Since an understanding of divorce does not necessarily guarantee emotional acceptance of divorce, questionnaires were employed in order to assess both children's understanding of divorce and their feelings about divorce. The subjects were white, sole custodial parents, both male and female, and their children. It was found that the children did not have problems with divorce adjustment in terms of their understanding of divorce. However, their feelings about divorce were negative. Results were similar at the two-year follow-up. There was a positive relationship between divorce adjustment and overall personal adjustment. Parents' evaluations of positive child divorce adjustment were related to children's positive feelings about divorce, not to their understanding of divorce. Parents saw the children as well adjusted and stronger as a result of the divorce.

Correlates of a positive adjustment to parental divorce were found to be greater length of time since parental separation, increasing age, internal locus of control, and good interpersonal reasoning. The children's negative feelings about divorce were not related to age. Both locus of control and interpersonal reasoning were predictive of children's divorce adjustment independent of age. That is, the more well-adjusted children had an internal locus of control and good interpersonal reasoning skills whether younger (initial assessment) or older (two-year follow-up). According to Kurdek et al., these findings provided "direct empirical evidence" (p. 576) for Hetherington's (1979) suggestion that differences in social and cognitive competencies account for developmental differences in younger and older children's divorce adjustment (Virginia Longitudinal Study of Divorce and Remarriage). It was concluded that child perceptions of parental divorce are best understood by the knowledge of the child's implicit ability to infer the thoughts, the psychological status, and the interpersonal relationships of other people.

Earlier research suggested a variety of influences on divorce adjustment of children. Walsh and Stolberg (1989) concluded that "divorce is a dynamic, multifaceted phenomenon whose effects vary over time" (p. 267) and elected to investigate the relationships among parental and environmental variables, behavioral, cognitive, and affective adjustment of children, and time since separation (recent, intermediate, or distant). Parental hostility, parenting skills, time since separation, and child reports of good and bad environmental events were significantly related to children's cognitive, affective, and behavioral adjustment to divorce in the following ways. High levels of overt interspousal hostility were related to high levels of internalizing behavior pathology at distant separation. Increased interspousal hostility was also related to externalizing behavior pathology and anger in children from recently separated families and to low levels of anger in children at distant separation time. Parenting skills were related to both internalizing and externalizing behavior pathology in children.

For boys, higher levels of child-reported good events were related to lower levels of internalizing and externalizing behavior pathology, and were positively related to fears. However, for girls, the reverse was true. Higher levels of good divorce-related events were related to higher levels of internalizing and externalizing behavior pathology and were negatively related to fears. High levels of child-reported bad divorce-related events were related to low levels of misconceptions about divorce in children from recently divorced families and to high levels of misconceptions about divorce in children at distant separation time. High levels of bad events were also related to high levels of anger in children. While the impact of some variables, such as hostility or bad events changed with increasing time since separation, other factors, such as parenting skills, predicted child adjustment regardless of time since separation. It was concluded that prospective studies could investigate changes in the impact of environmental and parental variables with increasing time since separation.

Kalter, Kloner, Schreier, and Okla (1989) set out to test, within one sample, the major explanatory theories evolving from research and clinical literature on the effects of divorce on children. As a rationale for their approach, they cited an emerging consensus among researchers of different conceptual orientations. Results of many earlier studies indicated that parental divorce initially causes stress and disruption in social, emotional, and cognitive development in children. Earlier studies had also shown that although many children recovered and adjusted well after the first two years, others continued to have social, behavioral, and emotional problems that seemed related to the ongoing events of what was viewed as the extended divorce process.

For this study, six hypotheses based on factors explaining the effects of divorce on children were distilled from the research literature on children's adjustment to divorce. These factors included father absence (since maternal custody is most prevalent), economic distress, and multiple life stresses (more likely to cause adjustment problems than a single stressor) that might result from divorce, interparental hostility, parent adjustment, and a short-term crisis view to explain children's initial reaction to divorce. The subjects were maternal custody children between seven and 11 years of age and their mothers. Correlational and multiple regression methods yielded similar results. The parent adjustment hypothesis received the strongest support. Positive adjustment in children was related to positive adjustment in the parents. The multiple life stresses hypothesis was supported only for boys' adjustment. Mixed results for the economic distress hypothesis suggest that while lower income is associated with greater adjustment problems in girls, higher income is associated with greater adjustment problems in boys. Father absence, short-term crisis, and interparental hostility hypotheses were not supported.

Concerning the parent adjustment findings, it is suggested that the well-adjusted custodial parent can buffer children from the stresses of divorce, mediating the effects of stressors such as economic hardship, parental conflict, and single parenting. Conversely, the child is negatively affected if the custodial parent is too disturbed to cope with these stressors. Therefore, consistent with earlier studies, this is also an interactional view of divorce effects on children. However, the role of other factors typically associated with children's adjustment to divorce is subordinate to that of parent adjustment. Just as Kurdek et al. (1981) claimed to provide empirical support for clinically generated hypotheses from the Virginia Longitudinal Study of Divorce and Remarriage (Hetherington, Cox, & Cox, 1982), Kalter et al. claimed their results provided "clear empirical support" for the clinically derived parent adjustment findings of the California Children of Divorce Study (Wallerstein & Kelly, 1980).

Amato and Keith (1991) concluded that the body of research on the effects of divorce on children's psychological adjustment, social competence, and academic achievement, and on parent-child relationships had yielded contradictory and inconsistent results or results that had failed to attain significance. Therefore, they undertook a meta-analysis involving 92 earlier studies (and over 13,000 children) to determine the magnitude of differences in the adjustment of children from divorced versus intact families, the level of statistical significance of pooled differences, and whether there are larger differences for some outcomes than for others. The meta-analysis also identified study characteristics (such as type of analysis or sample) that could affect variations in effect sizes.

Cumulative evidence was used to test hypotheses for three theoretical perspectives explaining the effects of divorce on children's adjustment. The first perspective is parental absence, which suggests that the loss of a parent to divorce would have a deleterious effect on children's adjustment, since parents play an important part in a child's development. The second, economic disadvantage, assumes that the decline in economic well-being which often results from divorce would negatively affect the adjustment of children of divorce. The third perspective makes the assumption that the conflict between parents who are separating and divorcing creates extreme stress for children, which adversely affects their adjustment.

Results of the meta-analysis that were related to issues of research methodology indicated that differences between children from divorced versus intact families were smaller in methodologically stronger studies than in methodologically weak studies (i.e., studies that employed no control variables, employed convenience rather than random or clinical samples, used smaller sample size, used single-item versus multiple-item measures).

Concerning the parent absence perspective, it was hypothesized that the loss of a parent through either death or divorce would have a similar effect on children. However, children of divorce scored significantly lower on measures of academic achievement and well-being than children who experienced the death of a parent or children in intact families. Additionally, children living with a stepparent had more problems (psychological adjustment, conduct, social relations, and self-esteem) than children in intact families and, on measures of psychological adjustment, had more problems than children in single-parent families. Therefore, a second hypothesis, that remarriage of the custodial parent would result in fewer problems in the children, was not supported. Remarriage of a custodial parent, which theoretically provides a second parent as a resource, did not alleviate problems in the expected manner. While there was evidence of better adjustment in boys in stepfather families, stepfathers may not affect or may negatively affect the well-being of girls.

It was hypothesized that maintaining frequent contact and close relationships with noncustodial parents would improve adjustment. There were mixed results on the quality of the relationship and level of contact with the noncustodial parent. That is, some studies showed higher levels of well-being with frequent contact, others found no relationship between these variables, and others found an increase in problems associated with more frequent contact. The researchers concluded that the parent absence hypothesis received only weak support.

Statistically controlling for income reduced significant differences between children of divorce and those from intact families, lending some support to the economic disadvantage explanation. Remarriage of custodial mothers (with improved financial status) did not improve their children's well-being as hypothesized. This finding does not support the economic disadvantage hypothesis. It was hypothesized that the father's generally higher income would ameliorate the effects of economic disadvantage that is often the case in the maternal custody arrangement. Father custody children were higher in all outcomes (academic achievement and adjustment) than those in mother custody families. Although this supports the economic disadvantage hypothesis, there were significant interactions with gender, where boys in mother custody families did more poorly than girls, while girls in father custody were less well adjusted than boys. (In contrast to these findings, a 1981 study by Kurdek et al. failed to find children of opposite-sex custodial parents less well adjusted than those of same-sex parents.) Overall, the economic disadvantage hypothesis received limited support.

Levels of well-being were lower for children in high-conflict intact families than for those in low-conflict intact families or even divorced families, lending strong support to the family conflict perspective. Additionally, it had been hypothesized that improvement in children's adjustment should occur with the passage of postdivorce time if family conflict accounted for these adjustment problems. This hypothesis received little support. That is, while results of longitudinal studies indicated improved adjustment with the passage of time, results were not similar in the cross-sectional studies under analysis. It was hypothesized that longitudinal studies might be more powerful because of their within-subject design. The third conflict hypothesis, that there is an inverse relationship between children's well-being and postdivorce parental conflict, was supported.

In summary, family conflict received the most support, but the two other perspectives, economic disadvantage and parent absence, also received some support. It was concluded that no single conceptual framework accounts for effects completely and that all are necessary for an understanding of the effects of divorce on children's adjustment.

The above chronology provides an overview of the course the research has taken over the past two decades. Earlier clinical techniques generated theories and hypotheses about factors assumed to affect children's divorce adjustment. These hypotheses were subsequently subjected to quantitative analyses in studies that focused on one or two variables (e.g., age, gender, etc.). More recently, a combining of theories and a summarizing of all previous work has resulted in the testing of multiple variables and the pooling of data in order to gain a better understanding of the complexities that emerged from the earlier work. While age, developmental status, economic stress, parental conflict, parent absence, and parent adjustment have all been identified as important variables in predicting effects of divorce on children, all researchers seem to agree that the issue of children's divorce adjustment is complex and that adjustment will depend on many dynamic, interactional factors.

Wallerstein (1991), one of the earliest investigators, sums up the current state of the research: "No single thread is linked throughout these studies to long-term outcomes, whether good or poor. Moreover, factors associated with good outcomes cannot be inferred by simply reversing those linked to poor outcomes. Instead, complex and shifting configurations of multiple and interacting factors govern the shadings at each end of the adjustment spectrum. . . . Taken altogether, these studies reflect a complexity that was unanticipated when the work of divorce research began. The findings by their very ambiguity shed light on the complexity of interacting family processes" (p. 359).

AGE/DEVELOPMENTAL STATUS

A developmental perspective on the study of the effects of divorce on children can be traced to the California Children of Divorce Study (Wallerstein & Kelly, 1980). Wallerstein and Kelly looked at different age groups in order to examine age-related effects on children of divorce. Their results (discussed above in Effects of Divorce on Children), suggesting developmental differences in children's adjustment following divorce, led to other investigations of the role of age and developmental factors in children's postdivorce adjustment.

Kalter and Rembar (1981) studied the significance, with respect to psychological adjustment, of a child's age at the time of parental divorce. The subjects were latency age (seven to $11\frac{1}{2}$ years old) and adolescent (12 to $17\frac{1}{2}$ years old) boys and girls. Age at the time of parental divorce was not related to later overall adjustment. However, age at parental divorce was associated with several specific behavioral and emotional problems. Divorce when a child was two and a half years old or younger was associated with problems separating from parents during latency. If divorce occurred during a child's

oedipal phase, differential effects during adolescence included inhibition of
aggression toward parents for adolescent boys and aggression toward parents
and academic difficulties for adolescent girls.

In a study of the direct and indirect effects of a variety of factors on children's divorce adjustment, the subjects were children from seven to 13 years
of age (Stolberg & Bush, 1985). One of the findings (reported more fully
below, in Interparental Conflict and Parent Adjustment) was that younger
children had higher levels of environmental life change events, which in turn
were associated with higher levels of external pathology and fewer social
skills.

Preadolescent, early adolescent, and midadolescent children from divorced and intact families were compared on measures of internalizing and
externalizing problems and cognitive and social competence (Forehand,
Neighbors, & Wierson, 1991). Boys were more likely to be less competent and
have internalizing problems than girls at preadolescence, and to have fewer
problems and be more competent, relative to girls, by midadolescence. That
is, for girls, there is an increase in internalizing and externalizing problems
and a decrease in cognitive competence from preadolescence to midadolescence.

The following are findings from more recent research that focuses exclusively on the divorce adjustment of adolescents. Good parent-adolescent relationships had a buffering effect on adolescent boys (Wierson, Forehand, &
Thomas, 1989). That is, the adolescents with good relationships with both
parents were functioning significantly better than those with poor relationships with their parents. Similarly, positive father-adolescent relationships
were associated with lower levels of internal psychopathology in adolescents,
while poor father-adolescent relationships were associated with adolescents'
higher levels of external psychopathology (Thomas & Forehand, 1993).
Frequent paternal visitation in high interparental conflict families enhanced
adolescent's cognitive competency (Forehand, Wierson, Thomas, Armistead,
Kempton, & Fauber, 1990). Results of another study suggest that disrupted
parenting skills and poor parent adjustment are related to poor divorce adjustment in adolescents (Forehand, Thomas, Wierson, Brody, & Fauber,
1990). Adolescents were found to be better adjusted than the clinical standardization sample and only slightly less well-adjusted than the nonclinical
standardization sample for the measure of behavioral adjustment employed
in another study (Abelsohn & Saayman, 1991). This led the researchers to
conclude that parental divorce is not necessarily catastrophic for adolescents.

The above studies address divorce effects for children as young as two
and a half years of age, but there is almost no research on the effects of divorce on infants. In a study assessing the effects of postdivorce parent
access (Hodges, Landis, Day, & Oderberg, 1991) on child development in
infants and toddlers (from birth to 36 months old) in maternal custody, preseparation conflict between the parents correlated with irregular visitation

of noncustodial fathers. A poor visitation pattern was related to language development delays. There was also a significant relationship between poor visitation patterns and delayed gross motor development, with boys' gross motor development significantly poorer than that of girls. These results suggest that divorce may have important consequences for child development, and these consequences might indirectly impact on psychological adjustment.

In summary, differences in children's adjustment to divorce may be related to a child's age at the time of divorce and to developmental tasks pertinent to that age. Infants may experience delays in language and gross motor development. Preschoolers may initially be more upset by parental divorce than older children and may or may not suffer more enduring effects. Early-latency-age children may become immobilized and regress, and may experience fears, sadness, and anger. Later-latency-age children may suffer a shaken sense of identity and may engage in activities designed to foster a sense of mastery and to overcome feelings of powerlessness following parental divorce. Late adolescence and young adulthood may bring problems with heterosexual relationships for young women facing the developmental tasks specific to their stage of development. However, research on developmental differences in children's adjustment to divorce is very limited and results are inconsistent. The divorce adjustment of children of different ages seems to be mediated by (among other things) gender differences. That is, in the process of socialization, boys and girls may respond differently to divorce, according to different expectations based on sex roles.

SEX OR GENDER EFFECTS

Many of the findings concerning sex differences have been discussed above. In an extensive review of the literature on sex differences, Zaslow (1989) concluded that, for the global hypothesis stating that boys do worse than girls following divorce, results are inconsistent. It is suggested that research move to a more differentiated view of outcomes. For example, boys in maternal custody, unremarried families may be more negatively affected immediately and for some years following a divorce, and girls may do worse in father custody or in stepfather families. Issues such as family configurations, ages, and developmental levels need to be considered when assessing divorce effects on children.

In the California Children of Divorce Study cited above, it was noted that sex differences for young children surfaced at the 18-month follow-up postdivorce (Wallerstein, 1984). Boys, whose psychological adjustment had been slightly worse than girls at the time of divorce, became significantly worse in all life settings at this later point in time. Although no significant differences were found between boys and girls in overall adjustment at the 10-

year follow-up, the distinctive sleeper effect in young women (described above in Age and Developmental Status) was characterized by the emergence of anxieties that may earlier have been repressed, especially concerning heterosexual relationships (Wallerstein & Corbin, 1989).

In Hetherington's Virginia Longitudinal Study (1979, 1989), boys continued to have adjustment problems and problems in relationships with their mothers two years after divorce. Boys from divorced families versus boys from intact families were more noncompliant, antisocial, coercive at home and school, acted out more, and had more problems with academic achievement and peer relationships. In contrast, girls from divorced, nonremarried families had positive relationships with custodial mothers and were functioning well. At the six-year follow-up, mother-son relationships were problematic, while mother-daughter relationships were untroubled except in early maturing girls or families with high levels of conflict.

Concerning stepfathers in the remarried families, boys' behavior improved with stepfathers, while girls' behavior deteriorated. Amato and Keith (1991) also found better adjustment in boys in stepfather families, while stepfathers had either a neutral or negative effect on girls' adjustment.

Hetherington's (1989) cluster analysis of her results yielded three times as many boys as girls in the maladaptive, aggressive-insecure cluster described above (see Effects of Divorce). The children in this cluster were girls whose mothers had remarried and boys whose mothers had not remarried or had recently remarried. There was a nearly equal number of boys and girls in the opportunistic-caring cluster. The caring-competent cluster was made up of mostly girls, with the only boys in the cluster from divorced, nonremarried maternal custody families. It was hypothesized that the children's increasing responsibilities following divorce had a positive effect on girls that was cancelled out for boys by the maternal custody factor (i.e., problematic mother-son relationship and father absence).

Another study found that children's gender was not significantly correlated with divorce adjustment (Kurdek, Blisk, & Siesky, 1981). It was hypothesized that the differences between boys and girls may diminish as the children reach "levels of equilibrium" following the divorce, but that this process may be more protracted for the boys.

In a longitudinal study comparing boys and girls in first, third, and fifth grades from divorced and intact families, children from intact families performed better on measures of social-behavioral and academic competence than did the children from divorced families (Guidubaldi, Cleminshaw, Perry, & McLaughlin, 1983; Guidubaldi & Perry, 1984, 1985). Boys did less well on measures in both areas than did the girls. The differences between the children of divorced versus intact families were greater for boys at higher grade levels, while fifth grade girls from divorced families differed only slightly from girls in intact families.

In a study conducted by Forehand, Neighbors, and Wierson (1991) described above (see Age/Developmental Status), girls and boys differed in social and cognitive competence and in internalizing and externalizing problems. Preadolescent boys were less competent and more likely to have internalizing problems than girls. Boys were more competent and had fewer problems than girls by midadolescence.

Sex differences were found in a study assessing a number of major theories based on clinical and research literature (Kalter, Kloner, & Schreier, 1989). In regarding how parental adjustment and multiple life stresses predict adjustment in children of divorce, Kalter et al. (1989) concluded that boys might be more responsive to specific concrete events in their mothers' lives, while girls might focus on their mothers' feelings or internal experiences. Finally, gender differences emerged when data from many studies were reanalyzed. A meta-analysis of 92 studies (Amato & Keith, 1991) resulted in the findings that, in mother custody families, boys were less well-adjusted than girls, while in father custody families, girls were less well-adjusted than boys.

The question of preexisting conditions is raised in prospective studies, which report conflicting findings concerning gender differences. For example, three studies (Block, Block, & Gjerde, 1986; Cherlin, Furstenberg, Chase-Lansdale, Kiernan, Robins, Morrison, & Teitler, 1991; Neighbors, Forehand, & Armistead, 1992) reported that boys' academic and/or behavioral adjustment problems predated parental separation and that girls were less affected by predivorce stressors. However, in another prospective study (Shaw, Emery, & Tuer, 1993), boys and girls did not differ in predivorce adjustment problems, but boys had more adjustment problems than girls following divorce. Another prospective study included four marital status groups—divorced/nonremarried, divorced/remarried, always harmonious, disharmonious (Jenkins & Smith, 1993). Behavior change from predivorce to postdivorce status was assessed. There was a slight increase in the emotional and behavioral problems of boys in the divorced/nonremarried group. When averaged (pre- and postdivorce) scores were analyzed, boys were significantly more behaviorally disturbed than girls. Children's self-reports of emotional and behavioral disturbance were highest for boys in the divorced/nonremarried group.

Although there is a need to account for many other variables that may mediate children's adjustment following divorce, studies to date suggest that boys in maternal custody may do less well in their adjustment and in their relationships with their mothers than girls in maternal custody. However, girls may be less well adjusted than boys in father custody families and in stepfather families. Differences in adjustment between the sexes may diminish in adolescence and, in late adolescence and young adulthood, girls may experience more adjustment problems than boys.

INTERPARENTAL CONFLICT

Emery (1982) reviewed the literature on the effects of marital conflict on child adjustment and reported on research that indicated that poorer psychological adjustment was found in children in both intact and divorced families where levels of parent conflict are high. Children in high-conflict families have more behavioral, social, and emotional problems, including aggression, fears, and internalizing problems. Hetherington (1979) found that children in low-conflict divorced families were better adjusted than children in high-conflict intact families. A better adjustment to divorce in children was related to a low level of postdivorce conflict (Hetherington, Cox, & Cox, 1982; Wallerstein & Kelly, 1980). Children in Hetherington's (1989) maladaptive, aggressive-insecure cluster were from homes with high levels of conflict, negative affect, and poor conflict resolution styles that involved verbal or physical attacks, withdrawal rather than compromise, or assertion of power.

In a study of boys and girls in either mother, father, or joint custody (Walsh & Stolberg, 1989), interspousal hostility was significantly related to behavioral adjustment to divorce. Witnessing hostility between parents led to aggressive behavior in children for several years following divorce. Anxious, depressed, and withdrawn behavior began to appear in these children several years postdivorce. There was an inverse relationship between interparental hostility and parenting skills. Hostility apparently interferes with co-parenting ability.

In sole or joint custody families involved in chronic custody disputes for a period of one to four and a half years (Johnston, Kline, & Tschann, 1989), the children with more frequent access to both parents had more behavioral and emotional problems. Parents more often perceived these children to be depressed, withdrawn, and aggressive and to have more somatic symptoms. The researchers hypothesized that high parental conflict places the children in the middle of disputes and at risk of being used in those disputes. The more overt the parental conflict, the more disturbed the children are likely to be. The more frequent the contact with both parents in distressed families (i.e., families involved in ongoing custody and visitation disputes), the more disturbed the children were, even with low levels of parental aggression. A number of behaviors were clinically observed, including attempted alignment with one or both parents, attempted maintenance of complete fairness with each parent, conflicted loyalties, withdrawal from the dispute, a feeling of being important as the object of parental disputes but accompanied by a fear of rejection and a sense of burden created by the parents' requests for nurturance or support.

The researchers point out that a vicious cycle can be created in that the child's symptoms and disturbance can further fuel the custody battle. Older children with increased cognitive capacity became more involved in parental disputes and, therefore, more likely to suffer loyalty conflicts and to be asked by parents to take sides. If such an alignment occurs, the older child may refuse contact with the parent who is rejected.

Overall, girls did not do better than boys, but there were some sex-linked differences. Girls' more frequent access to both parents had a more negative effect on their emotional and behavioral adjustment. Boys' behavioral adjustment was not affected by frequent access, but they were more likely to be used and caught in the middle of parental disputes, and to suffer disruption to social competence and school performance. However, in another study (Kalter, Kloner, Schreier, & Okla, 1989), no support was found for the hypothesis that interparental hostility affects child adjustment and, consequently, child development.

In a sample of infants and toddlers (birth to 36 months) in maternal custody (Hodges, 1991), preseparation conflict between parents was linked to less regular visitation with the noncustodial father, and less regular visitation was related to developmental delays in language and gross motor skills. Children exposed to preseparation conflict were seen by their mothers as less dependent on their mothers and more tense with their fathers.

In order to deal with the complexities of the effects of interactional variables on children's divorce adjustment, more recent studies have employed multivariate techniques. Stolberg and Bush (1985) studied the direct and indirect effects of background factors (marital hostility, time since separation, number of children in the family, mother's education and employment status, child's age and sex), custodial parental divorce adjustment, and child-rearing environmental factors (single parenting skills, environmental life change events for the child, time spent with noncustodial fathers) on adaptive and maladaptive child adjustment. In a path analysis, it was found that marital hostility directly (i.e., unmediated by any of the other variables) predicted children's higher levels of internal and external psychopathology and their lower levels of social skills.

In another path analysis (Fauber, Forehand, Thomas, & Wierson, 1990), parental conflict indirectly affected children's adjustment to divorce through its disruptive effect on parenting skills. Three conflict-engendered disruptions in parenting behavior (lax parenting, psychologically controlling parenting, and parental withdrawal from or rejection of the child) were hypothesized to result from divorce and were found to mediate the relationship between parental conflict and children's divorce adjustment. Of the three, rejection/withdrawal was most consistently associated with child adjustment problems.

The simultaneous (path) analysis of factors relevant to children's behavioral problems and emotional adjustment following divorce (Tschann, Johnston, Kline, & Wallerstein, 1990) included both preseparation factors (parental conflict, child attributes affecting ability to handle stress, parent-child relationship) and postseparation factors (parental loss, parent-child relationship, social and environmental changes). One of the most important findings was the indirect effect of marital conflict through the mother-child relationship. That is, conflict before separation affected mothers' warmth and acceptance in their relationships with their children. Hypothesized reasons for this effect include changes in family roles that could discredit parental authority or result in children assuming parent roles or taking sides in loyalty conflicts. The divorce process can lead to diminished capacity in competent parenting skills. The ongoing conflict may result in parents modeling poor controls and problem-solving abilities. It was concluded that all of the consequences of conflict yield problematic parent-child relationships.

Other recent studies again relate divorce adjustment to interparental conflict. Borrine, Handal, Brown, and Searight (1991) found that adolescent adjustment was related to the adolescent's perceptions of family conflict. Lower levels of postdivorce conflict were associated with children's adaptive divorce adjustment (Brown, Eichenberger, Portes, & Christensen, 1991), while higher levels of interparental conflict were related to more problematic parent-child relationships (Forehand, Wierson, Thomas, Fauber, Armistead, Kempton, & Long, 1991). Among a variety of parenting practices evaluated in a prospective study of both divorced and intact families, parental conflict was the only variable that consistently predicted poorer adjustment in children across both time and gender (Shaw, Emery, & Tier, 1993).

In the meta-analysis of 92 studies (Amato & Keith, 1991), one of three major groupings of factors affecting children's divorce adjustment was the family conflict perspective. Strong support was found for the family conflict perspective in that children in high-conflict intact families did more poorly than those in low-conflict intact families and those in divorced families.

Interparental conflict seems to be an important variable deserving of further study. Its relationship to children's postdivorce psychological adjustment may be complex. Kelly (1988) suggests that parental conflict affects children's adjustment not only directly, but indirectly as well, through its influence on frequency of contact with noncustodial fathers, custodial mothers' adjustment, and custody determination and implementation. Additionally, Kressel (1988) concludes that little is known about the diversity of parental interactions (including conflict resolution style and problem-solving and communication skills) and the differential effects that these diverse interactional patterns may have on children's adjustment.

PARENT ADJUSTMENT

Although research on the effects of parent adjustment on children of divorce is very limited, some studies have shown a relationship between various measures of custodial-parental adjustment and their children's adjustment

(Guidubaldi & Perry, 1985; Kurdek & Berg, 1983) and academic achievement (Mednick, Baker, Reznick, & Hocevar, 1990). At a five-year follow-up, Wallerstein and Kelly (1980) found serious academic, social, and behavioral problems in children of psychologically disturbed custodial parents. Kalter et al. (1989) reported that their study provided clear empirical support for Wallerstein's and Kelly's earlier work, which had been based on clinical methods rather than on standardized measures. In testing six hypotheses to explain the effects of divorce on children's adjustment, strongest support was found for the parent adjustment hypothesis. It was suggested that well-adjusted custodial parents provide effective parenting, which facilitates healthy adjustment in their children and buffers them from the stresses of divorce. On the other hand, it is also possible that the significant relationship between mother and child adjustment is the result of children's adjustment problems creating adjustment problems in mothers.

In the Stolberg and Bush (1985) study described above (see Interparental Conflict), a path analysis was employed to assess the direct and indirect effects of background factors, childrearing environmental factors, and custodial parental divorce adjustment on adaptive and maladaptive child divorce adjustment. Mothers with more children self-reported better divorce adjustment, and more well-adjusted mothers had better parenting skills. In turn, better parenting skills were associated with better social skills, more prosocial activities, and less internal psychopathology in children.

Forehand, Thomas, Wierson, Brody, and Fauber (1990) hypothesized that divorce disrupts parenting ability or is associated with poor parent adjustment or both. This, in turn, results in poor adjustment in adolescent children of divorced parents. Cognitive and social competence were poorer and there were more internalizing and externalizing problems in adolescent children of divorced parents than in children from intact families. In a path analysis of the variables under study, marital status was indirectly related to adolescent functioning through parent functioning as well as parenting skills. Divorce was associated with poorer parent functioning and parenting skills which, in turn, were associated with poor adolescent functioning. However, marital status was also directly related to adolescent functioning, indicating that marital status by itself is worthy of consideration as a factor affecting children's divorce adjustment.

Another factor related to parent adjustment is the parent-child relationship. Kalter et al. (1989) point out that the well-adjusted custodial parent will effect "a developmentally facilitating parent-child relationship" (p. 617). They hypothesize that future research that accounts for this relationship will be more predictive of outcomes for children of divorce than currently employed divorce stressors such as conflict, father absence, or economic disadvantage. It is assumed that poor parent adjustment that may result from divorce will have a negative impact on parenting skills and on the parent-child relationship. Conversely, the parent who is well adjusted following divorce employs effective parenting skills and has a positive parent-child relationship. Based on these assumptions, all of the following studies focus on findings concerning parent-child relationships (including noncustodial parent-child relationships and visitation issues).

One such study more recently investigated the relationships among mother-daughter empathy, the quality of the parent-child relationship, and children's postdivorce behavioral functioning and emotional adjustment (Mutchler, Hunt, Koopman, & Mutchler, 1991). There was a significant positive relationship between custodial mothers' high levels of empathic understanding of their daughters and daughters' adaptive personal and social adjustment. Mother empathy was also associated with high quality of adjustment in the parent-child relationship.

Adolescents from divorced families who had good relationships with both parents did not differ in their functioning from adolescents in intact good relationship families, and functioned significantly better than did adolescents who had poor relationships with their divorced parents (Wierson, Forehand, & Fauber, 1989).

A prospective study assessed predivorce parenting practices and found that divorced parents had more problems with predivorce parenting than did nondivorced parents (Shaw, et al., 1993). These included less parental concern, and higher levels of parental stress and parental conflict, which have been associated in other studies with poorer parent-child relationships.

Parent-child relationships were discussed above in every section, mediating or explaining effects of divorce on children. Information about this complex subject can be found in discussions of overlapping issues such as father absence, relationships of mothers with their sons or daughters, relationships of fathers with their sons or daughters, relationships of stepfathers with their stepsons or stepdaughters, relationships of children with noncustodial parents, and remarriage. The following gives a sense of the complexities of this issue, although it is somewhat of an oversimplification of Hetherington's 1989 findings on parent-child relationships. Mother-son relationships for nonremarried mothers were problematic, while nonremarried mothers enjoyed satisfying relationships with their daughters, except in the case of early maturing girls. There were high conflict levels between remarried mothers and their daughters in the first two years after remarriage. Stepfather-stepdaughter relationships were problematic. Relationships between remarried mothers and their sons and between stepfathers and stepsons were problematic for the first two years, then were more improved than the relationships between stepfathers and their stepdaughters.

Wallerstein (1991), in a comprehensive review of research on the long-term effects of divorce on children, expressed surprise that "major upheavals" in the relationships between parents and their children resulted from the great changes in the marital relationship. "What is clear is that the multiple economic, social, and psychological life stresses of being a single or visiting or a remarried parent, together with the unanticipated psychic reverberations of the broken marriage contract, have combined to weaken the family in its child-rearing and child protective functions" (p. 359). Some of the more recent research described below has addressed the issue of the impact of multiple factors on parent-child relationships and children's divorce adjustment by means of multivariate analysis.

In a study described above (see Interparental Conflict), the mother-child relationship mediated the effect of marital conflict on children's behavioral and emotional adjustment to divorce (Tschann et al., 1990). Changing family roles following divorce might result in child assumption of parent roles, child loyalty conflicts, diminished parenting skills, and parental modeling of poor controls and poor problem-solving ability. The researcher concluded that all of these consequences of conflict can have a negative effect on the parent-child relationship.

Another study also found that parenting skills mediated the effect of parental conflict on children's divorce adjustment (Fauber et al., 1990). Conflict was associated with three maladaptive parenting behaviors—psychologically controlling parenting, parental withdrawal or rejection, and, to a much lesser extent, lax parenting.

The impact of parent-child relationships on children's divorce adjustment is indirectly apparent in a study of family functioning factors (Brown et al., 1991). Children were better able to adjust to divorce when custodial parents maintained family rituals, provided a sense of emotional security and support and when postdivorce parental conflict was minimal.

In a longitudinal study, the parent-adolescent relationship did not improve or deteriorate between the first and second year postdivorce (Forehand, Wierson, et al., 1991). Higher parental conflict levels were associated with problems in parent-adolescent relationships, and the parent-adolescent relationship was the best predictor of school functioning.

The following describes findings concerning noncustodial parent-child relationships and visitation. Kelly (1988) reviewed the literature relevant to long-term adjustment in children of divorce. She concluded that the relationship with noncustodial parents deteriorates as a result of decreased contact, while stable and frequent contact with the noncustodial parent is associated with better child adjustment, unless the noncustodial parent is poorly adjusted. However, frequent visitation with noncustodial parents was not related to positive divorce adjustment in one study (Kurke, Blisk, & Siesky, 1981). Hetherington et al. (1989) concluded that frequent visitation is advisable only if interparental conflict is low. Johnston et al. (1989; see

Interparental Conflict) found more behavioral and emotional problems in children with more frequent contact with both parents. The researchers hypothesized that high levels of interparental conflict accounted for these results. That is, the children are placed in the middle of or are at risk of being used in parental disputes. Healy, Malley, and Stewart (1990) found there are no simple answers concerning the positive or negative effects on children's adjustment of frequent contact with noncustodial fathers. Both age and gender influenced the effects of ongoing contact. Younger children, and especially boys, experienced enhanced self-esteem and more behavior problems with frequent contact, while girls and older children had lower self-esteem and fewer behavioral problems.

Forehand et al. (1990) investigated the interaction of paternal visitation and interparental conflict in order to determine its effect on children's divorce adjustment. Contrary to the conclusions of Hetherington et al. (1989) and Johnston et al. (1989), frequent paternal visitation in families where conflict was high enhanced adolescents' cognitive competence. That is, frequent visitation was a protective factor for these adolescents.

Among several paternal variables investigated (parental conflict, parental mood, visitation, father-adolescent relationships), only father-adolescent relationships predicted adolescent functioning (Thomas & Forehand, 1993). More positive father-adolescent relationships were associated with less internal psychopathology in the adolescents, while poorer father-adolescent relationships were associated with higher levels of external psychopathology in their adolescent children.

If parent adjustment or other factors impact on the parent-child relationship in the ways described above, these interactional effects would explain seemingly contradictory conclusions concerning frequent visitation with noncustodial parents. Parent adjustment and other factors may mediate the effects of frequent contact on the noncustodial parent-child relationship and, in turn, the effects of the noncustodial parent-child relationship on child adjustment.

In summary, there is some evidence that parent adjustment is related to children's adjustment following divorce. Parent adjustment may have an impact on children's postdivorce adjustment by affecting the parent-child relationship, which is very complex and can be affected by the many changes in family circumstances and family configurations associated with the ongoing divorce process. It may be that the well-adjusted parent fosters a healthy parent-child relationship that has protective value for the child facing the stresses of divorce, while a psychologically disturbed parent has a negative effect on the parent-child relationship, which in turn leads to maladjustment in the child.

CUSTODY DISPOSITIONS

The emergence of joint physical custody brought with it an initial enthusiasm for this arrangement as the solution for everyone, especially the decision-makers (i.e., the court). In 1982, Ilfeld, Ilfeld, and Alexander were finding the relitigation rate for joint custody was one-half that of sole custody families, and they concluded that joint custody was "most beneficial," relevant to reduced interparental conflict subsequent to divorce.

With the passage of time, enthusiasm has been tempered, and it is no longer clear that joint physical custody works for everyone. Some reviewers of the literature emphasize the inadequacies of joint custody research (Clingempeel & Reppucci, 1982) and raise doubts about the assumption that joint custody engenders cooperation between the divorced parents (Derdeyn & Scott, 1984). Others conclude that there is no single custody determination that is best for all children and that decisions should be made on a case-by-case basis (Schwartz, 1987). Some of the initial research, with conclusions favorable to joint custody, might have overlooked the heightened motivation and healthy adjustment of the parents who preferred and chose this option, and who participated in those early studies. However, this early work fails to account for court-ordered joint custody, where interparental conflict is high (Johnston, Kline, & Tschann, 1989). The degree of cooperation required of parents in the joint physical custody arrangement, not to mention the contact between parents, could create many problems for parents already in conflict.

The earliest studies on joint custody relied almost exclusively on interviews, lacked control groups, and employed small sample sizes. Four joint custody families were interviewed by Abarbanel (1979), who concluded that the joint custody arrangement was "at least as good an arrangement as any other" (p. 328). She found children were able to manage the shifting between homes and discrepancies between parents without loyalty conflicts, and that they were able to maintain strong attachments to both parents without the sense of loss characteristic of children of divorce in single-parent custody. Among 40 divorced fathers interviewed by Greif (1979), the fathers with joint custody were more involved in and had more influence on their children's development than fathers with sole maternal custody arrangements. Ahrons (1981) interviewed divorced parents and found those with joint custody to be satisfied with the arrangement, while noncustodial parents were less satisfied with their custody dispositions.

In 1981, Steinman employed "clinical, semi-structured interviews," and studied parents who chose joint custody and who actually shared time with their children in an approximately 50–50 arrangement. (Many studies do not closely control for actual amount of time the child spends with each parent.)

While Steinman found that parents were generally satisfied with the arrangement, children had some concerns: disrupted activities for older children, anxiety and confusion in preschoolers concerning shifting between residences, loyalty conflicts, and concerns about fairness to each parent.

Results of a combination of interviews and parent and teacher ratings of latency age boys in joint custody or sole maternal custody indicated that boys in joint custody had fewer behavioral problems than those in maternal custody (Schiller, 1986). It was concluded that while these results might indicate joint custody to be superior to sole custody, it was also possible that they were due to the strong parenting skills of these joint custody parents who had reared them from birth.

In a study involving multivariate analysis techniques and follow-ups at one and two years, Kline et al. (1989) found no evidence that joint physical custody was different from sole physical custody in terms of postdivorce child adjustment. Specifically, custody arrangements were not significantly related to children's behavioral-emotional and social adjustment. Factors that were associated with children's adjustment included age, gender, number of children in the family, parents' initial depression/anxiety, and parents' conflict at the one year follow-up. Boys and latency-age children were more vulnerable to behavioral and emotional problems regardless of the custody arrangement. Negative adjustment in children of divorce was unrelated to custody disposition, but was the result of the cumulative effect of family factors initially and postdivorce.

Pearson and Thoennes (1990) conducted a reanalysis of interview data from a large sample of joint and sole custody parents who had originally been interviewed in earlier studies. Joint custody was found to be a "favorable arrangement for parents who chose it and for their children" (p. 233).

An investigation involving children in families who were involved in ongoing custody and visitation disputes for an average of four and a half years (Johnston et al., 1989) found no evidence that either sole or joint custody is related to better adjustment in the children. However, joint custody was significantly related to access to parents, and children with more frequent access were found to be more emotionally and behaviorally disturbed. This study, discussed more fully above (see Interparental Conflict), has implications for court ordered joint custody where interparental conflict is high.

The same issues that were raised in the discussion of the effects of divorce on children's adjustment (see above, Effects of Divorce on Children) are relevant for the research on joint custody as well. A multivariate approach is needed in order to assess the cumulative effects of the many factors (i.e., characteristics of the child, interparental conflict, parent-child relationships, and other family variables and environmental factors) that play a role in the ongoing process of divorce. In a review of the literature on child adjustment following divorce, Sorensen and Goldman (1990) concluded that judges are moving toward consideration of these specific factors in custody decision-making.

RESILIENCE (FAVORABLE OUTCOMES)

The studies mentioned thus far have focused on the maladaptive behavior of children following divorce. The focus of interest for some researchers has been the resilience of children in the face of adversity (Garmezy & Rutter, 1983) and, more specifically, on favorable outcomes versus maladaptation in children of divorce (Gately & Schwebel, 1992).

A multivariate investigation (Stolberg, Camplair, Currier, & Wells, 1987) of the divorce adjustment of children resulted in two independent dimensions of divorce adjustment—maladaptation and enhanced functioning. Life-change events for children best predicted their maladjustment, while good single parenting skills and low levels of predivorce marital hostility determined children's enhanced functioning. Hetherington (1989) found that whether or not children suffer long-term maladjustment depended on the cumulative positive or negative effects of a variety of factors, including the child's individual characteristics such as temperament, family relationships, and extrafamilial factors such as school and peers.

Gately and Schwebel (1991) proposed the Challenge Model to account for all outcomes of divorce, positive, neutral, or negative. They suggested that valences of outcomes are determined by the nature of the challenge that a child faces and by moderating variables, including intrachild characteristics (gender, age, cognitive and social competence, temperament) and available coping resources, including family, environmental, and social-cultural factors.

Adolescents from divorced, mother-custody families had only slightly more behavior problems than did the normal, nonclinical standardization sample of the behavioral adjustment measure employed in a study conducted by Abelsohn and Saayman (1991). Additionally, they were better adjusted than the clinical standardization sample. The researchers concluded that divorce is not necessarily catastrophic, but is "within the realm of normative adaptation" (p. 189) for many adolescents.

As Gately and Schwebel (1992) observed, the research methods employed thus far are more likely to detect negative rather than positive outcomes. These methods include the use of measures that detect weaknesses; the use of clinical (more maladjusted) samples; the reliance on data from parents, teachers, and clinicians who all overestimate negative effects of divorce on children; and the failure to use the children themselves as sources of data. More research is needed to identify the nature of favorable outcomes and the sources of strength and protection for children who thrive in spite of parental divorce.

PREEXISTING CONDITIONS (PROSPECTIVE STUDIES)

Noting thz at earlier research had failed to account for preexisting conditions, researchers more recently have focused on what was true for children of divorce before the divorce occurred. In a longitudinal study (Block et al., 1986), the entire sample was initially made up of intact families. Data about children of divorce became available some time later when some of the previously intact families experienced divorce. Boys in the divorced families exhibited characteristics normally thought to be associated with divorce (aggression, uncontrolled impulses, and excessive energy) up to 11 years before parental separation. Predivorce stress factors in the family, including conflict and inaccessibility of parents, were cited as possible sources of the behavioral characteristics. Girls were less affected by the predivorce stressors than boys had been.

A more recent prospective study yielded results similar to those of Block et al. (1986). Neighbors, Forehand, and Armistead (1992) found that the academic functioning of boys from families who subsequently divorced was poorer than the academic functioning of girls whose families subsequently divorced and boys from intact families. There was a decline in the academic functioning of girls in divorcing families that began before the divorce and continued after the divorce. However, girls' postdivorce academic functioning remained higher than the academic functioning of boys in divorced families.

In an examination of intact family parents who subsequently divorced (Block, Block, & Gjerde, 1988), prospective and concurrent analyses were employed to study the relationship between marital status and parental functioning. As much as 11 years predivorce, tension between spouses existed and parents were unsupportive in the parenting of their children. Concurrent analysis findings were similar to those of many of the studies cited above. That is, mother-son relationships were troubled, while mother-daughter relationships were more positive.

Another prospective study assessed the effects of divorce on children's behavior and academic achievement by means of national longitudinal surveys in both the United States and Great Britain (Cherlin, Furstenberg, Chase-Lansdale, Kiernan, Robins, Morrison, & Teitler, 1991). The effects of divorce on boys' behavior and achievement was substantially reduced when predivorce levels of achievement and behavioral and family problems were taken into account. Effects of these problems were somewhat reduced for girls. It was concluded that "much of the effect of divorce on children can be predicted by conditions that existed well before the separation occurred" (p. 1388).

Data from the New York Longitudinal Study (Chess & Thomas, 1984;

Thomas & Chess, 1977; Thomas, Chess, & Birch, 1968) were employed to investigate the relationships among predivorce parenting practices, child adjustment, and marital status. The subjects included boys and girls who were anywhere from less than a year old to 22 years old at the time of parental separation. Contrary to the findings of Block et al. (1986) and Cherlin et al. (1991), boys did not differ from girls in level of predivorce behavior problems. However, boys had more behavior problems following divorce. Lending support to the results of Block et al. (1988) are the findings that divorced parents had more predivorce child care problems (less parental concern and higher levels of parental rejection, parental conflict, and economic stress) than non-divorced parents. These parenting problems were found more often with boys than with girls, with the exception of parental conflict, which predicted child adjustment consistently across gender and time. It was concluded that the behavior problems often found in boys following divorce are related to parenting problems that begin prior to divorce.

More recently, a prospective study investigated behavior change in children from predivorce (time 1) status to postdivorce (time 2) (Jenkins & Smith, 1993). The four marital groups under study included divorced, divorced/remarried, always harmonious, and always disharmonious. Compared with children from always harmonious and always disharmonious families, children whose parents divorced did not increase significantly in behavioral disturbance following the divorce. When mothers' behavior ratings of their children for time 1 and time 2 were averaged, there were significantly more behavioral problems for children in disharmonious families and those in divorced/nonremarried families than for those in harmonious families. Boys were significantly more behaviorally disturbed than girls. These differences in results obtained for change scores versus average scores were attributed to higher levels of disturbance present at time 1 in children from divorced or disharmonious families than in those from harmonious families.

Based on child reports of emotional and behavioral problems at time 2 only, children in divorced/nonremarried families and in disharmonious families had the highest levels of disturbance of the marital status groups, with boys in divorced families at the highest levels of disturbance. Researchers concluded that results support the findings of Block et al. (1986), that behavioral disturbance exists in children prior to parents' divorce, and the findings of prior research demonstrating higher levels of behavioral disturbance in boys in disharmonious families than in girls.

As limited as the research is on the effects of divorce on children, almost nothing is known about children's predivorce adjustment and its relationship to postdivorce adjustment. Prospective studies are also needed on familial factors affecting children's predivorce adjustment, including interparental conflict, parental adjustment, and parent-child relationships.

METHODOLOGICAL AND CONCEPTUAL ISSUES

A number of methodological problems make it difficult to interpret the research on the effects of divorce on children's adjustment. Definitions of variables are a problem. For example, father absence studies often do not differentiate between conditions of father absence due to divorce, death, desertion, or imprisonment. When the effects of father absence were studied in conjunction with reason for father absence (death versus divorce), boys from divorced homes were found to engage in more aggressive play than boys from widowed homes (Santrock, 1977). This suggests that more specific definitions might yield results that have been obscured by more global definitions.

Many studies do not differentiate between children's differing age levels, and some lump together a wide span of ages, as though divorce affects children similarly, regardless of age. Very little work has been done on developmental differences and their impact on adjustment. It is often assumed that adjustment and predictors operate in the same fashion at different developmental levels. The same is true for sex differences. That is, some studies combine data for boys and girls and fail to take into account what has emerged as a very significant variable, gender differences in response to divorce. Studies of gender differences should account for differences in the socialization process of the sexes (i.e., different coping strategies and behavioral responses to stressors for boys versus girls).

Some factors, such as parent adjustment and socioeconomic status, are not well documented or controlled. In a recent study of poor, inner-city children, negative divorce-related events and one belief about divorce (fear of abandonment) were significantly related to both parents' and children's reports of child adjustment problems (Wolchik, Ramirez, Sandler, Fisher, Organista, & Brown, 1993). The children's reports of their adjustment problems, negative divorce-related events, and beliefs about divorce replicated findings of earlier studies employing white, middle-class children. On the other hand, the relationships found between both parent and child reports of child adjustment and negative events and beliefs about divorce had not been found in earlier research.

Most samples, consisting mainly of middle-class, white subjects, are not representative of the divorce population at large. McKenry and Fine (1993) recently investigated differences in black and white custodial mothers' single parenting experience following divorce. Although there were no racial differences in parent involvement with children or authoritarian parenting behavior, black mothers had higher expectations than white mothers regarding children's control of their tempers, independence, and compliance with parental requests. There were no differences in black or white mothers' satisfaction with the role of custodial single parent. However, black mothers perceived children's well-being more positively than did white mothers. Therefore, there may be important racial differences, although similarities in the parenting experiences of these black and white mothers outnumbered the differences.

Frequently, sample size is small. Often, no control groups or comparisons are employed. Since maternal custody has been the most prevalent arrangement, most studies have employed the maternal custody arrangement and many of them have involved the effects of divorce only on boys.

The measures employed in these studies are often of questionable reliability or validity. Emery (1982) points out the inadequacy of measures of marital and child problems and contends that the difficulties concerning these measures become more serious when correlations among several measures of different reliabilities are compared. Zaslow (1989) suggests that currently used outcome measures may not be appropriate for measuring girls' responses to divorce and that "an apparent sex difference in children's response to divorce, with boys manifesting more negative effects, may be an artifact of the particular outcome measures selected for consideration" (p. 121). Emery (1982) notes problems with nonindependent data in which the same raters rate both the child and the marriage or the raters of child behavior are aware of the status of the marriage. An expectation that divorce causes behavior problems in children may influence the ratings of child behavior by parents, teachers or mental health professionals who have knowledge of the marital status.

There is a need for more prospective and longitudinal studies, since most of the previous work has involved cross-section designs and retrospective techniques. One of the most serious criticisms is that the use of cross section designs and univariate or bivariate techniques leads to an oversimplification of the interpretation of children's responses to what are the cumulative, interactional, and dynamic stresses created by divorce. Multivariate analyses have only very recently come into more widespread use in research on the effects of divorce on children. There is a need for more use of multivariate approaches that account for the interactions among social, intraindividual, and intrafamilial factors over time. Studies have focused on intrafamilial factors and have overlooked how these factors can interact with intraindividual factors such as coping style, temperament, and developmental level. A multivariate approach would provide a means of addressing the ways in which children in the same family can be differentially affected by divorce (Monahan, Buchanan, Maccoby, & Dornbusch, 1993).

Kurdek (1988) explored current conceptual and methodological practices and made some conceptual recommendations for future research. For example, he suggests looking at family processes related to adjustment rather than family structure (e.g., single parent versus intact two parent) since even families with the same family structure can differ in many ways (e.g., parent conflict, parent adjustment, etc.). He suggests a continuum approach in which families are defined by processes that facilitate adjustment regardless of their family structure. In this regard, Wood and Lewis (1990) found, in a regression analysis, that family status (divorced versus intact) was not a significant predictor of problem school behavior in second, third, and fourth grade children. Rather, quality and frequency of coparental interaction better predicted children's school behavior than did their parents' marital status. Emery (1988) reflected on the research and also concluded that it is not divorce but family processes (e.g., parental conflict, parent adjustment, parent-child relationships, etc.) that begin before separation and continue after divorce that best predict children's adjustment.

Further conceptual refinement of intraindividual factors might provide some fresh perspectives. For example, a recent study sought to explain the differential effects of divorce on children by assessing factors that can differentially facilitate children's adaptation to negative divorce events (Mazur, Wolchik, & Sandler, 1992). Hypothesizing that a child's responses to stress are influenced by the child's interpretation of an event, the authors based their work on two related areas of research. According to Beck's (1967, 1976) model of depression, depressed people make negative cognitive errors, exaggerating the significance of negative life events by overgeneralizing, personalizing, catastrophizing, and selective abstraction. Another research approach has focused on the distortion of reality in mentally healthy people who are unrealistically optimistic. Their distortions, or positive illusions, include enhanced self-esteem, the exaggerated belief of personal control over outcomes, and more optimism about the future than is likely.

In the Mazur et al. study, children's higher levels of negative cognitive errors were significantly related to higher levels of self-reported adjustment problems and to their mothers' reports of child behavior problems. Children's higher levels of positive illusions were significantly related to their self-reported lower levels of aggression and anxiety. Negative cognitive errors and positive illusions accounted for children's adjustment outcomes, even beyond that which was explained by actual divorce events in the children's lives.

Some other conceptual issues include accounting for favorable outcomes and the factors that differentiate between children's positive and negative adjustment following divorce. As Gately and Schwebel (1992) have pointed out, "(T)he way science has addressed the questions of children's outcomes" (p. 62) has limited the identification of favorable outcomes. That is, the content of the literature to date has been shaped in part by the fact that pathological and stress models guided the research to search for unfavorable outcomes. Secondly, the research methods most often employed are likely to detect negative rather than positive outcomes (e.g., measures that identify weaknesses and the use of clinical samples). Additionally, prospective studies that determine preexisting conditions (i.e., predivorce) can further shape the way that research questions might be asked and advance our understanding of children's divorce adjustment.

Overall, the challenge for the custody evaluator is to use data from the research literature to accomplish two tasks. One is to match the research findings with existing legal criteria set forth to guide custody decision-making, e.g., the standards in the UMDA. We are directed to consider all "relevant factors" including (1) the wishes of the parents; (2) the wishes of the child; (3) the child's vital interrelationships with all significant others; (4) the child's adjustment in home, school, and community; and (5) the mental and physical health of all critical persons.

The second challenge is to fine tune the research data into forms that can be used in individual cases, i.e., forms that transcend the rather global markers yielded by the research data one would have to depend on to make meaningful custody assignments, such as age, sex, number of children, etc.

Our aspiration was and is to supplement the usual postdivorce research data by creating tests and tools that more directly reflect the legal criteria set forth in the UMDA.

The PORT, BPS, PASS, and PPCP represent our way of operationalizing especially the issues referred to in items (2) and (3) above, the "real" desires of a child, and the nature of a child's vital interrelationships with other critical figures, especially with each parent. These tools also address, although in a more limited way, items (4) and (5), adjustment factors of both the parents and the child.

Chapter Three

Congruent Communications: The Vital Roles of Symbol Systems and Information-Processing Strategies

WHAT ARE SPECIAL TARGETS FOR THE CUSTODY EVALUATOR?

This chapter details why we believe an approach to custody decision-making that aims to determine the *effects of a particular parent's behavior on a given child* makes more sense than one that concentrates directly on "parental behavior," an entity we claim does not in fact exist until impacting a child's organism.

In describing what our teams gradually came to see as the two variables that most usefully describe why a particular parent turns out to be helpful (or hurtful) to a given child as compared to another parent, we will demonstrate how interviews, conventional tests, even most observations, are only partially helpful in measuring such variables.

Symbol systems and information processing strategies are offered as concepts highly useful to both the practicing as well as the theoretical evaluator. To the former they can act as orienting principles in evaluating obtained observations and to the latter as variables to guide research on the construct validity of tests useful to a custody evaluator.

Consider the following scenarios. In each case, assume that what is related is an important part of the information you have, and your job is to come to a conclusion as to which piece of parental behavior, the mother's or the father's, is, as is frequently said, "in the child's best interests."

In other words, as you read through these scenarios, imagine that you are performing a custody evaluation and have had an opportunity to do a home visit at each parent's home, where you have observed the following scenes. The assignment is to consider how you would use the information offered to make a judgment as to which parent is doing the better job for the child in each situation.

An 11-year old boy approaches his father and asks how the air conditioner works. The father responds as follows: "There are three parts of the air conditioner you should know about. There is a compressor outside and its job is to cool down the air. In the basement of our house, there is what is called an air-handling unit. Its job is to pump the air throughout the house. In the living room there is a thermostat. It has two jobs. One of its jobs is to tell the compressor what in fact the temperature of the living room happens to be. The other job is to send a message to the compressor, and that message is to tell the compressor what the person setting the thermostat wants the temperature to be. In general, an air conditioner can do about 15 degrees better than what the outside temperature is at that moment."

Had this child approached the mother with the same question, she might have gently taken him by the hand, and led him over to the thermostat in the living room. She would say: "Here's 'on' and here's 'off.'"

If you were grading the performance of each of these parents, how would you grade the father's response? Would you give him an 'A'? Or maybe a 'B' or 'C' or even 'D'? Is his response too technical or pedantic? How about the more condensed response of the mother? How would you rate this?

Consider the following scene. A nine-year-old boy approaches his father and asks for help with his math homework. The father responds as follows: "Damn it! Can't you ever do anything on your own!? Come here, give me that!" Following this, the father sits the child down and proceeds to give him very clear and detailed help with his math homework, explaining the broader concepts as he does so.

Had the same child approached his mother, she might respond as follows: "I have total faith in you, honey. I know that when you put your mind to things you do them very, very well. I know that if you give yourself a chance to think about that homework a little bit longer on your own, you'll come up with very, very good answers."

Which response is in the child's "best interests"? Which one is truly likely to be more helpful to this child?

We will return to these examples later.

INTERVIEWS, OBSERVATIONS, AND TRADITIONAL TESTS

I performed my first custody evaluation around 1959 while on the faculty of the Jefferson Medical College of Philadelphia. In those days I worked closely with Dr. Zygmunt A. Piotrowski, by occupation a world-famous expert in projective techniques, by avocation and interest an expert in the history of ideas, art, and architecture. We coauthored a book, which involved the original research in developing the scoring scheme for the *Hand Test* (Bricklin, Piotrowski, & Wagner, 1962), and several articles on prognosis in schizophrenia. I also studied—much more briefly—with Dr. Emanuel Hammer, whose vast and amazing personal collection of projective drawings does not gather anywhere near the attention and merit it deserves. I also had the opportunity to share an office and have lengthy conversations with Dr. Robert Waelder (who among other things introduced me to Anna Freud); Dr. Waelder, a psychoanalyst, was also interested in the history of ideas in general, and the history of scientific ideas and methodologies in particular. He began his career in the study of physics. He was a co-editor, with Sigmund Freud, of the very first psychoanalytic journal.

Hence, I was well grounded in the theories, practices and research bases of the psychological world. At the same time, I began cooperative work with Michael Halbert, one of the early experts in Operations Research, which entailed understanding how to ask the world research questions that lead to useful and meaningful answers.

In spite of having instant, relaxed, and prolonged access to all of this talent—in days when medical colleges had plenty of money and there was lots of time to sit around discussing science and philosophy and one's research projects—it was no easy matter, even with the assistance of these distinguished persons, to tease useful information out of the existing clinical tools, the so-called traditional psychological tests along with interviews and observations, for custody decision-making.

These difficulties launched a series of research endeavors (the main thrust of which is described in Chapter Five on the development of the *Perception-of-Relationships Test* or PORT). Three main facts emerged almost simultaneously from these research endeavors.

Pitfalls of the Interview

One fact was that we could not depend upon interview data to yield accurate information, especially when the interviewees were engaged in disputes. Parents caught up in custody battles fail to realize that much of what their children tell them is what they, the children, believe the parents want to hear. And this is usually that the other parent is indeed a scoundrel. Such parents, believing they are hearing "facts," become even more entrenched in their negative positions.

There are other pitfalls to be wary of with the interview. Sadly, many parents simply lie when supposedly reporting facts. Far too many mental health professionals believe they are experts in the detection of lying. I wrote my very first book on the inside of a maximum security prison, gathering data for the original scoring scheme of the *Hand Test* (Bricklin et al., 1962). One of the most shocking things in my young life was how "normal" and "ordinary" the inmates of this prison could be in given contexts. Murderers, thieves, and rapists, when queried about their lives, could put on oh-so-sincere faces and proceed to lie through their teeth. They appeared relaxed, friendly, and intimate. The impression was conveyed that it was wonderful to have finally found someone, some trustworthy psychotherapist, to whom the whole "truth" could finally be told. In the most sincere and convincing ways they would then give completely false accounts of their lives.

Ekman and O'Sullivan (1992) documented this same finding: Neither mental health professionals nor forensically trained psychiatrists nor courtroom judges (among others) were very good at detecting lying through watching and listening to people speak.

Another serious flaw with the use of the interview has to do with its iatrogenic properties. As mentioned, the interview is what co-creates the "negative incident model," a parent's belief that the way to prevail in a custody dispute is to amass a huge number of negative incidents about the other parent.

Now I am certainly aware that one cannot conduct a comprehensive custody evaluation without using interviews. No participant would follow any proffered plan if he or she did not feel thoroughly "listened to." I am also aware that clinical judgements based on variations of the interview can be quite sophisticated. (See the important article by Shedler, Mayman, and Manis, 1993, which details how that much maligned entity, "clinical judgement," may have far more to offer than is realized in some circles.)

So we deal with a matter of proportional emphasis. The emphasis in the interview must be *away from* anything that highlights each participant's list of horror stories, and *toward* a search for parenting skills.

Pitfalls of Observations

The second fact to emerge from our research endeavors was that observations, whether conducted in the home or the professional's office, were equally tainted as sources of information.

The difficulties with observation as a clinical tool can be approached from two perspectives. The first is common sense; the second follows from an important piece of research by McDermott and his colleagues in 1978.

From a commonsense perspective, it is important to remember that parents do not behave typically either in mental health professionals' offices or in their own homes when they are being visited by the professional. I can recall a mental health professional offering what she took to be important testimony on a father whom she had evaluated as part of a custody evaluation. She described how his five-year-old child had fallen down and scraped his knee in her parking lot. She said in court: "The father ministered to this boy in the most tender and caring way." She went on to base many of her conclusions on this observation.

I wondered if she really believed she could take at face value this piece of the father's behavior as representative of what he would have done if he were not being observed. I do not think one has to be a genius to realize that parents are not going to behave typically in situations where they know they are being observed.

Some mental health professionals think they can get around this dilemma by instructing their secretaries to observe parents in the waiting rooms and out in parking lots. In addition to being a dubious move legally— a secretary is not trained to make clinical observations—I submit that parents know there is a very strong probability they are being observed when they are anywhere near a mental health professional's office and would exhibit restraint that may not at all be characteristic of their behavior patterns when not being observed.

Some mental health professionals would answer this by saying that they do not observe naive things such as a parent "tenderly ministering to a child," but rather sophisticated psychological things like "bonding patterns."

In reality, in the absence of multiperson observations and recordings of standard situations with one-way mirrors, it is quite difficult to recognize a "bonding pattern." I have seen children in whom it was proven that there had been physical and sexual abuse cling lovingly to the fathers who had perpetrated these abuses. Children have many reasons to cling lovingly to parents— even parents who have seriously mistreated them. For one thing, there is at work the very powerful process of denial. These children cannot tolerate the fact that they have been treated in this manner and will often act in ways that simply deny what happened. There is also at work here the fervent wish on the part of the children that things be returned to normal.

Secondly, abused adults, as well as most children, assume a known port in a storm is superior to an unknown one. Further, they often internalize a victim-role. When children visit an evaluator's office, even an evaluator they have seen many times, they will still feel threatened and challenged, knowing that many important decisions hang in the balance. They have the sense that they might be separated from a parent on whom they have depended. Children know they are called upon to act as though things are okay when this is really not the case. Further, even or especially in sex abuse cases, they know that their reactions could very well cause a depended-upon parent to go to jail. In such instances, they may know that they not only could lose a parent, itself intolerable, but also food and rent money.

One cannot assume that because a child clings "lovingly" to a parent or sits "lovingly" on a parent's lap it is safe to come to any conclusion as to the real relationship between this child and parent in other contexts. I had occasion to observe a father with a five-year-old child in my waiting room. She sat in a seemingly relaxed fashion on his lap, hugged him, and looked at him with what looked like love in her eyes. Over the previous months, this father had repeatedly tied the child down and repeatedly pushed his finger into her anus, and otherwise beat and terrorized her.

I have spent 35 years working with patients in clinical settings; I doubt there was anything anyone could have observed in this waiting room situation that would have given any idea of the magnitude of horrors that had occurred between this father and child.

This is not to say that observation has no value. To my way of thinking, observation, to be useful, must take place within a very controlled setting where mental health professionals have opportunities to document the actual interaction patterns that take place between given people. This might include the number of times the child approaches the parent to ask for help, to ask for support, to request other kinds of aid, etc. Of importance, is the fact that *there must be choices available to the child in these situations; if there is only one parent present with the child, no reliable or valid conclusions should be drawn about the observed interaction patterns and especially whether or not they would be similar in other contexts.*

It might be argued that this (each parent "alone" with the child) is what we are trying to predict. That is, the child will no longer be interacting with both parents simultaneously after the parents are divorced. So why not observe the very thing we are trying to predict—the child alone with each parent?

This is a true, but misleading argument. First of all, we are trying, with our evaluations, to predict how the child will fare in *many* contexts: in school, with friends, relatives, significant others, etc., while in the care of each parent separately.

Second, and more to the point, seeing the child with each parent alone simply brings into the picture the operation of too many confounding variables, e.g., a child usually will make the best out of whatever choice is available. The child knows what he or she is doing is a "performance" and will "perform" with whoever is present; the process of denial and the above mentioned abuse-scenarios could be in operation. In fact, when a child is nasty or withdrawn in the presence of a given parent, he or she has probably been programmed to fear this parent or is punishing the parent, usually for some trivial and momentary reason.

I am not saying the "child alone with each parent" scenario should not be used for observational purposes. I am saying the evaluator should be aware he or she might have gotten very different results by using a scenario in which more choices were open to the involved child. Note, however, that in the midst of a custody evaluation even when *both* parents are present with a child, the child will often cooperate more with the parent he or she most fears.

The difficulties with observations have also been documented in an important piece of research by McDermott and his colleagues (1978) who sent trained investigators to observe children in their homes. All of the following obstacles were encountered: The expert's presence induced overly tolerant and overly considerate behavior; the up-and-down variabilities in children's behavior patterns were difficult to interpret; it was almost always impossible to verify reports of abuse; it was difficult to discover a child's "real preference" since young children could not express their feelings and older children were bribed or consciously confused by loyalty conflicts; reports from parents were frequently in conflict or inconclusive in important aspects, as was information from relatives, doctors, neighbors, and schools; there was great difficulty in evaluating parental sincerity, emotional stability, and general parenting ability; it was impossible to ascertain the effects certain environmental conditions would have on specific children at specific times in their development; it was impossible to tell if certain parents were exposing a child to unwholesome situations (e.g., drug abuse, prostitution, etc.); there was doubt about the ability of a parent to help a child with a specific, perhaps serious, problem; it was difficult to assess the long-term effects of religious fervor on the part of a parent. Hence these investigators were not very impressed with the validity of so-called "home visit observations."

McDermott and his colleagues went on to fashion an assessment tool of their own creation; interested readers should consult their article for more information on this tool.

Pitfalls of Testing

The third fact to emerge from our initial research endeavors was that we could find no consistent relationships between critical sequences of parental behaviors and the impacts of these behaviors on a given child. While there is ample proof that parental pathology impacts children negatively (Guidubaldi

& Perry, 1985; Kalter, Kloner, Schreier, & Okla, 1989; Kline, Tschann, Johnston, & Wallerstein, 1989; West & Farrington, 1973) it is usually difficult to use such information in an individual case. This issue is particularly complex in situations where an evaluation is needed, since it is frequently the case here that the parents seem evenly matched in "pathology." This is, of course, a global observation, since there is no universally accepted way to compare "pathologies" in any event. The difficulty of assessing the meaning-to-a-child of parental pathology seemed to us true not only for the standard classifications of psychopathology, e.g., anxiety, depressive moods, obsessive compulsive patterns, but also for other types of parental behaviors usually considered critical in child rearing, such as yelling.

Rigid strictness, for example, could be devastating for a free-spirit child who thrives on an ability to robustly explore his or her environment. On the other hand, for boundary-impaired or otherwise out-of-control children, this kind of rigidity could be highly useful.

Depressive moods in a parent could cause devastating effects in one child, while in other cases we found that children of depressed parents appeared somehow motivated by the parental depressions to pull back from the relationships and discover and develop enormous resources internally.

Long, detailed explanations were experienced as nurturant by some children, while others took this as a sign that they could not be trusted to come to their own conclusions.

Simply put, there are few parental behavior patterns that can be assumed to have universally good or universally bad effects on given children. Children have wildly different needs and filter systems. A child who has a strong need for a certain type of parental behavior may find it possible to filter out the "package" in which this desired commodity is offered.

We began to see that an emphasis on testing parents, although yielding a fair amount of data, left us with no clear way to make sense of what all the resulting information meant in terms of a particular child. (A comprehensive look at the uses and misuses of psychological testing in custody evaluations is presented in an important article by Brodzinsky, 1993.) Further, while traditional test data *may* predict judges' decisions, they cannot identify unique parental assets for specific children.

The more we became involved with the research that led to the *Perception-of-Relationships Test* or PORT (Bricklin, 1962, 1989), which involved the careful observation of parent-child interactions under controlled circumstances, the more it became clear to us what it was we needed to find a way to measure. This research (see Chapter Five) involved prolonged one-way mirror observation of parents interacting with their children. A substantial number of variables were tracked and recorded as a child was given various tasks, puzzles and tests to solve, and allowed to "use" one or both parents for help. These included which parent was approached for help, whom the child spontaneously moved closer to, smiled at, listened to more attentively, seemed to understand more clearly, etc. We also eventually administered our tests to children on whom copious family therapy notes were available.

The variables our research teams concluded we needed to know about—let's call them for now those variables that determine the congruence with which a parent communicates with a child so that the child is able to take in and profit from these communications—were only indirectly and inconsistently related to standard measures of parent (or child) psychopathology.

Each parent has a way of deciding when and how and in what amounts to offer information, a way of deciding how questions and answers are to be phrased, of demonstrating competency skills (implicitly and explicitly), of when and how love or sympathy or empathy are to be offered, of deciding when and how to practice and demand consistency, of modeling admirable traits, etc. All such communications are offered in ways in which not only direct verbalizations may or may not be involved, but also subtle facial expressions, tones of voice, body postures, and so forth. And all of these variables interact with a child's totally unique set of needs, coping styles, and filtering systems.

We observed also the very important point that parental skills are highly contextualized. This is an exceedingly important notion for the custody evaluator to grasp, because it may be that a given parent can be, for example, exceedingly patient with young children, while demonstrating much the opposite when dealing with older and possibly more aggressive children. A parent who remains very calm and collected when giving information about homework may be a whining, irritable, demanding person when offering information about dating. What this means is that the fact that the custody evaluator discovers what he or she may think of as a good "trait" in one parent does not guarantee that this behavioral disposition, the trait, will be available to this parent in all situations and contexts.

MARITAL COMMUNICATION

While the research on custody decision-making was proceeding, I was also involved in a long-term investigation on the differences between effective and ineffective marital communication (Bricklin & Gottlieb, 1961). It was becoming obvious that the same variables that resulted in effective marital communication were those operating in effective parent-child communication (although I did not, in those days, use the terminology employed currently; more information is offered in Chapter Thirteen on this topic.)

These variables can be conveniently clustered in two categories. One category I call "symbol systems." A symbol system refers to the manner in which an individual assigns meaning to his or her world. This is a concept well known even to elementary students of psychology, that "meanings" are highly personal and idiosyncratic, but I doubt that many realize the full complexity and importance of this concept in custody evaluations.

The second category involves information processing variables. Our particular focus is on the congruence between how a communicator offers information and how the receiver takes in and uses this information. Simply put, many parents (as well as many spouses) offer information *in ways that are either highly likely or highly unlikely to be taken in and usefully assimilated and employed by the receiver of these communications. Further, when there are marked disparities in how one individual offers information and how the other takes in and utilizes information, prolonged contact between these people will create enormous irritability in both.*

SYMBOL SYSTEMS

An individual's symbol systems refers to how he or she assigns meaning to another person's behavior. This would include words spoken and simple actions (which would involve facial expressions and tone of voice), as well as complex actions and entire sequences of behavior. We use the word "symbol" because an individual typically looks at these different stimulus elements in his or her life and assigns meaning to them; in countless instances these meanings have very little to do with what the person who is doing the communicating thinks he or she is getting across. As we will see presently, matters can become very complex in this area. We use the word "systems" to refer to the fact that people assign symbolic value or meaning to other people's behaviors, and their collective systems of symbols determine a good bit of the psychological worlds in which they come to live.

Symbol systems may be quite simple. For example, if you are talking to someone and not looking at this person while you are talking, he or she will very likely assign the following meaning to this behavior: "This person does not care about what I am saying." In other words, eye contact is pretty much taken as a universal symbol of "paying attention." The truth is that a person may look away from a speaker for a variety of reasons, some psychological and others having to do with the way the brain processes information. It may be that the person who is looking away is paying very definite attention to a speaker's words, but the greatest likelihood is that the speaker will assume the looking-away behavior "means" a lack of attention.

Symbol systems can also be quite complex and may even involve the sensory system with which a person chooses to communicate. I remember a time that I mildly yelled at a co-worker for being tardy in returning a patient's phone call. I could see that she was deeply upset that the big cheese had yelled at her. I immediately began reassuring her in words: "You know how much confidence I have in you and how much I value your work. You know how much I like you and care about you as a person, and so on."

I could see from her facial expression I was getting nowhere. I delivered a small hug. I could feel her relax. This had the meaning to her that I *meant* what I was saying. What it also told me is that very likely, when interacting within her family of origin, she distrusted auditory information (words) and placed much more confidence in kinesthetic information, e.g., a hug. In other words, when a person would deliver a message to her kinesthetically, she assigned it a much higher probability of being true than if the same message were delivered via words.

The truth is that no selected sensory system is inherently more "accurate" than any other. As a matter of fact, if someone were trying to convince me of something and hugged me in order to make the point, I would probably say, "Yecch, get away from me. Stop that slimy stuff and explain your point." This would mean that I distrust kinesthetic information and assign a much higher accuracy potential to auditory information.

Symbol systems can be exceedingly unpredictable. I remember one very sad case where a surgeon was telling me that his wife was emotionally cold toward him. I had watched them interact, and this was not the impression I had of this woman toward him. I asked him to give me an example of what he meant. He responded as follows: "I recently performed a procedure that did not go well. The patient did not die, but I was very upset. My wife couldn't have cared less."

At this point, I said to this man, a man for whom I myself had sincere affection: "If I wanted to show you that I really cared about you and was concerned about how you felt, tell me exactly what I should say or do so that you would believe this is what I felt, genuine care and concern."

He said: "Well, that's obvious. If you wanted to show you cared, you'd ask me technical questions about the procedure."

This, as they say, blew my mind. He actually was asking me to show care and affection by asking him questions such as what kind of scalpel did you use, what kind of sutures did you use, and what actually went on in the procedure.

Here is a personal example. Our family has a long musical tradition. My wife's grandfather worked with John Philip Sousa; her mother was a well-known opera contralto. Both she and I have sung in operas. The Beatles crossed us over to the world of rock and roll. Two of our children went on to enter the field of popular music. This culminated in a band that was able to sign with a major record label, write sound tracks for several movies, and go on tour with big name bands. In the early part of their careers, I managed their band, and I often toured with them. My love for music manifested itself in a great deal of attention to this area.

At some point, my two daughters approached me and collectively said: "It's so obvious that you love the boys more than us."

At first I thought they were joking. I asked what they meant. The answer was: "You tour with the boys, you talk about nothing but music, you pay very little attention to what we do."

There was much truth to these charges *behaviorally*. I thought everyone in the family was fascinated not only with music, but with the whole *field* of music—touring, playing nightclubs, etc. I had taken the girls out with the band countless times. It had never dawned on me what symbolic message my activities had had for them.

Since I knew in my heart how much I love them, I still thought they were joking. I answered: "The truth is I hate all of you; I just happen to like music. If it wasn't for that, I wouldn't talk to any of you."

But I could see that they were not joking at this point. I knew they knew I loved them, and vice versa. But I developed a fairly hopeless feeling inside and was rather saddened and shocked to know that they could not know the "truth." I realized there is no way I could demonstrate the feeling I have inside myself as proof of my love. You cannot open your chest cavity and say: "Look at this; can't you see all that love in there!" For this is what most people mean when they speak of what they "mean": some subjective inner sensation that is experienced and to which they assign a verbal label. But, of course, the object of the feeling experiences only what the feeling person actually does, and even *that* is totally through the filter of some symbol system that could hardly be articulated.

Knowing about symbol systems, I realized it would be pointless to have an argument about how much "love" I had. I felt fairly certain, going by subjective feelings and the willingness with which I would have made sacrifices, that I loved them all equally. However, honoring my knowledge of symbol systems, I had to ask them: "If I loved you more, what would I be doing?"

They responded in a way that, in retrospect, I realized was quite logical: Talk about things other than music, talk about things that they are specifically interested in, and involve myself more in things that are important in their lives. I tried my best to do this; I do not to this day know how successful I have been, but at least I attempt to honor the requests.

The moral of the story is this: if a parent does not operate within a child's symbol systems, it really does not matter one bit what "the truth" happens to be or what a parent "feels."

INFORMATION-PROCESSING STRATEGIES

Through information-processing strategies, our various research teams refer to the manner in which an individual organizes and offers, and takes in and ultimately utilizes information. This concept makes no hard and fast assumptions about the roles of genetic, structural, physiochemical, or neonatal factors in determining the manner in which a person's responses are to be understood.

The parent attuned to the importance of these factors would know or intuit whether or not, for a given child, it's important to: get to main points quickly; assume the child can plan meaningful sequences of actions independently; pause to let the child speak first, prior to offering any important information; honor the time of day, nature of preceding behaviors, degree of "crankiness," and subsequent challenges facing the child before deciding to speak; regulate the pace of speech; allow or not allow interruptions; allow or not allow eye wandering.

The parent who was born with, or has acquired, these skills: watches a child carefully as he or she speaks, bases what is said on what the child has just said (or done), stops offering information if the child talks or is distracted. The "super" good parent in these regards also encourages independence by offering information only when the child has verbally (or nonverbally) asked for help. It is *always* a good sign if a parent with more than one child reacts differently (albeit positively) to all of them, since that suggests a sensitivity to critical differences among the children.

Note well that parents whose behaviors reflect the operation of these skills can *not* typically articulate them consciously or formally. The disposition to respond with this degree of sensitivity is acquired unconsciously. In the very best parents, the acquisition of these skills comes from information gleaned via interactions with a given child. In other cases, it stems from how that parent just happens "naturally" to communicate, i.e., there is a "lucky" congruence between a given parent's range of styles and a particular child's ability to profit from these styles.

We have two points to make here: (1) the quality of parent-child relationships is far more affected by misalignments in variables such as these than is commonly realized, (2) difficulties are greatly exacerbated when one or both (e.g., the parent *and* the child) suffer organizational difficulties. Based on data gathered when collecting information for a book, *Bright Child-Poor Grades: The Psychology of Underachievement* (Bricklin & Bricklin, 1967), the number of children suffering such deficits is probably between 30 and 40 percent of a general population. When a parent with either organizational problems similar to his or her own child, or an inflexible style, interacts with a child with such problems, there is the potential for enormous conflict. The conflict is hard to resolve because the problem is *not* with the "content" of whatever is being argued or debated, but in the very style with which the latter is addressed by each. Thus, increased communication, by itself, rarely helps such disputants. It usually makes things worse. The more people with widely different information processing strategies "discuss" or "argue" about things, the worse matters get.

(It is interesting to note what happens to adults with organizational deficits. They are often diagnosed as "procrastinators," "disorganized," "lazy," and, in many instances, "borderline.")

Because a parent's ability to operate within a given child's symbol systems and information-processing strategies resides at an *unconscious level* in the better parents, the decision was made not to attempt to measure such parental knowledge directly. That is, even though certain of our tools in fact assess a parent's awareness of various aspects of parent-child communication interactions, our main approach has been to measure them "in action" via the manner in which a child is able to profit from parental actions.

CRITICAL CONCEPTUAL TARGETS: MEASUREMENT APPROACHES

The differential sensitivity—originating mainly at less conscious levels—with which a parent is able: (1) to respond to a child in terms of that child's unique way of symbolizing his or her world, and (2) to structure offered information in ways that take into account how a given child best *profits from* information, (and to have the skills to optimally comprehend how a child offers information) provides a useful way to understand much of what our teams have come to think of as "good" or "effective" parenting. All communication interchanges can be addressed via these two variables.

While these critical parental sensitivities (to a child's symbol systems and ways of using information) certainly interact with other variables (e.g., parental anxiety, etc.) in codetermining what will emerge in actual behavior at some particular time, the observations and data collected in forging the custody evaluation instruments described later indicate the consistent superiority of those parents who demonstrate heightened levels of these skills. Further, when there *are* other factors in operation (e.g., parental anxiety or depression), these factors tend to affect children negatively not only by the children's conscious or unconscious perception of such factors directly, but *in the degree to which these forces distract the parent from being an attentive communicator.* The more anxious and/or depressed a parent, the more distracted this parent will be. The more distracted a parent, the less likely is this parent to have the kind of "attuned sensitivity" required to become consciously or unconsciously aware of a child's symbol systems and ways of processing information. In other words, factors such as warmth, on the positive side, or tension and irritability, on the negative side, are important in large part to the degree that they facilitate or impede a parent's attunement to a child's symbol system structures or information-processing strategies.

Because parental sensitivity to symbol system and information-processing variables interact with other personality factors in real-life situations, and because custody evaluators will rarely get hidden or "disguised" opportunities in which they can observe these skills in relative isolation, our data-based tools sample them in highly specific real-life situations as well as in more global ways. Others sample them more directly. Another way of saying this is that an inspection of the items in our tools will not reveal what we believe to be the important variables underlying congruent parent-child interactions, i.e., the parent's ability to respond to a child in terms of that child's symbol systems and information-processing strategies.

To give the flavor of the variables to which we wish to draw attention, let us spell out how a parent especially adept at putting the described sensitivities into action actually functioned in a research setting.

The parents, Molly and Jim, were in their thirties. Both were professionally employed. They interacted with each of their two children separately, first with son John, eight years of age, and later with daughter Mary, six years of age. As will be described later, the children in the PORT study were presented with a series of puzzles, games, and tasks to "solve." No specific instructions were given about the roles of the parents. The family groups were essentially left alone in a room, although the parents did know they were being observed from behind a one-way mirror so the observing "mental health professionals" could learn some things about "how children interact with their parents."

If one were to summarize what happened, Molly, the mother, offered information quite differently to each of her two children. Jim's communication patterns were similar with each child. Interestingly, when questioned later, neither Molly nor Jim displayed any conscious awareness of how or what each was personally doing, other than that each was "trying to help." Especially interesting is the fact that Molly had no conscious awareness that her patterns were quite different toward each child.

The different patterns of each parent are best seen in the contrast between these patterns. Jim, whether offering information to his son or daughter, typically initiated all exchanges (i.e., spoke before waiting to see what help was requested or indeed even wanted), tended to offer rather invariant amounts (rather lengthy) of information to both children regardless of how stuck each seemed at the moment, and always explained why what he was offering was relevant (i.e., attempted to give background information with all proffered strategies).

Molly's pattern with daughter Mary was similar to Jim's, but contained many elements of her way of responding to son John. It was in connection to John that her pattern was quite different—different from her own patterns with Mary and different from Jim's style with John. In relation to John, she almost always waited until he asked for help before saying much of anything; gave small amounts of information whenever she in fact did speak; always waited for further questions before adding supporting details; always got quickly to the main point of her information when she did speak, offering no background information unless requested; never explained in advance why a given strategy was being offered.

Further, with both children, Molly's facial and body muscles were relaxed and in "neutral gear" just about all of the time. Jim showed visible signs of tension (and would jump in with help) whenever one of the children seemed even mildly perplexed or stuck on a given task.

It is interesting to note that Molly was the parent-of-choice (POC) for both children on both a very early version of the BPS and the PORT. However, that is not the point to which we wish to draw your attention at this moment. Here our intention is to illustrate by means of a case in which the patterns were rather clear-cut what we mean by a parent who is unconsciously attuned to the unique and different manner in which each of her children can take in and profitably use information. It was our team's unanimous understanding that at some intuitive level Molly saw daughter Mary as having a wide and flexible range of patterns in which she could receive and use information. Without realizing it, she utilized quite a different style with John, being aware at some level that his utilization patterns were very different from Mary's.

This is a good point to mention that our teams do not believe that the factors of which we speak in this chapter, symbol systems and information-processing strategies, are important in all interchanges. It may even be the case that in 90 percent of the interactions a given parent has with a given child, these patterns are not critical. After all, sometimes the interactions between a parent and a child are brief and to the point, as in "Mom, can I go out to play," to which Mom would reply either yes or no.

Even if there are only 10 percent of situations in which these factors are critical, our belief is that when they are critical they are exceedingly critical.

These concepts, symbol systems, and information-processing strategies are also highly useful in making operational sense of the notion of a child's "special needs." For this is what things will all boil down to in any event. Whether a child is diagnosed as suffering an "attention deficit disorder" or is labelled "delinquent" or "impulse ridden" or whatever, when all is said and done, the critical question will involve the effectiveness with which each parent can take into account a particular child's idiosyncratic ways of dealing with information.

In this same sense, these concepts operationally address the need to understand a child's "developmental status" (Bray, 1991). Picture a funnel in its typical upright position. Regardless of the developmental forces entering at the top, the critical output feature can be usefully described in terms of how these forces will affect a given child's way of taking in and using information, and the manner in which meaning is assigned to his or her world. Whether one is seeking to understand how a divorce situation will affect a child or how commodiously a particular parent will interact with this child, developmental factors will be important to the degree that they impact on this child's way of using and symbolizing information. Stated from the reverse perspective, it is to the degree that an evaluator remembers to think about these variables that he or she is likely to consider relevant developmental information.

Let us now return to the parent-child interaction examples offered at the beginning of this chapter, and review a few of them in light of an appreciation for symbol systems and information-processing strategies. As we attempt to show that one of each of the responses is a better response—for a particular child!—than the other, we are certainly *not* claiming that a single interaction of the type detailed would be critical in a child's development. We do wish to suggest, however, that *a steady accumulation of experiences of these kinds can be ultimately very hurtful or very helpful for a given child.*

In reviewing these examples, note that we could use each to illustrate several different of the critical points we wish to illustrate rather than only a few. It is best at this point to opt for the latter, simply for the sake of clarity.

Let us first review the example of the father's response to the 11-year-old who asks how the air conditioner works. (I must admit that this is an example from my own life, and illustrates how I would typically *always* answer such a question—until I got to appreciate the differences among my various children—at which time I would answer each very differently.)

"There are three parts of the air conditioner you should know about. There is a compressor outside and its job is to cool down the air. In the basement of our house, there is what is called an air-handling unit. Its job is to pump the air throughout the house. In the living room there is a thermostat. It has two jobs. One of its jobs is to tell the compressor what in fact the temperature of the living room happens to be. The other job is to send a message to the compressor, and that message is to tell the compressor what the person setting the thermostat wants the temperature to be. In general, an air conditioner can do about 15 degrees better than what the outside temperature is at that moment."

My wife's response to this question would typically be to take whichever child asked the question over to the thermostat in the living room, point to it, and say: "Here's on, and here's off.'"

We can use this example to illustrate some of the most important issues of which we speak. And we will see that some have to do with information-processing variables, and some with symbol system variables.

An exceedingly important information-processing variable is the amount of information offered at any given time. We will see in this example, as in those to follow, that it is relatively impossible to know which of the two responses would be better without knowing something about the child's way of assigning meaning to the world and the child's way of taking in, organizing, and using information.

If, in fact, I had offered that air conditioning response to my son, Scott, who happens to have a good capacity to take in rather substantial amounts of information, a person who could magically read his mind and heart following this interchange would find that Scott finds this kind of response helpful, nurturant, and interesting. Scott has an instantly arousable sense of curiosity; he can become quickly fascinated with how something works; the more information he is offered, the more secure he feels. Giving him a good bit of information—and here we begin to deal with symbol system variables—means to him that the speaker finds him worthwhile to care about and worthwhile to take the time to enhance his sense of security.

However, our other children are definitely what we would call need-to-know people, especially a particular daughter. She prefers to be given information in very small doses. She will then greatly expand on this initial base by the asking of questions. She learns best on a need-to-know basis. My wife's response, the "Here's on and here's off" one, would definitely be the better response for this daughter. Note that the need-to-know child typically responds to small pieces of information with a series of questions, each one emerging after the prior information has been digested.

There is absolutely no difference in intelligence between these children, just in the manner in which they best receive and use information.

Note, also, that for the latter child, the giving of great amounts of information at any time seems to mean to her that she is not trusted to come to conclusions on her own. Whenever she is given even mildly long explanations, her response invariably is: "Don't you trust me to be able to figure anything out on my own!?"

One can see from this example that any given parent-child interaction can be assessed in terms of both categories: the parent's appreciation both for how a child best uses information *and* for how a child will assign "meaning" (i.e., react "emotionally") to the interchange.

Let us move on to the next example. A nine-year-old boy approaches his father and asks for help with math homework. The father responds as follows: "Damn it! Can't you ever do anything on your own!? Come here, give me that!" Following this, the father sits the child down and offers clear and detailed help with the math homework, explaining the broader concepts as he does so.

Had the child approached his mother she would respond as follows: "I have total faith in you, Honey. I know that when you put your mind to things you do them very, very well. I know that if you give yourself a chance to think about that homework a little bit longer on your own, you'll come up with very, very good answers."

When we offer these choices at our lectures and workshops to mental health professionals, members of the audience invariably vote in a nine-to-one ratio in favor of the latter being a better response than the former. In the majority of cases, the mother's response probably would be optimal. The symbolic meaning of the father's behavior would be so negative and devastating to most children, that most children would hardly hear the detailed and clear advice offered.

However, it has been our experience in working, over a span of many years, with children who are learning-disabled in all degrees of severity, very mild through moderate to severe, and with their regular and extended families, that these children, who actually comprise a huge number of the total child population, would in many instances do better with the father's response. Some children so desperately need clear and structured information that they develop very effective filtering systems in their quest to find it. They either develop highly adequate strategies to separate the important *pre-organized* information they so urgently require, from the "emotional packages" in which this information is given them, or else typically find the trade-off (useful information in return for some emotional bruises) an adequate trade-off in favor of the pre-organized information.

Keep in mind that these different parental behavioral dispositions have wildly different utilities for involved children. What constitutes an adequate trade-off for one child may be an atrociously inadequate trade-off for another. At some deep unconscious level, there is certainly a priority of needs for a given individual; these vary quite a bit more than people are likely to realize. In our tests and observations, it was quite clear that children with rather substantial information processing deficits did exceedingly poorly with open-ended or vague or unstructured people. Their inner worlds become easily disorganized, which not only leads to a fragmented feeling within but to fragmented external behavior, which is usually responded to by others in highly negative ways.

Hence, in the example above, the symbolic meaning—which would probably be negative for just about anyone—that may come to the child by virtue of the father's yelling is more than compensated for by what accrues to this child by virtue of the structured and clearly detailed information. One might say that in return for the few emotional bruises the child gets from Dad, he or she is lessening the bruises that will accrue in the course of daily life (i.e., lessening the amount of negative feedback he or she gets from peers and teachers).

SUMMARY

From scenarios such as these, it became clear to the members of our various research teams that interviews, unstructured observations, and traditional tests were limited in their potential to generate data useful to a custody evaluation.

Information about how parents behave, though important (enormously so when a law has been broken, e.g., abuse), could never tell the custody evaluator the most relevant thing he or she needs to know, the *usefulness* of parental behavior for a given child.

Two concepts, symbol systems and information-processing strategies, emerged as exceedingly helpful to describe the congruence (or lack thereof) of an effective and nurturant parent-child communication interchange.

As you read about some of the tests and tools that have been developed, keep these concepts in the back of your mind even though they are not explicitly utilized in the scoring schemes.

Chapter Four

Bricklin Perceptual Scales (BPS): Child-Perception-of-Parents Series

CUSTODY DECISION-MAKING: VITAL TEST PROPERTIES

Putting together what was learned from our ongoing research projects (described briefly in Chapter Three) in developing the Perception-of-Relationships Test, it became clear that for a test to be maximally useful in custody decision making, certain guidelines would have to be followed in its development.

1. The test would, in the main, have to be based on a child's nonverbal perceptions, rather than on parental behavior, not only because parents possibly engaged in adversarial procedures are very likely to misrepresent themselves, but also because parental behavior can best be understood in terms of its meaning and utility to a particular child.

2. The test, although reflective of a child's complex observations, thoughts, and feelings, would ideally be capable of helping to suggest a one-person POC (parent-of-choice) out of a two-person field, often where such determinations are close, as in choosing a POC in situations where the par-

ents are pretty evenly matched, since this is exactly what judges have to do all the time. However, equal emphasis would be placed on identifying areas of unique usefulness that a given parent may have for a child. (We use the term, parent-of-choice or POC, to refer to a child's *choice* as determined by a single tool, e.g., the BPS. The term, primary-caretaking-parent (PCP), refers to the *role* of the primary caretaking, or custodial parent, even in situations where joint *legal* custody may prevail.)

3. We wanted the BPS to allow each parent to be rated in each area covered by the test. Hence, instead of forcing a child to give a response predicated on the following type of assessment, "In situation A I would prefer Dad over Mom," we wanted to afford the child an opportunity to express, "In situation A Dad would do 'this' well and Mom 'that' well."

4. The test would have to avoid asking the child direct questions, because this approach is exceedingly vulnerable to bribing and coaching. As we will see, the BPS discourages coached responses by the manner in which similar items for the mother and father are separated, and by the absence of any possible guidelines for the child to use to remember where prior responses were made. Later, further steps will be detailed for dealing with children who are consciously championing a certain parent. (This is easier for the child to do with the BPS than with the PORT.)

5. The test would have to avoid asking the child to make a direct choice between his or her parents (to be primary caretaker) so as to avoid or at least lessen guilt. Asking children, even children 14 or 15 years of age, with whom they would prefer to live not only can induce terrible guilt but also elicits unreliable information. Koppitz (1968, p. 128) remarks: "Even a deprived and abused child will rarely if ever denounce or accuse his parents...." I would take this a step further and say that in our experience when a child does denounce a parent, in almost all instances he or she has been coached, often explicitly, or else the child has some other covert agenda. Children will, of course, list complaints e.g., "She makes me go to bed too early," but will rarely do more than this kind of mild complaining, especially to the strangers with whom they perforce are asked to share their feelings in custody disputes. Chapter Thirteen considers in more detail the issue of directly asking children about a preferred custody arrangement. Some professionals believe this practice of asking children has some positive benefits, allowing the children a feeling of participation and control over their lives.

6. The test would have to reflect those vital child care areas in which there is a significant discrepancy in how a child views and responds to each parent.

7. Only tests are really adept at measuring children's deep perceptions, because such perceptions are essentially private. A parent's work history, financial stability, recreation patterns, etc., are, so to speak, in the public do-

main, where judges and other decision-makers at least potentially have access to them. Not so the child's deep-set attitudes and perceptions—perhaps the most important data to be considered.

8. The test would have to be based primarily on unconscious rather than conscious responses, since conscious decisions are not only more prone to bribery, coaching, and guilt, but—more important, to my way of thinking—are also inadequate to handle the job of making custody decisions. The amount of data that must be considered and somehow assimilated often overwhelms the conscious apparatus. So, too, would the welter of guilt, confusion, divided loyalties, appreciation for parental weaknesses, etc. Further, young children lack a vocabulary sufficiently differentiated to express what is going on in their deep-set feelings. This is not to say that a conscious choice cannot represent unconscious considerations, but rather that it is more useful to get the child's "answer" from the horse's mouth, the deep inner "gut," whenever possible.

This would be a good point to spell out why both the BPS and PORT rely essentially on nonverbal responses. Nonverbal responses are more closely aligned with, and reflective of, unconscious mental sources than with conscious sources. They can reasonably be thought of as "whole-organism" or "gut-level" responses. This is not to say that such responses cannot be overridden or "dominated" by more conscious responses. In fact, as we will detail later, this is something about which the evaluator must be alert.

In the sense intended here, the unconscious is seen as our inner computer, that part of us that collects the thousands of interactions we have with others, "weights" them according to our own special and unique value systems, and yields what we all experience as gut-level dispositions. These dispositions are the result of some unique process that takes place outside of awareness and is obviously the result of countless interactions filtered and weighted by our own unique personalities. Such unconscious attitudes are perhaps more accurately called action tendencies, because they define how we are more likely to act in certain situations, but not necessarily what we would consciously or verbally say about these same situations.

We realize that such conceptualizations are simplifications. No response is derived in full from either conscious or unconscious sources. So when we refer to an unconscious response, we refer to a response that in greatest part is mediated by processes outside of regular awareness.

Nonverbal responses are much more reflective of a child's actual interactions with a parent than what he or she has been told about that particular parent.

Further, the verbal apparatus is simply inadequate to express a child's feelings about his or her parents. In fact, children use very few words to describe their parents. You will rarely encounter words other than "great," "good," and "not so good." Children hardly ever use really negative words about their parents spontaneously—even abused children.

While both the BPS and the PORT (see the following chapter) rely on nonverbal responses, the PORT would be the test-of-choice where it is suspected that a child is running all or most of his or her responses from a non-spontaneous, conscious level.

Keep in mind that with both the BPS and PORT it is assumed that the child has had sufficient contact with each parent to have formed a conception of that parent based on *actual interactions* with the parent (not on hearsay information). This issue is covered in the manuals of the two tests. A "standard" custody arrangement (e.g., spending at least every other weekend with the noncustodial parent plus some vacation time) is more than enough contact to yield measurement information in accord with our research-based clinical and life history data. However, this is not a hard-and-fast rule. Much less contact, a few days every three to four weeks, seems to suffice.

AN OVERVIEW OF THE BPS

The test consists of 64 questions, 32 of which pertain to the child's perceptions of mother and 32 to perceptions of father. The child responds to each item twice. After a verbal response is recorded, the child responds nonverbally to a continuum line that ranges from Very Well through Not So Well.

Each parent is assessed in the same 32 areas. A parent-of-choice (POC) is declared in terms of which parent, the mother or father, gains the most items. It is assumed that this parent is the parent better able to operate in the child's "best interests" in the widest variety of situations as measured by the BPS.

An item that measures a child's perception of Mom's competence is: "If you were having a problem with a school subject, how well would Mom do at helping you to understand and deal with what it is that's troubling you?" The Dad question, which is positioned in the sequence of items to be maximally separated from its Mom counterpart, is worded essentially the same. (The wording can be changed for younger children, as long as the *same wording* is used on both the Mom and Dad card for the same item.)

An item that measures perception of supportiveness is: "How well does Dad do at making you feel really loved?" Another is: "When you feel real angry, how well does Dad do at helping you calm down?"

An example of perception of follow-up consistency is: "If you tried to stay up real late, way past your regular bedtime, how often would Mom make sure you got to bed at your regular bedtime?"

An item that measures possession of admirable traits is: "If you had a pet, how well would Dad do at taking care of it if you had to go away for a few days?"

Next, with the card in front of the child, the question for that card is read aloud in a slightly different phrasing: "If this (pointing to end of line marked 'Very Well') is Dad doing very well at helping you to calm down, and this (pointing to end marked 'Not So Well') is Dad doing not so well at helping you to calm down, where on this line would Dad be?"

The child uses a stylus to punch his or her responses on the card.

A scoring grid, printed on the reverse side of the card, is later utilized for automatic scoring. The questions are also printed on this side of the card.

The items are sequenced to insure maximum separation of types of content and of similar mother and father items. The same 32 questions are asked in relation to both parents, so the test essentially allows the child to respond to each parent in 32 key circumstances.

The wording used to ask the questions was chosen very deliberately and should in most instances be followed precisely.

THE BPS GROUPINGS: COMPETENCY, SUPPORTIVENESS, CONSISTENCY, AND POSSESSION OF ADMIRABLE TRAITS

The groups themselves, and the frequency of items in each, were chosen to approximate the proportionate degree to which each is mentioned in attempts to define "in the best interests of the child." The BPS Manual has an extended discussion of attempts to define this concept, as does *Solomon's Sword* by Schutz et al. (1989). Chapter Nine gives further information on our understanding of the areas that should be targets in a comprehensive custody evaluation.

It should be understood at the outset that the test does not measure a parent's actual competency, or even, in all instances, the child's perception of parental competency. Although some items directly ask about this, the degree to which a child perceives a parent to be competent, it is more accurate to think of the BPS as revealing how a child wants to be presented with, or taught, or have modeled for him or her, the skills of competency. This same line of reasoning applies to the other areas assessed as well, for example, to any so-called "special needs" on the part of a child. If a child has a problem with his or her school work, the custody evaluator might be particularly interested in identifying the parent better able to help the child in school-related areas of deficiency. But one must heed what was said above; the custody evaluator is not necessarily looking for his or her own notion of the parent better able to address these issues, but *should be* looking for that parent whose style is congruent with the child's ability to take in and profit from parental information. In other words, the BPS is designed not to show who is truly (whatever that would mean) the more competent parent in this area, but the parent who has greater utility for the child in the involved area. Of course, ideally, these two aspects could be identical, i.e., the parent who possesses the more school-related information of the two parents might also be the parent whose communication style is most optimal for the child.

BPS DATA AND THE SELECTION OF A PRIMARY-CARETAKING-PARENT (PCP)

The BPS yields two types of scores, an Item Score and a Point Score. An Item Score refers to the number of items gained by each mate. An Item Difference Score refers to the difference between items gained by Mom and those by Dad. The BPS POC (POC, remember, means parent-of-choice, and is used in reference to the indication from a single device, e.g., the BPS) is the parent who gains the most items overall (out of a total of 32). Additionally, Item Difference Scores can be computed for the four separate areas of perception measured by the BPS: competence (11 items), supportiveness (11 items), follow-up consistency (3 items), and admirable traits (7 items).

The parent who garners the higher scores on the greater number of items is declared the parent-of-choice (POC), the premise being that it is this parent's range of styles that is best adapted to the involved child's needs in a wide variety of situations.

The BPS and PORT have been validated in several ways (see their manuals). I have always considered their high agreement rates in suggesting PCPs with choices arrived at by mental health professionals with access to two to seven years of independently generated clinical and family history data on each family (a 90 percent agreement rate) to be the most important.

Chapter Five

The Perception-of-Relationships Test (PORT)

AN OVERVIEW OF THE PORT

The Perception-of-Relationships Test (PORT) illuminates areas of psychological functioning particularly useful to the custody evaluator.

The drawing placements of the various PORT figures reflect the degree to which a child seeks psychological "closeness" (interactions) with each parent in varying situations.

The differential adequacies with which the figures are drawn in various contexts suggest the types of action tendencies—dispositions to behave in certain ways, e.g., assertively, passively, aggressively, fearfully, etc., adaptive as well as maladaptive—the child has had to develop to permit or accommodate interaction with each parent.

Hence, the PORT is particularly helpful in custody decision-making because it sheds light on the degree to which a child actually *seeks* interaction with a given parent, and reflects the degree to which he or she has been able to work out a comfortable, conflict-free style of relating to each parent.

Like its companion test, the BPS, the PORT is a data-based projective test where the data base has been developed specifically to assist informed custody decision-making. The majority of children in the data base were four years and older. Special instructions are given for children between the ages of three years, two months and four years. I have used several PORT tasks with children as young as two years of age.

If the examiner's purpose is to determine which of a child's parents would be the better primary caretaking parent (PCP), the one who garners the greatest number of the child's PORT "choices" might be given consideration. The data base in terms of which this suggestion can be tendered appears in the test's manual. However, more information than this can be obtained from the PORT.

One of the very useful properties of the PORT is its ability to illuminate which aspects of a child's response originate in the main from unconscious sources, and which from conscious sources. This information can help identify when a child's stated preferences are not based on actual interactions the child has had with a given parent. In such instances, it is possible that the child's stated preferences are, in fact, based on what the child has been explicitly or implicitly told about the parent. This scenario, which I call the NBOAI (not-based-on-actual-interaction) scenario, will be covered in greater detail later, since the so-called "parent alienation syndrome" is a subset of such NBOAI and NBOAI-like situations, and must be recognized as such. Whatever may be the situation in which a child is surrounded by pressuring or "alienating" parents, torn by loyalty conflicts, etc., our data indicate that this child's unconsciously determined responses will still be mainly reflective of what that child's actual interactions with a given parent have been like, i.e., are very resistant to manipulation. It is the PORT's ability to tap into these responses that gives it special utility in custody decision-making.

A DRAWING-BASED PROJECTIVE TEST

The PORT is a projective test based essentially on human figure drawings and their placements. Although its main use in custody decision-making stems from its data base, there are several general interpretive principles (which pertain to drawings) that expand its clinical usefulness.

For one thing, the action tendencies portrayed in drawings are "close" to motor expression (since that essentially is what they are, motor expressions). Human drawings are highly predictive of what people will show in their overt behaviors.

Second, action tendencies revealed in drawings are *self*-action tendencies (Piotrowski, 1950; Hammer & Piotrowski, 1953). For example, if a boy pictures his father in a very aggressive mode, it *may* mean that he sees his father as aggressive, but it *certainly* means that he, the child, has aggressive tendencies and that these are accessed in relation to his father. Stated another way, when a boy draws his dad, he in some way is drawing his "perception" of his father, but more fundamentally he is drawing himself *as he psychologically exists in relation to his father.*

Our clinical and statistical data argue that whatever it is that is accessed when a child is asked to draw a parent, the motor response, the actual drawing, portrays the autoplastic adjustments the child has had to make to insure a continuance of that relationship.

Clinical and research data that suggest the contexts illuminated by the PORT may be described as follows.

The scoring scheme for Task I—drawing each parent—reflects the autoplastic adjustments the child has had to make to accommodate interactions with each parent. The scheme illuminates the degree to which these behavioral dispositions, dispositions which will be carried forth in life, are positive or negative. (Autoplastic adjustments refer to self or inner adjustments. Alloplastic adjustments refer to things external to the self. A negative autoplastic adjustment, for example, would be where the child cannot say what is on his or her mind, fearing it would upset, or make angry, the parent with whom an interaction is taking place.)

Task II—drawing a self-representation on the same sheet as a drawing of Mom, and then of Dad—creates a context (psychologically, i.e., internally, *or* actually) of the child alone with each parent.

Task III does the same as Task II in regard to the child being in the simultaneous presence of both parents.

Task IV—drawing the entire family—taps into a "symbolic" or idealized family configuration.

Task V, the family doing something, taps into notions the child has of the family as a dynamic entity, and often will reflect the child's ideas of wished-for aspects of the self in relation to the expressed figures (and secondarily, wished-for dispositions of the portrayed figures). Responses to this task are best divided into structural elements, e.g., is the family doing something together, which reflect what the child sees the family capable of attaining as a dynamic, single entity, and content elements, e.g., the self-figure playing ball with Dad, which often reflect wished-for elements.

Task VI, picturing the house and two stables, for children 6 years of age and up, taps into more conscious layers of the child's personality.

Task VII, which pictures a little dog dreaming about Mom, and then Dad, accesses a child's conscious and unconscious (possibly idealized) wishes in relation to each parent.

Hence, when the clinician/evaluator interprets PORT indications of both the adequacies or skills a child is acquiring by virtue of interactions with each parent, and the "closeness" sought with each parent, these dispositions should always be thought of as existing in relation to certain contexts. Another way of saying this is that rare indeed is the parent whose psychological utility to a given child is "good" across the board. Strengths will be found in certain contexts and not in others. Both the BPS and the PORT can identify many of these contexts. (Each of these contexts represents some family subsystem.)

THE DETECTION OF PHYSICAL AND SEXUAL ABUSE WITH THE PORT

The PORT shows promise of being a helpful tool in the detection of the physical and sexual abuse of children by their parents. This promise stems from the PORT's sensitivity to the dynamics of parent-child relationships.

Some have argued that drawings cannot validly detect sexual abuse. This is misleading. What is true is that psychological tests cannot detect abuse directly; what they *can* detect are the *psychological consequences* of abuse.

Unfortunately, especially from a legal perspective, the nature of the psychological consequences created in a child by some external event is not necessarily related to the manner in which *society views* this external event.

The law is often *not* interested in whether or not sexual abuse creates psychological consequences; it is more often interested in whether or not abuse has taken place.

My experience is that some instances of sexual activity between parents and children do not create measurable psychological sequelae in some children, at least with existing scoring schemes.

I realize this is a highly complex (and emotionally charged) issue. It may be that negative sequelae will show up only after several years, or that the manifestations of such activity could be subtle indeed, perhaps in reduced interpersonal possibilities or in impaired psychophysiological function.

But it *is* demonstrable that "trauma" is, so to speak, in the eyes of the beholder. Further, many activities society might label "abuse" can be presented to a child as "just a game."

Hence, it is doubtful that current psychological tests or, more accurately, their scoring schemes, can be used to *rule out* the possibility of sexual abuse. They can be used, however, to detect the psychological sequelae of abuse. (However, one would *never* claim this directly or in a report, as will be noted in Chapter Thirteen.) And they can be used to measure the *impact* of the abuse in some meaningful ways.

A variety of techniques are now used to detect abuse: interviews, videotaped interviews (hopefully, to reduce the role of leading questions), interviews combined with anatomically correct dolls, children's descriptions and utilized vocabularies to describe alleged events, statement validity analysis and criterion based content analyses, and projective tests. The PORT comprises a useful addition to this list.

This last point, having to do with the disguised purposes of the PORT, is very important. For the PORT (or more particularly, its scoring system) in no way suggests to the child what the examiner is specifically interested in measuring. And as so many custody experts today realize, allegations of sexual abuse are more and more used as a threat that a mother can direct against a father (or vice versa) to prevail in custody battles.

We need all the tools possible that do not influence a child to give responses about sexual abuse that he or she believes the examiner is looking for.

It is exceedingly easy to get a young child to "say" or "reveal" what he or she thinks is being sought. One can get a child to change his or her answer to a test or an interview by simply saying, "What did you say?" Many a child interprets a mere request for clarification as a criticism and will change the proffered response.

There is no easy way to develop a test data base for the detection of sexual abuse, since few persons accused of it will admit to having done it. Even where there is *some* physical evidence, guilt is not always certain. Only in the wake of conclusive physical evidence and/or *meaningful* confession can one be certain it has taken place.

In all instances to date where we had an opportunity to examine children where abuse was claimed and reasonably substantiated, there were indications on the PORT that could be seen as such. However, we have no accurate idea at all of the number of false-negatives in our samples. (Out of more than several hundred cases, we were fairly certain that sexual abuse had occurred in sixty.)

Here is a summary of some of the ways in which sexual and/or physical abuse show up on the PORT. Most are illustrated in the PORT manual.

1. Wavy lines or severe breaks in a line show up on self- *or parent*-representations in the involved body area (hips, genital area, thighs, breasts).

2. A dramatic increase may be seen in the distance between the self-figure and (abusing) parent-representation (compared to self placement and the other parent representation) on PORT II or, sometimes, III. This may also happen on PORT IV or V, but the phenomenon is harder to notice here, since the intervening spaces can be filled with other people or objects.

3. Abused children often show evidence of abuse by manifesting a severe slanting (more than 45 degrees) in either self- or (abusing) parent representations (PORT I, II, III, IV, or V).

4. An abused child may place a protective boundary around the self-representation (most common) or the (abusing) parent-representation (less common). If asked about this "boundary" representation, the child will make light of what he or she has drawn ("Oh, that's nothing," or "It's his little bed," or "That's really a swing"). *Do not be put off by how a child reacts after-the-fact to any aspect of a drawing.* What is drawn is *always* more important than how a child *reacts* later to what is drawn or how a child verbally describes what has been drawn.

5. Whenever there is a dramatic difference between the two parent representations in how hands or fingers are portrayed, be alert to something specific (and negative) that was done with a hand. The distortion will usually be on *just one* of the hands. A hand of a physically abusive parent may be portrayed as a hatchet or hammer. When *both* hands on a given parent representation are unusually large, the clinical meaning is often positive (the child feels "empowered" by this parent), but if *only one* hand is large and the other small, the meaning is negative and may be specific to the (parent's) use of that hand. (It is also, in keeping with our interpretive principles, of consequence to the child's own experience of self in relation to that parent. That is, it means the child is conflicted in relation to the involved parent in action tendencies mediated via the hands.)

6. Explicit genitalia are exceedingly rare in children's drawings and always should be considered "red-flags."

7. Finally, one may find very idiosyncratic (and graphic) placements of a self- and (abusing) parent-representation in sex abuse cases, for example, where the child draws the self-figure's genital area directly over the face of a (fellating) parent.

The following clinical signs may also occur in instances of physical and/or sexual abuse. These signs are diagnostically not as "strong" as the aforementioned ones, being characteristic of *any* intense amibivalence within the child toward a parent. However, one should be alert for their presence.

A. Any abused child who feels he or she has a secret-that-must-be-kept (which is true of almost all abused children who are old enough to realize that what has happened is probably "wrong") may show some of the signs described later for the MMU or mind-made-up child. The "meaning" is the same—that in each case there are conflicted secrets and loyalty issues at stake. The examiner will find: responses that are given too quickly and/or with a rehearsed or "rigged" quality to them; answers proffered where no question has been asked (in favor of the parent who needs protection); a child who does *not* become progressively more comfortable as the shared time (with the examiner) increases; a child who avoids eye-contact and who does not respond to overtures of friendliness; verbal responses offered far too quickly, before the child could have allowed his or her "unconscious" to tell its story to the "conscious" mind.

B. The child may react to PORT I or II with a "frozen" look on his or her face when confronted with the need to draw the parent over whom the conflict exists. The eyes become fixed and stare straight ahead. This "frozen" response pattern usually disappears by PORT III.

C. Any significantly short *or* long reaction time to one parent in contrast to the times obtained in reference to the other parent should be taken as a sign that an in-depth consideration of abuse is warranted.

Remember that a complete investigation of sexual abuse allegations would involve information obtained from a huge variety of informants (parents, friends, relatives, teachers, live-in companions, almost *anyone* who has or had private contact with the child), medical data, thorough psychological and developmental investigations of all critical persons, a study of family dynamics, etc. (More information will be offered in Chapter Thirteen).

Validating such charges is a vexing proposition, since what the legal system often depends upon is an investigation by some children and youth protective service. Given the enormous variability in adequacy level of such endeavors (and an overreliance on the interview for data), this seems to me all too often like attempting to validate the accuracy of a thermometer (akin to tests) by holding one's hand to a forehead (the imprecision in interview data).

Please note that if a particular parent fares poorly on a child's PORT, as with marked distortions and other signs, but there are *no* signs of physical or sexual abuse, one is probably dealing with parental disinterest, a disinterest that is markedly hurting the involved child.

DEVELOPMENT OF THE PORT AND VALIDATION

A wide variety of psychological tests, tests we believed would illuminate significant aspects of a child's perception of the relationship(s) with his or her parents, were given to 30 children (a few volunteers and children from various private practices). The scoring scheme was designed so as to designate a "chosen" parent (mother or father) for each test item. For example, the circle-diamond figure of the *Bender-Gestalt Test* was among those employed. It was hypothesized (predicted) that a size-differential in these two aspects of the figure would be related to mother versus father choice, specifically, that those who preferred the mother would draw the circle larger than the diamond. Neither this assumption nor the opposite (that mother-preferrers would draw the diamond bigger) proved true, but this is what is meant when we say the scoring scheme was designed to yield a "chosen" parent for each item, i.e., the scheme was planned to show who the child was choosing as the preferred parent by his or her performance on that item.

Many test items were used, including drawing tasks (most of them original), *Rorschach* Plates IV and VII, certain *Bender* figures, and some sentence-completion type items.

A panel of three mental health professionals viewed from behind a one-way screen a one- to two-hour sample of family interaction. Standardized tasks (e.g., solving math puzzles, filling out answers to test questions, solving word problems, putting jigsaw puzzles together, building "block" constructions, memorizing poems, etc.) were given to the children and a checklist was used to itemize the number of times the child looked at each parent, requested information or help from each parent, and manifested positive affect (smiled, etc.), as well as to describe how the child positioned himself or herself physically vis-à-vis each parent, and the degree to which each child comfortably utilized what each parent offered. The child was allowed to "use" the parents as desired and the parents were instructed to respond as they wished. (The parents had simply been told we were investigating some of the ways parents and children interact.)

Since none of these parents were involved in custody battles, it was assumed that any nontypical reactions could be attributed to random psychological forces (to "look good," etc.), but not to any conscious desire to deceive for legal reasons. In other words, here, as in the future, our assumption is that we get optimally "honest" information from situations involving parents who are *not* battling each other and hence have no legal reason to lie or act atypically. (In support of this hypothesis, we should mention that when the 86-item "Parent Questionnaire"—a device that asks about who responds to the child's requests in the majority of instances while the family was intact—was used with an adversarial population, responses of 86 to zero in favor of the responding parent were not uncommon.)

The panel used the information generated in these controlled settings to designate either the mother or father in each family as the "preferred one" or POC in the eyes of the child, that is, the one who, if need be, would be the optimal PCP.

Seven items were retained for further study as best able to choose (postdict) the chosen POCs for PCPs. Our hope was that these measures were revealing which parent the child viewed as more supportive and better able to respond to the child's various needs.

A *pre*dictive study was done with 30 new subjects. The items predicted the independently designated PCPs (same overall design) with better than 90 percent accuracy. The PORT was also validated with clinical and life history information gathered over a two to five year time span. Further data are given in the test manual.

Chapter Six

The Parent Awareness Skills Survey (PASS)

The *Parent Awareness Skills Survey*, or PASS as it is abbreviated, is a clinical tool designed to illuminate the strengths and weaknesses in the awarenesses a parent accesses in reaction to typical child-care situations. Stated more technically, the PASS is designed to generate clinical hypotheses concerning the kinds of impacts a parent's communication strategies are having on a given child. It can be helpful in leading an evaluator to understand why a parent may or may not have done well on the PORT or BPS since the sensitivity (or lack thereof) a parent displays on the PASS will often help to explain why that parent was portrayed either positively (or not so positively) on those tests, which reflect a child's complex perceptions of the parent.

The PASS presents a parent with 18 child-care problems, and asks how he or she would respond to each. Specifically, each parent is asked what he or she would say and/or do in response to these situations. The parent is asked to assume he or she has children of the age mentioned in each situation.

Here is a sample of some of the PASS situations.

- Your three-year-old repeatedly grabs the toys of his older brother, age eight, without asking.
- How would you introduce your three-year-old boy to a new baby brother or sister?
- Your 14-year-old girl says: "I'll be home on time" but rarely is.

- Your 11-year-old girl is caught cheating during a test.
- A school decides your seven-year-old boy has some special problems and should be taken out of his regular class and placed in a special class.
- Your seven-year-old overhears you telling a lie. She says: "You told a lie."
- Your 15-year-old son grabs a kitchen knife during an argument with his 17-year-old brother, and acts like he might use it.
- Your 11-year-old daughter has taken money from Mom's purse.

The main purpose of our scoring plan is to sample in depth parental reactions that could apply to all situations and to children of all ages.

Hence, the PASS is scored in terms of the adequacy with which a parent becomes aware of critical aspects of childcare issues, and the effectiveness with which the parent is then able to communicate with the children about these issues.

"Awareness" is stressed in the name of this clinical tool because the process of responding adequately to a child begins with this all-important skill. A parent will be effective with a child only to the degree he or she is able to discern—*become aware of*—just what it is about a given situation that should or should not become a focal point of intervention. A parent's awareness of these so called "critical issues" is a main target of the PASS.

The PASS reflects, therefore, the kinds of skills a parent must have in order to be an effective parent *regardless* of the age of his or her children and regardless of the "content" specifics of any particular situation. The conceptual or "construct" world of the PASS had its origins in research conducted in the 1960's on marital communication (Bricklin & Gottlieb, 1961).

These early notions were supplemented by those of John Grinder (McMaster & Grinder, 1980) with their emphasis on "outcome frames." The conceptual world of the PASS was further enhanced by already cited utilization concepts of Milton Erickson. This orientation essentially says that if you are communicating to someone and that person does not seem to be getting what you are communicating (i.e., is not responding as you wish), this person is not necessarily "resisting" or "fighting you"; it is rather that you are not offering the message in a way that the other person can use it.

Perhaps the greatest influence on the PASS was the PORT-generating research described in Chapter Three, where we had to watch and record how children responded to their parents.

The PASS yields scores that mirror a parent's awareness of:

1. the elements one should in fact address—or *ignore!*—in various situations to bring about positive solutions, a recognition of what we call the *critical issues* involved;
2. the necessity of selecting strategies *adequate* to bring about positive solutions;

3. the need to respond in words and actions *understandable* to the child;
4. the desirability of *acknowledging the feelings* aroused in a child by various situations;
5. the desirability of *taking a child's unique past history into account* in deciding how to respond;
6. so-called *feedback data*, a recognition that an effective communicator pays attention to whether and how an offered response is in fact coming across to the child.

Scores are computed for responses given under three separate conditions.

The first is called "Spontaneous Level" (SL) responses. These are the parent's spontaneous, uninterrupted responses to the various child-care dilemmas.

This is followed, for eight of the items, with two separate "Probe Level" (PL) questions. The first set of PL questions are very gentle and nondirective. The second-level probe responses are quite direct.

Probe Level responses, by allowing parents an opportunity to reveal what they know but did not think to express spontaneously, mirror thoughts and subsequent actions likely to find their way to motor expression only under favorable circumstances, e.g., situations in which a parent has had time to think things over, is not upset about something else, etc. Further, the probe questions result in a much greater dispersion of parental responses, allowing finer and more precise distinctions to be made among respondents.

Although we have compiled and listed samples of responses from members of the Bricklin Associates research team considered adequate in two of the scoring categories, the decision was ultimately made that final judgments of the adequacy of parental responses to the PASS must be in the hands of the evaluator. The flexibility inherent in this process insures maximum fairness to a parent responding to the PASS, for it allows the evaluator, in judging the adequacy of any given response, to take into account the respondent's unique background—cultural and economic factors, level of education, local standards, etc. We soon realized in developing the PASS that local community standards can vary even from neighborhood to neighborhood. For example, in some neighborhoods it is standard procedure to scream and punish, while a few blocks away this may not be the norm at all. When it is the case that it is possible to evaluate one parent only, the evaluator can use his or her own experience to judge minimal standards of awareness adequacy.

From a scientific perspective, we use the PASS to generate hypotheses about the information derived from the data-based tests, the BPS and PORT.

Additionally, one can use the PASS to strengthen parental communication skills by simply allowing (or mandating) that certain parents read the

PASS manual. In having an opportunity to think about the sample responses offered by members of the Bricklin Associates research team, the parent can expand his or her available options.

ADDITIONAL USES FOR THE PASS

As we have suggested, a reading of the PASS Manual helps an individual to realize many of the ingredients in successful and nurturant communication.

The PASS has also been used in several research projects involving parent-child communication. When one is using the PASS for research, it is recommended that the *actual number* of each manifestation of the scoring categories be utilized for comparative purposes, (e.g., the *actual number* of critical issues identified, the *actual number* of adequate solutions mentioned, etc.) rather than the 2, 1, 0 scoring system suggested in the manual.

Chapter Seven

The Parent Perception of Child Profile (PPCP)

In denying Woody Allen custodĬy of his three children, New York Supreme Court Judge Elliott Wilk had plenty to say about what Woody did not know about his children. Under the headline "Judge Wilk's Scathing View of Woody Allen as a Parent," the *Philadelphia Inquirer* (June 8, 1993) had all of these things to report about what Judge Wilk found lacking in Woody Allen's knowledge of his children: He did not even know if one of his children, who suffered from cerebral palsy, had a doctor; he did not know the names of any of the children's pediatricians; he did not know the names of teachers or anything about academic performance; he did not know the name of the children's dentist; he did not know the names of any of the children's friends; he did not know the names of any of their many pets; he did not know which children shared bedrooms; he rarely attended parent-teacher conferences; he knew nothing about his adopted children's siblings.

A rather furious debate followed this denunciation of Allen in the press, in which guilty fathers who had about the same knowledge of their children as did Woody Allen defended this lack of knowledge as typical for fathers. It struck me as funny, but sad and poignant at the same time, that so many fathers were sitting around after reading Judge Wilk's "list" against Woody Allen wondering if they could answer many (or even any) of these same questions.

This whole debate underscores once again why we have taken the approach to custody decision-making we have. This approach essentially says that by itself, without the types of data generated by the BPS and PORT, or at least *similar conceptual data*, it is rather pointless to try to assemble a list of "good parenting traits" that can be meaningfully used in every case. It is conceivable to me that a Woody Allen–type parent (at least as he was characterized by Judge Wilk) could have a single behavioral disposition, for example, a capacity for vital interest in some area of mutual child-parent involvement, that might have such overwhelming value to a particular child as to render unimportant the many other "deficiencies" that might be true about this particular parent.

As with the PASS, the PPCP is best used in conjunction with the data-based PORT and BPS. Once the evaluator has some notion of the actual utility a given parent's behavior has to a child, the evaluator can then seek to understand why this is so.

The *Parent Perception of Child Profile* or PPCP, co-authored with Gail Elliot, offers a parent an opportunity to express what he or she knows about a particular child in a wide variety of important life areas.

Along with other aims, the PPCP was our attempt to operationalize the concept of "genuine interest in a child." When one speaks of the degree to which a parent is sincerely interested in a child, one should aim at measuring something more than what that parent feels subjectively. It is this inner feeling, perhaps a subjective experience of "warmth," that the average parent probably understands as some sign of his or her "interest" in a child. Still another parent might point to the number of things he or she *does* for a particular child as a sign of "interest."

While there is certainly merit in both these assumptions, the most important operational criterion of interest to our teams is knowledge. The truly "interested" parent is the parent who has taken the time to get to know a particular child. Only the knowledgeable parent can fine-tune his or her communications so that they can be truly effective for a given child. Further, this knowledge cannot easily be faked (as can a flurry of the do-good-things-for-the-kids kind of behavior such as typically occurs—curiously enough—right around the time of a custody evaluation); knowledge takes considerable time and effort to acquire. Doing-good-things-for-the-kids can sometimes be a cheap shot.

The PPCP can be evaluator-administered or self-administered. If evaluator-administered, by virtue of the large number of life-areas it samples and the detailed nature of its questions, the PPCP can serve as a springboard for the parent to express attitudes and feelings not only about the child, but about every person and activity having any significance whatsoever in a child's life.

Responses are gathered in eight categories: *Interpersonal Relations, Daily Routine, Health History, Developmental History, School History, Fears, Personal Hygiene,* and *Communication Style.* (A special *Irritability Scale* is described later.)

The evaluator decides on a case-by-case basis which PPCP items to administer and which to omit (for example, one would not administer the *School History* items in reference to a preschool child). In situations where a number of children are part of the evaluation process, the evaluator may select one or two of them as critical "target" children in reference to whom the PPCP questions would be asked.

Other Source (OS) Information

Some lines in the PPCP Q-book (question book) are preceded by the letters OS. The OS lines give the evaluator space to record corroborative information from other sources, such as teachers, pediatricians, babysitters, tests, documents, etc. Corroborative information would be important in cases where the evaluator is highly concerned about the accuracy of a parent's perceptions.

Other source (OS) or corroborative information is sought at the discretion of the evaluator, as the need for it varies extensively from case to case. In one situation, there may be very little concern about the degree of genuine interest and/or attentiveness of either parent, and hence the need for corroborative information could be exceedingly low. In another case, this same variable, the degree of genuine interest a parent has in a given child, could be the predominant issue. Here, the need to check the accuracy of one (or both) of the respondent's answers may be quite high.

Since it is obviously not necessary from a sampling perspective to corroborate *every* item (and also not cost-effective), the evaluator exercises case-to-case judgment as to which life areas should be sampled as a check on the accuracy of parental perceptions.

In one case, a child's school performance may be of major concern, while social relationships may predominate in another. In yet another instance, one parent may question the other parent's degree of attention to the child's physical health.

Recall Questions

Recall questions are contained on a special Recall Worksheet. Space is provided for the evaluator to record the respondent's "Recall Answers" for comparison with the original answers. They are used when the evaluator suspects a respondent's interest in a child is not sincere.

The Irritability Scale

Although called a scale (for eventual research uses), this part of the PPCP derives its usefulness from the fact that each response choice is described in exact, operational terms. (0 = No annoyance at all; 1 = Mildly annoyed but would not even say anything out loud; 2 = Annoyed enough to speak up, but would not yell; 3 = Would yell but not hit; 4 = Would yell and hit.) Hence, the evaluator can use the respondent's descriptions to red-flag areas where psychological assistance is needed.

Summary of PPCP Uses

1. The PPCP provides a way to gather and organize a parent's stated perceptions of his or her child in a wide variety of critical life-situations.

2. The PPCP affords a parent the opportunity to express attitudes and feelings toward just about every facet of the child's life.

3. The PPCP provides a framework for the evaluator to assess the accuracy with which a parent perceives a child. Parental responses can be checked in several ways.

4. A main use of the PPCP is to compare the responses of selected respondents, such as the two parents. Comparisons can be made in several ways, including *accuracy, depth of knowledge* in any given life area, especially one or several deemed critical to a particular child, and the feelings and attitudes expressed. Other areas of comparison include the *scope* of parental knowledge, the emotional tone of the descriptions (e.g., supportive or diminishing), whether or not any overall value or philosophy pervades all of the responses (e.g., cult-thinking), and areas needing special attention.

Another important comparison can be made when it is suspected that a separated or divorced parent is attempting to gain extended custody not out of genuine interest, but because his or her own parent, the child's grandparent, wants more time with the child. In these situations, one is typically dealing with a parent who picks up the child for his or her visit and delivers the child immediately to some other caretaker (usually the grandparent, but it may be a girlfriend or a childless baby-sitter who likes being with the child).

Administering the PPCP to the suspected real caretaker will show a performance on this person's part vastly superior to that of the secretly disinterested parent.

Another creative use would be in a situation where one parent claims that either a babysitter or a live-in companion with whom the child has contact when with the other parent is not a good caretaker. The PPCP can be used to forge a win-win solution, by either disproving the allegation or at the very least red-flagging areas of weakness that can then be strengthened to achieve a satisfactory level of comfort for the parent lodging the complaint.

Chapter Eight

Getting Accurate Information

The purpose of this chapter is to suggest some things an evaluator can do to maximize the attainment of accurate data. Some are formal/procedural, while others are more difficult to label. I refer in this latter regard to an attitude or "mood" the examiner creates in the respondent—a mind-body set that will either facilitate or impair the degree to which accurate data are offered.

In the discussion to follow, we are particularly interested in situations where it is important that a respondent's evaluation response be critically similar—the concept of an analogue comes to mind—to the response that he or she would have toward the parent in question in a real-life example of the context aimed at by the test item.

We will refer to the critical concept being developed here as a "state-of-arousal" and will abbreviate this as SOA. Defined very roughly, a state of arousal or SOA refers to a certain level of circumscribed and unique activity within the respondent's organism that codetermines the way (or process by which) incoming information will be registered and stored. Approximately speaking, incoming information is stored in accordance with (or "within") the prevailing SOA; the concept further hypothesizes that in order for this same information to be *optimally* retrieved at some later time, the individual would have to be in the same (or a highly similar) SOA as prevailed when the information was stored.

The above is greatly simplified, but will enable us to understand the concepts being developed. The usefulness of these notions is that they posit an underlying series of mechanisms that not only yield important tips on eliciting accurate test information, but further help explain some of the reasons why parents are either helpful or nonhelpful to their children. For a complete discussion of these ideas, see *The Psychobiology of Mind-Body Healing* (Rossi, 1986, 1993). (Some of these concepts, *from a different perspective*, are given in Robert Ornstein's (1991) work, *The Evolution of Consciousness: The Origins of the Way We Think*.)

Rossi begins by noting that James Braid (who lived between 1795 and 1860) originated the concept of what Rossi calls a state-dependent theory of mind-body healing and hypnosis. (Throughout his own discussion, Rossi refers to the processes of which we speak as "state-dependent memory, learning and behavior" and abbreviates this in the following way: "SDMLB" [p. 45]). I use the term SOA, which is shorter, albeit less precise and informative. Braid suggested that hypnosis be thought of as a situation in which a person who is hypnotized cannot remember upon awakening what occurred during the "sleep," but *could* remember what happened while in a similar state of hypnotism thereafter. Rossi (1993) says: "Modern researchers would call this a process of 'state-dependent memory and learning': What is learned and remembered is dependent on one's psychophysiological state at the time of the experience. Memories acquired during the state of hypnosis are forgotten in the awake state but are available once more when hypnosis is reinduced" (p. 36). Since the retrieval of the memories is dependent upon properties in action when they were stored, the memories can be called "state-bound information" (p. 38).

Perhaps one of the clearest statements of this concept is made by Fischer (1971) in pointing out that what we call experience comes about from the association of a particular level of arousal with a particular symbolic interpretation of that arousal. The experience would be referred to as state-bound. Hence, it can be reelicited either by factors that bring about the particular level of arousal in effect at the time of the initial encoding of the experience or by the appearance of some symbol of its interpretation—a visual image, a certain taste sensation, a melody, etc. He quotes a situation in which 48 subjects learned nonsense syllables when drunk. The critical factor was that these subjects could, in the future, recall significantly more of these syllables when they were once again drunk than they could during sober states.

Zornetzer (1978) wrote (paraphrased): Normally, in memory, a specific configuration of arousal that exists in the brain at some time of learning becomes a critical aspect of the stored information. The neural configuration of this state of affairs might have to do with brainstem acetylcholine, catecholamine, and serotonin systems. Such activities, activities which codetermine the instant SOA that happens to predominate at the time certain experiences are encoded, would need to be reproduced or at least approximated later in order for the encoded information to be available.

Milton Erickson capitalized on these concepts in his development of a technique that would permit people who had forgotten clinically relevant events to recapture them. He used a process in which he would orient them toward material being sought by recreating certain simple and complex configurations of the sensory stimuli that existed around the time the forgotten event was initially encoded (Erickson & Rossi, 1979).

This gives us a direct clue to what an evaluator might need to do in order to obtain accurate (analogue) data: somehow use the stimuli available to create in the person being evaluated the SOA that most frequently prevails in the contexts in which characteristic responses are sought. Hence, if a test item asks a child, "How well does Dad do at staying calm in an argument?" the hope would be that all of the variables that codetermine the child's response would create in the child a representative SOA of the child when he or she perceives Dad in an argument. In other words, what we *don't* want is a child's calm reflections, his or her verbal "summary opinions," about Dad's behavior during an argument. What we *do* want is for the child's test response to "emerge out of" the SOA prevailing when the child perceived Dad in an argument. A given SOA, remember, *codetermines the actual memories, resources, talents, and skills available to an individual at any given time.*

Only if an examiner working in concert with a given test item can access the relevant SOA will accurate information predictive of what a child would do in that kind of situation be elicited.

I am certainly aware that my use of the SOA concept is far less detailed than is Rossi's. Also, I have not presented his enormous array of empirical and theoretical detail on the subject that enables one to gain an appreciation for the many critical uses to which it, and similar notions, can be put. Further, Rossi's main intention is to promote mind-body communication and healing.

But Rossi's concept presents some clear advantages for the custody evaluator.

1. Essentially, it offers a better *and far more precise way* of understanding the factors surrounding the way information is encoded and (especially important for our purposes) made *available* (or not available) in both positive and negative ways.

2. It provides a clearer, more useful way of understanding another critical psychological concept, that of "context." Thus, in many ways, it may eventually prove more helpful to actually define a context in terms of a prevailing SOA, rather than describe "place" or "time" or other external characteristics. Indeed, if what is available to an individual is, in largest part, determined by an instant SOA, then *that* literally defines a specific context. For now, however, greater flexibility is maintained by keeping both

terms so that a certain context may be so defined or articulated as to encompass several SOAs.

3. Related to the above, the SOA concept reminds the custody evaluator that what a parent or child can access and use in one situation may not be available in others. This has special significance to the custody evaluator, who must understand that just because a parent can do something in one type of situation (e.g., be "patient") this constitutes no guarantee that the same resources will be available to the parent in another situation.

4. By understanding that each parent, in different psychological situations and thereby operating out of potentially divergent SOAs, stimulates different SOAs in the child, attention is drawn to how multitudinous are the ways in which parents propel children to either access—or *not* be able to access—given talents and resources. This must be understood not only when the evaluator thinks about differences *between* parents, but also when thinking about how the *same* individual may vary throughout the day.

5. The SOA concept provides a clearer understanding of why the resources available in a traumatized state (or a state that critically resembles a trauma state) are so limited, and why it is so hard to get "corrective" (or "curative") information into this system (i.e., change it).

6. The SOA concept helps sharpen our understanding of what an evaluator can do to maximize the attainment of accurate data.

Note that the SOA concept does not assume that the encoding of an experience is within a static structure. Certain ways of accessing an SOA can change it. In another sense, "...the structure of old learnings (already encoded experiences) reform in the context of more recent learning" (Barton, 1994, p. 9).

To the degree, then, that an evaluator is successful in the way certain words are emphasized, or in pacing or in tonal expression or in the general mood created in the respondent, the evaluator will access relevant SOAs in a child for given test items.

We cannot know all of the variables that make one evaluator more successful in eliciting accurate information than another. I do not think that this has solely to do with an evaluator's ability to create a state of "relaxation" in a given respondent, adult, or child. In the context of a custody evaluation, the evaluator *does* want to create a safe haven for the child, but *too much* relaxation may be a negative rather than positive state of affairs. I believe this because I think postdivorce children taking evaluations are confused at conscious levels, and to the extent that the evaluator is successful in getting a given child past this confusion, the data will be more accurate. Also, create too much of a joke-filled or fun or relaxed environment for a child, and the child believes he or she can get away with contrived or evasive answers. Further, nonrepresentative SOAs are accessed.

My own belief is that an evaluator who is authoritative while at the same time friendly and neutral will get better information than one who is simply friendly. *The attitude of the evaluator has to create an attitude of focused attention on the part of the child.* Words have to be spoken in a way that results in the *respondent creating vivid sensory reenactments of critical environments inside his or her mind.* Such reenactments would constitute the best bet for reliable access-codes to the responses desired, since the evaluator would have no way of knowing beforehand idiosyncratic "key words." I believe this approach can be exceedingly helpful in obtaining accurate information, particularly in situations where respondent answers are to be counterparts (analogues) of that which would happen in similar real-life situations. We see here the analogy to the work of Milton Erickson in retrieving forgotten events: the use of critical sensory stimuli to create appropriate contexts and frames of reference.

The authority of the evaluator must create the aforementioned safe haven for the child, in which the child can "dare" to recreate in the privacy of his or her inner mind the situations solicited by the BPS in a direct way, and the PORT in more symbolic ways. The evaluator who fully engages the child's attention, and conveys to the child that dissembling is not permitted, and then goes on to read the test questions in a way that enables the respondent in his or her inner mind to create vivid sensory reanactments of the contexts in question will be the evaluator who gets "good" data.

CONFUSING SOURCES OF INFLUENCE IN A CUSTODY EVALUATION

The custody evaluator must be wary of many forms of influence that could push a child into forming a consciously held conclusion about the superiority of one parent over another. Consciously voiced opinions do not always stem from "legitimate" sources. There is the further but more remote possibility that even unconscious test data might be emanating from tainted sources.

Among the forms of influence on a child that a custody evaluator might question would be both superficial and subtle forms of bribery—influences likely to be in operation particularly around the time of an evaluation.

Superficial bribes would involve offering a child ice cream, a chance to stay up late, etc. A subtle bribe would consist of treating the child more nicely than might typically be the case.

Some evaluators feel that a parent's ability to provide a child with a better school and a better neighborhood and superior forms of recreation and games are also bribes and could very well influence a child in that child's reactions toward each "competing" parent, i.e., to overvalue the parent able to provide such amenities.

Loyalty conflicts are another source of confusing data. Loyalty conflicts can manifest themselves in many ways, including a refusal by the child to make any choice whatsoever. For example, this child, when responding to the BPS, will make sure that all of his or her responses are exactly in the middles of the continua.

A child may feel threatened. Some parents threaten to leave the child's life if the child does not choose for that parent. There is always the possibility that a threat of physical violence is playing a role, as with a father who threatens to beat up either the child or the mother if the child does not choose for him.

A child may be motivated by a desire to save a parent perceived as impaired.

Of late, the use of alienation ploys on the part of one or both parents has crept into the awareness not only of custody evaluators but of all people who participate in the psycholegal custody decision-making system. Alienation ploys may be subtle or blatant. As a matter of fact, the pendulum has swung so far in this area of concern that it is often the case that a parent who is caught using an alienation ploy is automatically assumed *not* to be a candidate for primary caretaking parent—to me, as much an error as failing to note the operation of alienating ploys.

We will also consider the parent who might be on a sustained bribery campaign, that is, bribing the child in a consistent manner. This, in the opinion of some, could influence the child even at *unconscious* levels. The extent to which this might be possible will be considered below.

We will argue later that the critical solution to any or all of these possible scenarios is the ability of the evaluator to determine whether or not a child's response, be this a consciously voiced response or a response to a test, is in fact *based on that child's actual interactions with each parent* or on something other than actual interactions. We will further argue that if such information can be teased out of clinical and/or life-history data, so much the better; it was in this search for tools that could differentiate between conscious and unconscious responses that we developed the PORT.

Specifically, in order to investigate "suspect" forms of influence, the custody evaluator must ask himself or herself: "Are the responses emanating from unconscious sources of a child's personality telling the same story as are responses emanating from more conscious layers of the child's personality?"

Our position, then, is that responses stemming from unconscious sources are those predominantly based on a child's actual interactions with a parent, while those stemming from more conscious sources *may be* based on actual interactions but *are more susceptible* to bribery, loyalty conflicts, threats, alienation ploys, etc.

Keep in mind that no response emanates totally from either source. All reactions, including what we label "conscious," represent neurobiopsychological activity at all levels, and hence we deal again with matters of proportional contribution even with the C and U concepts.

An unconscious reaction may be thought of as a knee-jerk or gut level or whole-organism response. An unconsciously mediated response occurs automatically and relatively effortlessly. Based upon countless real-life interactions as filtered through an individual's unique need systems and information-processing strategies, they represent the deepest and most genuine sources of one's personality.

As we move through a discussion of "suspect" sources and the steps to be taken to reduce the possibility of evaluation errors based on such sources, it is wise to consider ways to recognize a child whose consciously sourced responses should be considered not reliable. When this is the case, PCP recommendations should be generated from less conscious sources of data.

Recognizing a Not-Based-on-Actual-Interaction Scenario

The not-based-on-actual-interaction (NBOAI) scenario occurs when a child's consciously offered responses are markedly different from what is revealed by the less conscious layers of his or her personality. The mind-made-up (MMU) configuration is a prominent indication of a possible NBOAI scenario. The MMU child has a very definite opinion as to who should be seen as the "better" or "winning" parent and is trying very hard to convey this impression.

We call this child the MMU child to draw attention to the fact that the child has a definite viewpoint on who should be the PCP even though the evaluator does not necessarily know the source from which this "definiteness" is emanating.

There are blatant as well as subtle signs of the MMU condition. Keep in mind that although this MMU child is often the child who has been bribed or coerced or alienated, he or she could also be simply a child who knows his or her own mind and is trying to make sure that this consciously held opinion is heard and respected.

First of all, many of the MMU child's responses and utterances have a rehearsed or rigged quality to them. It often sounds as though the child is repeating lines that have been rehearsed (perhaps internally, perhaps externally).

The MMU child will volunteer information. This is rarely the case with children who are being evaluated in situations about which they are ambivalent (the usual scenario in custody disputes). Children do not usually even like to respond to questions, especially if they think their answers are going to be used to judge their parents. The MMU child will not only volunteer information, but may do so when no specific questions have been tendered. This is indeed atypical for children at large. These utterances may take the form of exceedingly positive information about the campaigned-for parent, or extremely negative information about the nonchampioned parent.

The MMU child usually responds exceedingly quickly to the BPS, often before full questions have been asked. Also, with non-BPS engendered queries, there is often no pause between question and response, particularly along the lines mentioned above, i.e., quickly offered positive information about the campaigned-for parent, and quickly offered negative information about the other parent.

When the BPS is being administered, almost all responses for the candidate of choice will be placed at the "Very Well" end of the continua lines.

Interestingly, the MMU child does not tend to relax as the testing session progresses. The typical happening is for children taking tests to have quite a bit of tension at the outset of the examination. As the examiner uses his or her (hopefully) considerable skills at creating the aforementioned "safe haven," the involved children tend to become somewhat more comfortable as time progresses. The child who is campaigning for a certain parent does not follow this progression. Tension will remain throughout the evaluation. The child often anxiously watches the evaluator, (probably to see if his or her "message" is getting across). This scenario applies even when the evaluator is a neutral participant in the custody decision making procedure, or indeed *has been hired by the parent consciously favored by the child.*

The child further will avoid eye contact. He or she will resist overtures of friendliness.

There are many reasons why the MMU child does not relax as testing progresses. Primarily, the child feels ambivalent about what he or she has undertaken to accomplish and needs to cover up this ambivalence. As mentioned, there may also be performance anxiety, i.e., "Am I getting my point across?!" Further, the child feels guiltily dishonest.

Perhaps the most interesting sign of the MMU child is that the verbal portion of a response is frequently rushed in prior to the completion of the unconscious or whole-organism, deep, gut-level response.

Normally, the human organism responds as follows. A stimulus is offered. It is processed first at unconscious levels. The entire organism takes part in this. One might say that the inputs are being "weighted" by the individual's own personality (including anatomic-skeletal and "chemical" dispositions) and assigned "meaning" and/or "significance" (in terms of the associations available). The result of all this is some whole-organism, gut-level, knee-jerk reaction. This process ordinarily has a smooth and effortless quality to it; it is the way things normally happen. A resultant verbal response is in part based on the conscious mind's ability to "read" what the whole organism has had to say. One can note this progression in even the most trivial of instances, for example, when a person is trying to decide between a steak sandwich and a cheese sandwich or voicing an opinion based on a reaction to a movie, a lecture, or almost anything.

Stated simply, a normal verbal response incorporates a hopefully accurate reading by the conscious mind of what the unconscious mind has had to say. In common language, people may talk about such whole-organism responses as "feelings," but this is not to say an individual is consciously aware of the entire whole-organism process.

This progression is typically violated by the MMU child, who must use the verbal response to override the unconscious response, so desperate is he or she to make sure that the campaigned-for parent is properly represented.

The skilled evaluator can detect when a child is interfering with the natural progression of bodily responses. The body, via its muscular-skeletal system, has to have the freedom to operate in an unencumbered manner if the information from the unconscious is to be made available to the conscious mind. Subtle body movements, changes in skin colorations, different breathing patterns occur, and *then* the verbal response is offered. This is why the MMU child sits so rigidly; it is almost as if the child must restrict his or her body from having its full range of "vibrations" or movements available. A natural progression has a graceful quality to it because the child is allowing the process to operate according to its own "unconscious" principles. The verbal response, in largest part, is a summary of the information contained in the entire process. The opposite is true with the MMU child, who is promoting (or dispromoting) a certain parent.

Test-based signs of a NBOAI scenario are recognized when the PORT unconscious indicators (PORT U) tell a different story from the PORT conscious indicators (PORT C). The POC on the BPS will be for the consciously championed parent. When there is a NBOAI scenario, the PORT U are used to suggest a PCP.

Bribes and Misinformation

The critical aspect in whether or not a parent can pull off a piece of "bribery" is to be found in how sincerely and how long the parent can sustain the behavior. If it *is* sustained, one should not think of it as "bribery." Keep in mind that a child's unconscious mind (like an adult's) is *exceedingly attentive* to hypocrisy, that is, where a person is telling one tale out of one side of the mouth and a completely different one out of the other. Bribery can indeed affect a child's conscious decision-making apparatus but it has quite a different impact on the unconscious, which is open and attentive to conflicted and mixed messages.

And what of a parent who "campaigns" for himself or herself? We live in an era where a vigorous, even aggressive use of self-advertisement is blatantly at hand, even with the most positive of role models, including presidents, senators, and other high-level politicians. We see it with movie stars and movie studios seeking Oscar nominations. In other words, it is no longer looked down upon for a person to campaign vigorously in his or her own behalf.

Hence, the critical questions with a bribing parent are to be asked about the individual nature of what was done, the stability of the behaviors over time, the degree to which the "bribes" are consistent with other data emanating from that parent and, ultimately, with their impact on a given child. Further, the practical, test-based question has to do with whether or not responses the clinician feels are "suspect" are consistent with the remaining body of responses.

The Parent Perceived As Impaired

It is important for the custody evaluator to recognize when a child is consciously championing a parent who is seen by the child as needing help.

In this scenario, there will be many of the MMU signs mentioned above. The child is actively seeking to make his or her choice of the "impaired" parent known to the evaluator. Less frequently, one can encounter a child without MMU signs whose choice is based on a perception of parental weakness. The remarks to follow should help spot this possibility.

Basically, the unconscious indicators will tell a different story than the conscious indicators. For example, if one is using the PORT, the perception of impairment will show up by distortions in drawings of the parents. This frequently occurs on Port task I, and will manifest either as one of the standard impairments listed in the PORT Manual, most frequently a slanting of the figure, or as some other distortions. This may also occur on any of the PORT drawing tasks (IV and V), in which parent figures occur.

It is frequent on family drawing tasks for the perceived-as-impaired parent to be shown in very passive positions, for example, lying down.

Often, in response to Port VII where the child is asked to make up a dream about each parent, a story will be told in which there is an outright mention of a need to help a parent. This may take the form of a parent perceived as sad: "Dad is crying because he cannot see his kids." This, of course, also appears in manipulative not-based-on-actual-interaction scenarios. Basically, the custody evaluator should always be on the lookout for a parent perceived as impaired when there are either distortions in the drawings of a given parent figure or that parent is pictured in sad or passive or exceedingly compliant positions. Frequently, there will be direct mention of a need to help this parent.

THE NOT-BASED-ON-ACTUAL-INTERACTION SCENARIOS: ALIENATION STRATEGIES

We use the term, not-based-on-actual-interaction (NBOAI), to draw attention to what we believe is the essential diagnostic task: the need for the evaluator to recognize when a response on the part of a child is not in fact based on his or her actual interactions with a specific parent.

The evaluator must not believe that the way to balance the merits found between a given mother and father is to diagnostically downgrade the parent who seems to be using more "alienating" strategies. Alienation strategies come in many sizes and shapes; often the ones who do it subtly are the ones who do the most damage and escape detection.

The fact that we call attention to the NBOAI aspect and not to the alienating strategies themselves is not in any way to minimize the (negative) importance of the latter. We will address this issue in a moment.

It is also our intention to underline the fact that the parent who is seen as doing the most obvious alienating should not automatically be selected as the parent of non-choice. The critical issue should always be the degree to which a parent overall is helping versus hurting the child. The notion that a child is best served by having access to both parents is, of course, the presumption. *This presumption remains to be proven in given cases.* A corollary of this line of reasoning is that it is the task of the custody evaluator to be able to identify the sources, including suspect sources, of a given child's responses.

We use the phrase NBOAI also to draw attention to the fact that the evaluator should not assume there is a one-to-one relationship between the extent to which a parent is using alienation strategies and the impact of these strategies on a given child. Whatever a given parent does that may be considered abusive differentially impacts the various strengths and weaknesses of any given child such that a good bit of abuse may have minor psychological effects in one child while the reverse may be true for another. This, again, is why it is so valuable to have tools that can help to identify the actual impact a given parent is having on a child rather than to have diagnostic attention focus more on what a given parent is doing. One must know the overall effects a given parent is having on a child rather than getting drawn into the assumption that a particular piece of behavior deemed odious by the evaluator is going to have exactly the negative effects the evaluator believes.

Alienation Strategies

Ward and Harvey (1993) have written an excellent piece on alienation strategies (see also Gardner, 1987, the originator of the concept) and their impact on children. In addition, they offer a very definitive (and quite aggressive) series of remedial strategies.

They accept as a definition of parental alienation the creation of a singular relationship between a child and one parent, to the exclusion of the other parent. The child who has been completely alienated does not wish to have any contact at all with the other parent and will express only negative feelings about that parent and only positive feelings for the other. The authors label the parent who attempts to create this singular relationship the "alienating parent," and the parent who is excluded the "target parent."

The following are identified as mild categories of alienation strategies.

One is where little regard is held by the alienating parent for the importance of contact with the other parent. This may show itself in a sort of disguised way by a parent's saying something like the following: "Well, you're certainly welcome to go off with your dad; I'm not going to stop you and I certainly won't force you to do this." In this category, the alienating parent does not encourage visits, shows no concern over missed visits, and shows no interest at all in what happened when the child was visiting the target parent.

The authors then identify what they call a "lack of value regarding communication between visits." Here there is no encouragement of phone calls or any other form of communication between scheduled visits, and little awareness of the feelings this may engender in the child if a visit or phone call is missed.

Next they identify a situation where there is a lack of ability in the alienating parent to tolerate the presence of the other parent even at events that are obviously important to the child, like ball games and dances and school presentations. The parent may actually say: "I'm not going to go if (the other parent) is there."

In this category, the authors also include a disregard on the part of the alienating parent for the importance to the child of the relationship with the other parent. This may manifest itself as an open willingness to apply for and accept a new job far away from the other parent.

The authors identify the following as "moderate" forms of alienating strategies: a communication of dislike of visitation ("You can visit with your dad, but you know how I feel about it"), a refusal to hear anything except negative news about the target parent, a refusal to speak directly with the target parent, a refusal to allow the target parent physically near (as in a visitation drop-off), doing and undoing statements—negative comments about the other parent made and then denied ("There are things I could tell you about your dad, but I'm not that kind of person"; "Your dad is an alcoholic —Oh, I shouldn't have said that"), subtle accusations ("Your dad wasn't around a lot when you were little"), and destruction of memorabilia of the target person.

Ward and Harvey (1993) next mention the category they label "overt": statements about the target parent that are delusional or false (for example, when a statement is made that the target parent drinks too much or uses drugs or does not pay support when there is no evidence to support these charges), inclusion of the children as victims of the target parent's bad behavior (as when it is claimed that the target parent abandoned "all of us"), overt criticism of the target parent (as when it is claimed that the target parent endangers the child's health), requiring the children to keep secrets from the target parent, direct threats of withdrawal of love if the child persists in his or her relationship with the other parent, an extreme lack of courtesy to the target parent.

Finally, they identify what they call "severe" cases in which the child has become so enmeshed with the alienating parent that he or she has completely adopted the party line.

Keep in mind that although Ward and Harvey provide a continuum along which the alienating behavior goes from pretty bad to gruesome, they do show an awareness that it is important to consider the effects on the child. One should not make the assumption that the psychological damage to a particular child will necessarily follow the same continuum as do the alienating strategies. As mentioned, very subtle alienation strategies may have a devastating effect on one child and not on another. A unique aspect of Ward and Harvey's recommendations are the aggressive remedial strategies suggested. They are spelled out in detailed, operational language; they are precise behavioral prescriptions, with built-in consequences for noncompliance.

The Four Most Common NBOAI Scenarios

The four common scenarios that can be seen in our test and observation data consist of the following: the first is the classic "parent alienation syndrome," a situation in which a parent is attempting to alienate a child from a target parent and is succeeding; the second scenario is one in which it may not be recognized that alienation strategies are being used because the child is not overtly on the campaign trail; the next two categories embrace situations that look like a parent alienation syndrome because alienation ploys are being used, but these cases are best seen as something different from the classic manifestations.

The classic NBOAI situation, the one typically referred to by people in the field as the "parent alienation syndrome," is one in which the child is being systematically programmed, subtly or blatantly, by one parent to hate and or fear the target parent. The alienation strategies are seen as achieving their purpose. Typically, in this situation, the alienation ploys are not subtle, but quite overt. The MMU signs on the part of the child are blatant; it is obvious the child is campaigning for a particular parent. The POC or parent-of-choice on the BPS will be for the championed parent. Most of the child's responses will be extremely positive for the alienating parent and negative for the target parent. However, it will be noted that the child cannot justify many of these BPS responses (in either direction). It will be noticed that when the child responds to examiner questions, the tone of voice will sound rehearsed or rigged or overly anxious. Very often the child will accompany his or her response with spontaneous comments to justify the response; this is highly uncharacteristic of children and rarely occurs unless there has been programming, e.g., "Yeah, Dad is a great guy." However, there are some exceptions (see below).

Although the BPS POC will be for the championed parent, the child will not be able to justify many of his or her responses, with real-life examples. Further, the child's unconscious hand movements to the BPS continua will tell a story that is different from the final, offered response. That is, when the child is responding in a negative way against the target parent, it will be seen that many of the hand movements are first toward the "Very Well" end of the continua. Most importantly, the PORT responses will show a divergence between the conscious and unconscious indicators. The story told by the unconscious indicators will be much more favorable for the target parent then would be expected by the child's conscious responses. *If this particular sign is not present, you are probably not dealing with a genuine NBOAI scenario.* Thus, if the child's unconscious reactions in relation to the campaigned-against or target parent indeed are as negative as is being reported, one is not dealing with a true "parent alienation syndrome" regardless of whether or not the alienating parent is attempting to create this scenario. Stated another way, it may well be that the alienating parent is attempting to alienate the child from the target parent, but if the unconscious indicators are negative it would mean that in addition to this going on, the child's *actual interactions* with the target parent have indeed been negative. This would mean that the alienating parent's strategies are wrong-headed, but perhaps justified. They may have negative implications—the child is being made to feel even worse about a parent toward whom he or she already feels badly to begin with—but the alienating parent should be seen to at least have reason for his or her position.

The next NBOAI scenario may go undetected, especially if the evaluator depends exclusively on interview and observation data, since the effects of the alienation strategies are much more subtle, and their results may show up only on a test that can differentiate conscious response sources from unconscious sources. This kind of strategy on the part of the parent may depend upon momentary parental facial expressions, tones of voice, etc. Since one of the features of this category is the absence of MMU or "campaigning" signs, it may not be obvious that the child's conscious responses are at odds with those derived in the main from unconscious sources. Hence, in this category there is an absence of MMU signs, although a test with the aforementioned capacities will show the conscious/unconscious split between conscious and unconscious indicators. A test such as the BPS will be for the alienating parent, and once again the child will not be able to justify many of the extremely positioned responses.

In the next scenario, one that is very rare, there are usually some obvious but muted MMU signs. It may look like a parent alienation situation, but the data will show a wise and thoughtful child who simply knows what he or she wants and is campaigning for this choice. Other data will support the child's choice. The child will justify BPS or other such responses with real-life examples reported in speech patterns appropriate to the child's overall development. The PORT or data derived similarly will be consistent with the child's POC, that is, the unconscious indicators will paint the same portraits as do the conscious indicators. This child will rarely make extremely negative remarks against the non POC. If MMU signs are extensive, you are probably *not* dealing with this particular classification.

The last situation indeed looks like a parent alienation syndrome and is, at least in the sense that alienation strategies are being used. However, this is a very complex situation and the basic essence of it is that a parent is campaigning against a parent who perhaps should be campaigned against. This is not to say that therapeutic maneuvers would not be aggressively directed toward stopping the alienation strategies; it is to say that this is a unique situation and should be understood differently than a classic NBOAI scenario. What we have is a situation where a parent is actively campaigning against another parent *and* the child's entire history of actual interactions with the campaigned-against parent has indeed been very negative. I have often found this scenario in cases where the campaigned-against parent had a criminal history including various forms of abuse. It is important to recognize this category of situations. An evaluator must not assume that the use of alienating strategies by a parent is a sufficient condition to rule out that parent as a potential PCP. In this scenario, there will be strong MMU signs and consciously derived responses will be in expected directions. *However*, the child will be able to appropriately justify his or her conscious responses against the target parent. (However, the child may not be able to sustain all positive statements for the alienating parent.)

The most important thing is that unconscious indicators concerning the target parent will be indeed as bad as the child is claiming.

MAXIMIZING ACCURATE DATA

Whenever possible, the evaluator should arrange for the two parents themselves or a neutral individual, mutually agreed upon by both parents, to bring the child to the evaluator's office for the first visit.

Since I consider PORT and BPS (or similar) data to be at the heart of the custody evaluation, I want to have maximally uncontaminated responses to such tests. Therefore, I do not want either parent physically in my office while the involved children are given these tests. (I ask them to leave the office area and return at the appropriate time.) This is not necessarily to say that a parent's presence in a waiting room or parking lot causes a child's test responses to be biased. However, since this issue is frequently brought up in court, it is best to minimize the possibilities of its occurrence. (This issue, a thorny one, will be covered in more detail in Chapter Thirteen.)

Also, the evaluator subsequently should still choose to see any involved child with each parent alone and, if possible, in other arrangements.

The evaluator's attitude should be friendly and reassuring but authoritative. It is my clinical guess that a "good" examiner's attitude should convey the following message to the child: "You can trust that I care about your welfare. I also want you to know I am totally neutral in this evaluation and that I will not easily put up with being lied to or deceived." This, of course, cannot be put into words. It should be conveyed by a calm seriousness of purpose.

Naturally, great flexibility is warranted. In some highly contested cases a child may have already been placed through the ringer and know exactly why he or she is in the evaluator's office. When the look on the child's face says, "I am so tired of all this fighting, and really don't want to have anything to do with deciding between my parents," it might be desirable to say something like the following, especially if the child thinks he or she is going to be asked to make direct, guilt-inducing choices: "I will not ask you any direct choice questions about your parents."

(Keep in mind that all of this assumes issues of confidentiality have already been covered.)

The evaluator should remember what was said about SOA or state-of-arousal research. The evaluator should phrase and voice all questions slowly and pregnant with meaning. Keep in mind that the evaluator's task is to evoke vivid sensory representations in the mind's eye of the child. This is to maximize the probability of accessing the SOA that is characteristic, or at least representative, of the context sought. Regardless of the test used, key accessing words can be repeated as many times as the evaluator deems necessary (so long as the exact same wording is used for both mother *and* father stimulus presentations).

When a child is obviously campaigning for a certain parent, the evaluator can do a number of things to maximize accurate data. In this situation, contrary to what was just said, the evaluator might directly ask the child whom he or she would like to be with. We feel that the gains in this maneuver outweigh the liabilities, since the child is trying so hard to convey his or her choice to the evaluator anyhow. This would be followed by saying something like the following: "You have told me whom you want to be with and that is very, very important information. This (whatever test you are currently doing) is simply designed to give us other information." The message you want to give the child is: You are free to relax now and be honest. You have carried out your mission admirably. If you are campaigning for someone, your message has been heard and noted. You are now free to relax and give spontaneous, honest answers.

When giving the BPS or any other tool that asks direct questions about a child's response to a parent's behavior, and you believe the child is answering not from the gut, but too quickly, and out of a desire to campaign, gently challenge responses by asking for examples.

Be suspicious when the child uses adult words or other words not developmentally appropriate for that child. However, keep in mind that some children are taught at very young ages to use adult terminology.

Remember not to be put off by what seems to be a lack of internal consistency in child-directed test items. People operate in highly contextualized ways; a parent who is a good recreational companion may be a poor companion in a situation that involves teaching.

Some of this material will be summarized in Chapter Ten, along with an actual checklist of activities that can be used to consider the accuracy of the evaluation data.

THE SPECIAL PROBLEM OF COLLATERAL-SOURCE DATA

Some custody evaluators (e.g., Honor, 1994) believe it is prudent to interview an extensive array of persons who might provide what is typically called "collateral" information—grandparents, baby-sitters, neighbors, teachers, pediatricians.

While it is indeed crucial to do this, it should be noted that information so derived is especially difficult to assess for credibility. Most "collateral" individuals to whom the evaluator will have access will already favor one particular parent by the time an evaluation has been called for, even individuals one might think would be neutral, such as teachers, pediatricians, and other professionals. This siding with one particular parent will typically *not* be based on careful objective observations of parent-child interactions, but rather on outright bias or similarities in symbol systems and information-processing strategies, as well as similarities in other demographic variables such as age, sex, marital status, employment, etc. (Woody, 1977, pp. 11–18). The problem arises with the fact that once we humans have a special affinity for someone, we tend to attribute all kinds of desirable traits to this individual—the "good parent," for example.

Here are some suggestions for interviewing collateral-source individuals.

1. Always gather sense-based data, *not* conclusions. People will give conclusion-type opinions; you can't stop them. But make sure the heart of your data comes from this question: "If I were there (at the time of the incident you are describing), what *exactly* would I see and what *exactly* would I hear?" Along the same line, always gather data from specific incidents rather than from generalizations, and determine the conditions surrounding these incidents as well as the frequency of observations. (In ACCESS, A Comprehensive Custody Evaluation Standard System [Bricklin and Elliot, 1995], we deliberately ask opinion/conclusion questions and only later ask for corroborative sense-based data. This helps us to detect biased participants, i.e., persons who offer strongly positioned points of view about the competing parents and then fail to back up these positions with sense-based data.)

2. Ask several detailed questions about the precise relationship the interviewee has had with each parent. People generally side with whoever has treated them better.

3. As soon as you hear a "point of view" (e.g., mothers are more attentive than fathers), be skeptical about subsequent data. Directly ask if the interviewee has some "philosophy" of how children should be raised. If so, interpret subsequent data with caution and with this philosophy in mind.

4. Be alert for affinities based on demographic variables. Older people may tend to favor mothers as primary caretakers over fathers, and unmarried people may favor fathers (Woody, 1977).

5. Use suggestions coming from statement validity analysis. For example, the following raise the credibility of any description: unrelated details added, contextual embedding (when people lie they usually make up the lie, and do not concern themselves with how the contents of the lie mesh with surrounding events), reproductions of actual conversation, spontaneous corrections, raising doubt about one's point of view, admission of faults of a "favored parent."

Chapter Nine

Areas of Assessment

The major areas we suggest the custody evaluator should assess are derived from many sources, including the Uniform Marriage and Divorce Act (1979), state statutes that have attempted to delineate custody evaluation targets, and information derived from decisions handed down in family courts across the country. Of major importance in framing how to approach the task of assessing these areas was our own clinical experiences, particularly those we had in the PORT-generating research. Here is where we had extensive opportunities to observe children interacting with their parents in the situations described in Chapter Five.

One must keep in mind that one can never specify an absolutely ideal or ironclad notion of that which should constitute a "custody evaluation." The very same controversies that surround the expert witness who is addressing ultimate issues in a courtroom apply here as well. That is, there is the unavoidable operation of personally held values operating at every level. This is certainly evident when one attempts to designate a certain lifestyle arrangement or "outcome" as being superior to some other arrangement or outcome.

Consider the following example. When my wife, Dr. Patricia M. Bricklin, and I conducted a radio program in Philadelphia a number of years ago, one of the most frequently asked questions came from mothers who wondered how "hard" they should push their children to practice the piano.

Lacking any kind of empirical data, we launched a drive to interview world-class pianists. Some artists said they were pushed to practice (it was almost always by the mother) and were delighted with their careers. Others claimed that, although rich and famous, they believed the early parental pressure contributed very negatively to their overall lives and were doubtful the game was worth the candle, while still others, even though successful, were absolutely miserable and blamed the "pushing behavior" they were subjected to as children (as well as the stresses a world-class concert pianist must endure). (We encountered *no* cases in which a famous pianist practiced as a child without parental urging, although some did report that the mere threat of the withdrawal of the lessons was sufficient "urging" for them to agree to practice.)

What can we glean from this information (in addition to how difficult it is to decide what represents a good outcome)? Suppose you, as a custody evaluator, were faced with a situation where one parent pushed practicing and one did not. How would you rate these differing approaches? Do we deal here with examples of how a similar piece of parental behavior can lead to wildly different outcomes, or are we simply to say that there were other important differences among those who turned out accomplished *and happy* as distinct from those who turned out accomplished *and unhappy*? Is it that each piece of parental behavior not only interacts with many other pieces of parental behavior, but with the child's total developing personality as well?

We would suggest that *all* of the above are true, *and*, there is really no way to say with certainty which outcome is "best" in any case. Even if it were possible to predict which set of variables produced only accomplished *and happy* piano players (which might, after all, be possible only under a very limited set of conditions), there will still be decision-makers or judges who believe a little misery is not necessarily a high price to pay for world fame, while other judges may find such reasoning reprehensible.

For reasons such as these we must conclude it is impossible to specify an absolutely must-do evaluation. Evaluator judgment is and will probably always be required. Even if our predictions were one hundred percent accurate, this would still be the case.

(For those of you who may be wondering how we ultimately responded to our callers, this is what we said: "Even children who are obviously gifted had to be pushed. So push, but gently. Give it up if the child chains himself to a bed or radiator rather than practice.")

There are four major categories in which the custody evaluator might seek information: tests, documents, interviews, and observations.

We suggest the following as a mind-set for a custody evaluator looking at the data emanating from these various sources.

First and foremost, the custody evaluator should be on the lookout for information that yields data as to important congruences between parent and child. (At the end of the chapter, we will comment on a "family systems" perspective as a supplement to this one.) Keep in mind the usefulness of understanding parent-child interactions in terms of a parent's unconscious appreciation for a child's symbol systems and ways of processing and using information.

Be alert for all the many ways one can make available to a given child the best of what each parent has to offer (while at the same time protecting the child from the "worst" each parent has to offer). Remember that behavior is heavily contextualized. A parent who, for example, is very patient when offering homework advice may be nervous and irritable when offering dating advice. A father who is very supportive with a son who has fears about "going to the doctor's" may be very unsupportive if that same son backs down from a fight. It would be unwise for a custody evaluator to assume that because a parent is a "patient advice-giver" or a good listener in one context, he or she will necessarily act similarly in other contexts. Some parents who are very good with slow and placid children become nervous wrecks when dealing with into-everything, ask-about-everything types of children. Some parents who do very well with young children become impatient and argumentative dealing with older children.

Make special note of all important parental strengths. It is ultimately the custody evaluator's responsibility to find creative ways to make these strengths available to the children who need them *and can profit from them.*

The custody evaluator should keep his or her eye out for any special needs or problems a child has that may require special attention or special skills on the part of the parent. Generally, these would include physical and developmental factors, medical factors, educational factors, psychological factors, cultural factors, and especially communication needs and idiosyncrasies. Remember, too, that a useful way to think about "special needs" is in the way their manifestations relate to a given parent's ability to communicate within a given child's symbol system structure and information-processing strategies.

The custody evaluator should always be alert for what we call "override" factors. These would be negativities of such dimension that they would supersede any other considerations in arriving at a decision about time distributions. They would include major impairments such as psychoses and proven abuse, or any other factor that could produce either extensive periods of distractibility or intense, momentary periods, such that the child would be in harm's way.

The home visit, itself, can provide only a limited amount of information since it is unlikely that the custody evaluator will get to see any given home as it really exists day-to-day. However, the information from a home visit may indeed be important in a specific case.

In cases of suspected abuse, it is wise to remove the parents as far from the house as is possible (once rapport is established with the child). Following this, the evaluator should walk the child through every room and nook and cranny in the house, watching the child carefully while maintaining a neutral but very subdued flow of conversation to keep the child comfortable. In cases where physical or sexual abuse may have been confined to certain areas of the house, it is possible that the evaluator might be able to notice in these areas a sign of fear in the child's face or body. This may be a look of being frozen, as though the child's face were part of a freeze-frame stoppage in a motion picture. It is as if all movement suddenly stops. This is not just a startle reaction. A startle reaction is characterized by a rapid intake of breath. The look of which I speak is more like a deadening of all of the child's movements. There may be other obvious signs to be alert for, as when a child initially refuses to enter a certain area of the house.

TARGETS FOR ASSESSMENT

The targets for assessment will be described from two perspectives. The first presents a list of the areas we believe the custody evaluator should assess, along with mention of sources of data that could contribute to this assessment.

The second perspective will be from a "what to do" point of view; here we will outline a variety of instruments that yield the data and information for the targeted areas. Essentially, this section is a guide on how to gather data useful for a custody evaluation along with a consideration of the issues surrounding the gathering of this information.

Here, then, is a list of suggested areas for the custody evaluator to target for assessment. Our teams have always referred to these parental or interactional dispositions as a search for parental strengths, since this helps cast our entire endeavor in a positive or win-win light. This emphasis occasionally makes the terminology a bit awkward, e.g., "the *strength* or the *ability* to maintain zero instances of drug or alcohol abuse," but the search for *parental strengths* creates a better aura for the evaluation than one that may sound tilted toward a hunt for pathology (or its absence). In the discussion to follow, the term "interview" may refer to the parents (or other main disputants), collateral informants, or attorneys.

Legal Criteria of Dispute Resolution

The evaluator should have the involved attorneys detail the legal criteria for dispute resolution in the relevant jurisdiction, e. g., whether joint custody is presumed "best" unless proven otherwise.

The Custody Evaluator Should Seek Information on Any and All Prior Custody Determinations, If Such Exists

Through interview data and documents, the custody evaluator should seek to understand not only what led up to the need for the current evaluation but the entire history of any other custody issues with which the participants have been involved. This, of course, refers to the present case in the main, but also to any other.

The study of prior determinations is important in the instant case, since it is almost always the fact that if there is an already existing custody arrangement that was court-determined, this cannot be changed unless there has been a so-called "change of circumstances." That is, it is usually assumed that the prevailing custody arrangement is "best" unless it can be proven otherwise. The reasoning seems to be not just that if it isn't broken, don't fix it, but in the absence of evidence to the contrary, things-as-they-are, i.e., continuity, is in a child's best interests. (This presumption also cuts down court involvement.) Altering a custody arrangement would be considered only if something is presumed to have happened that in some significant way changed the facts as they pertain to a child's best interests.

The custody evaluator should come to understand all of the important issues that exist when a custody evaluation has been ordered or requested. The evaluator will hopefully come to understand the hidden as well as open agendas.

An understanding of the issues is important not only in structuring the evaluation, but also as an aid in keeping costs under control. It is only when all the issues are thoroughly understood that it might be seen that there really is only one or possibly two critical issues at stake. This may modify the evaluator's notion as to what needs to be accomplished, such as a need to make a decision about certain educational options for a child. (See Chapter Thirteen for a fuller discussion of this issue.)

Before deciding on what to include in an evaluation, the evaluator should talk to all major participants as well as to all involved attorneys. In many instances, it is possible to talk to an involved judge beforehand. The custody evaluator should attempt to obtain copies of the transcripts of prior legal courtroom hearings as well as any other pertinent legal documents.

Is the Child Really Wanted?

This is approached differently depending on the age of the child. A frequently asked question at various seminars we offer on custody evaluations is about what can be done to assess parental interest when the involved child is very young, say, under one year of age. There are a number of things the evaluator may choose to consider in such situations. The evaluator can consider the overall condition of the child. While the following information is by no means absolutely certain in implication, it is nevertheless important. We refer here to the child's vibrancy, to the child's sleeping patterns, and to other patterns that might indicate distress versus no distress. The evaluator should be charitable in such assessments and *not* assume that allergies and colic are necessarily "psychological" in origin. Next, the use of traditional tests with the parents could be approached from a perspective of looking for signs of exceptional immaturity. Clinical experience suggests that mothers who have difficulty conceiving and subsequently caring for children often show a pattern that could be described roughly as follows: to the extent that a new parent is not finished with being a child, that individual is not ready for parenthood. Interview and observational data can be scanned for this kind of information.

In a more structured format, and in relation to children one year of age and more, the PPCP and PASS are designed to offer information as to whether a parent truly wants a child. The PASS, measuring as it does skills useful in communicating effectively with children, will reflect whether or not the idea of being a parent was important enough to a given individual that he or she would wonder and think about ways to become "better" in dealing with children by reading typical books on child development. The PPCP is expressly designed to measure the degree of genuine knowledge and interest a parent has in a given child. It provides an operational equivalent of "interest."

What Is the Status of the Child's Physical, Educational, Developmental, and Mental Health?

Documents from physicians and hospitals, mental health professionals and schools, along with information from interviews, observations, and tests, will yield data on the state of the child's overall health. It is important to understand any critical relationships between parental activity and the status of the child's health, such as giving medications in a timely fashion and minimizing exposure to areas of vulnerability (allergens, etc.). It is important to recognize any special physical, medical, educational, developmental, or psychological needs of the child and to consider the capacity of each parent to respond to these special needs. A certain amount of subjectivity or bias may creep into some situations here—for example, when a child is suffering from allergies or asthma. Some evaluators may favor a parental response that is low-key and encourages risk-taking in the child, while another evaluator may favor a more conservative parental approach in which the parent keeps after a child to take suggested medications, steadfastly makes the child avoid places where allergens may be plentiful, etc. This conservative approach may be viewed as unnecessary and unhelpful by the other parent, as well as by certain pediatricians. The evaluator should attempt to match the child's condition at any given point with the prevailing living arrangement at that time, for possible clues as to what constitutes optimal caretaking configurations for that child.

This is as good a point as any to remind custody evaluators that they do not have to have a definitive opinion about every single issue that comes up in these cases. It would be quite acceptable to report *all* of the information available in a case that resembles the one just described, and leave it to the judge to consider which may be the better approach. That is, the evaluator would specify that parent A is very strict about where a child may play and about his or her using an inhalator and taking various medications, while parent B is more laissez-faire about the same issues. It would be helpful, however, to determine whether or not each parent has documentation from a reputable medical source to back up the point of view espoused.

Many of the items below will address the parental capacity to respond to a child's psychological needs.

Congruent Positive Emotional Stimulation

The custody evaluator would want to observe whether or not each parent offers the child congruent positive emotional stimulation. Here we refer to facial expressions, tones of voice, initiated touch, appropriate muscle tone when with the child, as well as the parental ability to match the pace of offered communications to a child's observed rate of assimilation. In other words, the custody evaluator wants to see if a given parent is in "sync" with the child. The evaluator may further observe the child's emotional responsiveness to others (does the child seem comfortable?) as well as the presence of any unusual fears. The evaluator would then seek to understand the relationship between parental behavior and these variables.

Congruent Mental/Competency Stimulation

The custody evaluator would be interested in the degree to which each parent offers the child congruent mental stimulation. Has each parent encouraged optimal intellectual growth? The evaluator would also be interested in the pacing with which mental stimulation is offered the child. Again, here and in all matters assessed, the astute custody evaluator is looking for the unique way in which a parent is able (or not able) to tailor his or her communications to the child's ability to take in and use this information. *It is not enough to know that certain communications are offered; this is only the beginning of what an evaluator needs to know.* We should be most interested in results, not intentions. The evaluator would want to see if the parent's efforts *lead to* smoothly initiated, competent behavior on the part of the child.

Time Availability

The custody evaluator must know each parent's time availability for the child, currently and in the future. Interviews, observations, and documents all contain information pertinent to this area. Here is another area in which subjective bias may play a disproportionate role. I know that certain evaluators look with disfavor on situations where a given parent is not able to spend a tremendous amount of time with a child. And yet, the literature offers no clear guidelines on this matter except in extreme cases, as where a child is left alone for long periods of time or with baby-sitters or emotionally unconcerned others for long periods of time.

This is an exceedingly important area, and the custody evaluator must think of a child's life with each parent in a highly detailed, minute-by-minute fashion. It is not enough to know in some vague way how a child will spend his or her day with each parent under competing arrangements. The custody evaluator must come to understand in great detail exactly how a child's day will be spent under each potential arrangement. The evaluator must know not only where a child will spend his or her time but must come to understand all of the persons with whom a child will interact in each situation. When there are Significant Others with whom a child will spend important periods of time, they must, of course, be included among the participants who are evaluated.

Related to the above, the evaluator must understand a parent's ability to furnish appropriate baby-sitters and day care. Interviews, observations, and documents will contribute useful information here.

Material and Financial Needs

The custody evaluator must understand each parent's ability to provide for a child's material and financial needs. These would include appropriate sleeping arrangements, on-time meals, developmentally correct toys, a decent setting in which to complete homework assignments, etc. Interviews, documents, and home visits will yield this information. It is obvious that some degree of subjectivity will play a role here, as the evaluator seeks to understand this issue. The evaluator should not make any hard and fast assumptions about the usefulness of money and what it can buy for a given child. As mentioned earlier, one custody evaluator said of a father she had evaluated that he only "seemed" better because he could provide a better home, a better school, a better neighborhood, better friends, and more of the things the child likes to do than could his mother. This custody evaluator actually saw the father's financial resources as a "negative." She offered her assessment of what seemed to make father "better" with derision. She offered nothing that made the mother seem better, other than her *not* having the financial resources of the father. Our approach would be to let the BPS and PORT help tell us what these things mean to an involved child. It is not wise to assume from our subjective biases what such factors might mean to a given child.

Continuity in Relationships

The custody evaluator must inquire into a parent's ability to provide for continuity in a child's already existing relationships. Here, the evaluator would consider areas such as the child's circle of friends, the child's school, religious affiliation, and other such variables, and assess the degree to which competing arrangements provide for continuity. Continuity is a factor usually considered to be very important by judges. I believe this area involves highly individual adequacies, and many children are far more flexible than some adult decision-makers assume. We deal with many more subjective factors here than is commonly realized, and there is neither time nor money nor desire to test out the efficacies of competing arrangements. If one votes for change where another might vote for continuity, one can build into the arrangement monitoring processes that insure optimal fine-tuning.

Things are, or course, different if one considers grandparents and extended families within this category. Here, the assumption of the importance of continuity is probably a lot more defensible. (However, some caveats are detailed in Chapter Thirteen.)

The evaluator should carefully inquire about any future plan on the part of a parent (e.g., relocation) that could separate the child from the other parent.

Relationship with Siblings

The evaluator must understand the degree to which each parent facilitates a given child's relationship or relationships with siblings. It is important for the custody evaluator to understand a given child's relationships with his or her siblings. There are some major issues to be considered here, and one of the most major, the splitting up of siblings, will be considered in Chapter Thirteen. In this category, we refer to a given parent's ability to facilitate and enhance a child's relationship with his or her siblings, or the absence of such skills in each parent. Interviews, observations, and documents can yield useful information in this regard. Keep in mind that not every sibling relationship is positive. The PORT or similar devices can be adapted to investigate a given child's relationship with any selected sibling.

Parent's Health

The custody evaluator should have information pertaining to a parent's ability to remain in good physical health. Interviews, observations, and medical/psychological documents will yield useful information here. Parental health must be looked at *only* as it impacts a child.

Prior Record as Caretaker

The parent's overall track record as a primary caretaker should be considered by the custody evaluator as judged from prior situations (if such exist). Interviews, observations, and documents will tell the evaluator some of the things he or she might need to know. One would inspect these sources of data for all of the many variables described in this chapter.

Possibility of Abuse and/or Neglect

The parent's ability to maintain zero instances of neglect, and/or physical and/or sexual and/or psychological abuse is of major interest to the custody evaluator. Interviews, observations, and documents will yield useful information in these areas. Traditional tests (of both parents and the child) are important. No test or device is infallible in this regard, and can be used only to yield important red-flag information. If needed, the evaluator can ask an attorney how to discover a possibly hidden criminal background on someone's part.

Drug and Alcohol Use

A parent's ability to avoid "drugs" and alcohol is of serious concern to the evaluator. Interviews, observations, and medical/psychological documents will be useful here. The evaluator must be exceedingly careful of subjective bias. I have seen individuals labeled "alcoholic" at the drop of a hat, often on the say-so of a tainted source. There are so many guidelines and tips issued by various pressure and/or interest groups describing what an "alcoholic" is as to make the concept almost meaningless. I have been involved in cases where an individual who had one drink a day was labeled an alcoholic. It was claimed by an angry informant in one such case that the "alcoholic" who had the single drink each day was indeed alcoholic because "he needed the drink," whatever this might mean. Her insistence in this matter had many professional participants in the case accept that the man had an "alcohol problem," even though there was no evidence whatsoever, medically, psychologically, socially or job-wise, to show even the slightest negative effects of this "alcoholism."

Unless drug or alcohol use leads to periods of irrational judgment or extensive periods of distractibility that have demonstrably negative impacts on the children, the evaluator must be careful of his or her own subjective biases on the "negative" importance of drug or alcohol use. There are several factors to be considered.

First and foremost, it must be demonstrated that any parental action deemed "negative," whatever be the source of this judgment of negativity, is in fact negative *in its implication for the involved child*. That is, a parental trait that is called "bad" by a custody evaluator, should be shown actually, not theoretically, to be impacting an involved child in a harmful manner. Ordinarily, this would come up in relationship to situations where periods of distractibility would be really dangerous (e.g., while driving) and might refer to mood swings, impulse control problems, etc.

Second, the evaluator must question the motivation of any individual who sounds the alarm. Michael J. Meyers (1991), a physician who serves as an expert witness in substance abuse cases, points out that a non-tainted complainer will be primarily interested in protecting the children, not in punishing the offender. There would be a willingness on this individual's part to go along with rehabilitation plans that maximize the offending parent's continuing (but protected) involvement with the children. (See the *Custody Newsletter*, Issue Number 8, for more information.)

Overall Attention to Needs

A major area of concern to the custody evaluator is a parent's ability to be attentive to the child's needs. Here we refer to the parental ability to be free of major physical and mental distractions and extensive episodes of irritability, poor impulse control, or poor judgment. The BPS, PORT, and PPCP all will yield important information here, since again, it is less helpful to know that a parent is engaging in a certain piece of behavior, and far more useful to know what kind of impact this behavior is having on a child. Traditional psychological tests, as well as medical, psychological, and psychiatric reports, can be helpful here. The evaluator should note the contexts in which the distractions or negativities occur, and *the frequency, duration, and intensity of given episodes*. It is not enough to state that a parent is, for example, mildly depressed. It is more helpful to state the conditions under which this is likely to occur, and information as to how such episodes seem to impact the child.

Negative data of this type should always be accompanied by recommendations for what could lead to improvement. Nothing a custody evaluator has to say should be written in a way such that a parent can take it as a condemnation. Here is an example of how a custody evaluator, in summary or brief form, might approach this issue: "Parent X becomes irritable when he/she feels overwhelmed by other things he or she needs to do. This currently is happening several times per day, the episodes are of moderate intensity and may last ten to fifteen minutes. When this happens, the involved child becomes afraid to approach the parent and may suffer a lack of needed guidance or empathy. Psychotherapeutic help specifically designed to enhance organizational skills may serve to reduce parent X's feeling of being overwhelmed. If parent X chooses to receive this help, it would be important to monitor progress in this very important area." Along these same lines, the evaluator might want to note areas of special strength, e.g., that parent X functions particularly well when talking to his or her child about any kind of long-range plans.

Parental Awareness

The evaluator should have some way of measuring a parent's awareness of the critical issues which may come up in day-to-day child-care situations. A parent's ability to recognize what aspects of a given situation should become a focal point of parental action—and just as important, to recognize when a given area should *not* be a cause for action—is a most important parental skill. The parent who understands just which aspects of a situation require action and which should be left alone is a parent who has the potential to make truly useful contributions to a child's upbringing.

The custody evaluator should have some knowledge of a parent's ability to generate adequate solutions in typical childcare situations. Interview and observation data can help; the PASS is specifically designed to reflect such awareness. Further, the more potential ways a parent has to address any given situation, the better. By having a storehouse of potential actions at his or her command, a parent can much better fine-tune a response to any given situation. This category would include limit-setting ability.

A parent should be aware of the desirability of acknowledging a child's feelings in many types of interactions. The custody evaluator should pay attention to the degree to which a parent is aware that emotional empathy is exceedingly strengthening to a child. Interviews and observations can help; the PASS is designed to reflect this skill.

The custody evaluator should understand the degree to which a parent is aware of the importance of taking a child's unique past history into account in dealing with current situations and in using words and phrases understandable to the child.

The custody evaluator should be interested in knowing the degree to which a parent is aware of the desirability of monitoring a child's reactions to any given parental communication. This awareness is an operational equivalent of "effectiveness" itself, since one can be aware of the effectiveness of *any* action *only* by monitoring the results the action is achieving. Here we also see the foundation skill behind flexibility, since the ability to flexibly adjust what one is doing is entirely dependent upon feedback data. Interviews and observations can help; the PASS is designed to reflect this exceedingly important trait. The prime tool of the flexible person is an awareness of the importance of monitoring, minute by minute, even second by second, feedback data. The truly flexible parent is keenly aware of the reactions he or she is generating in a given child.

The custody evaluator should seek to understand the degree to which a parent is aware of his or her child's interpersonal relationships. Interviews can be helpful here; the PPCP is designed specifically to reflect this important awareness.

The Child's Daily Routine

The truly concerned and interested parent is aware of his or her child's daily routine. The custody evaluator should be acutely interested in the degree to which a parent really "knows" his or her child. Nowhere is this more evident than in this important area. A paucity of knowledge about a given child on the part of a critical participant would argue that this individual's degree of interest in the child was not as great as might be claimed. Interviews can also be helpful here.

Health and Developmental History

The custody evaluator should inquire into a parent's awareness of the child's health history, developmental history, school history, fears, and personal hygiene habits. Interviews can be helpful, as well as test, observation, and document data.

Communication Style

The custody evaluator must know the degree to which a parent is aware of various aspects of a child's communication style. This is perhaps one of the most important parental strengths; it reflects an awareness on the part of a parent that much more is involved in getting a message across to a child than simply saying a group of words. Our belief in the overwhelming importance of this skill is documented in Chapter Three.

Parental Irritability

The custody evaluator should be interested in the degree to which a parent is aware of his or her own vulnerability to becoming irritable. It is fairly difficult for the custody evaluator to pick up this information from interviews and observations, even with tests, since parents taking part in custody evaluations are rarely, if indeed ever, truthful about the degree to which they become irritable. The *complete* evaluation is necessary to identify areas of parental vulnerability, and, as mentioned before, should yield information such that the evaluator is able to specify the triggers for such episodes, along with their frequency, duration, and intensity. I always consider it a "plus" if a parent admits his or her hot-buttons and has strategies to address them.

Solution-Oriented Parents

The custody evaluator must identify the degree to which each parent is solution-oriented and flexible, as opposed to adversarial and closed-minded. This is indeed among the most important of variables the custody evaluator should assess. It is difficult to get a good reading on these dispositions, since very few parents are directly honest about such attitudes. What the custody evaluator is essentially interested in is the degree to which a parent realizes the importance of, strives toward, and possesses mental tools appropriate for a cooperative relationship with the other parent.

Technically, the evaluator is looking for signs of two important skills: one is the capacity for nonadversarial communication (detailed in Chapter Eleven) and the other is the capacity for multiple-perspective-taking. This latter ability refers to an individual's skill at being able, so to speak, to "see things from the other person's point of view." Often, I consider it essential that someone teach this skill to parents caught up in custody disputes after all aspects of the evaluation and court dispositions are completed. Without this skill, it is unlikely that any kind of acceptable arrangement will ever be worked out. In the absence of other signs of serious information-processing deficits, a one dimensional house on the *House-Tree-Person* test, i.e., a house without any indication of multiple dimensionality, points to an *absence* of this skill. The same (negative) conclusion is warranted if the perspective used to draw the various parts of the house (e.g., roof, walls, etc.) do not logically mesh.

Parental Honesty

The custody evaluator should seek to understand the degree to which each parent is honest. This is not an easy behavioral disposition to measure, and common sense tells us it is highly contextualized. That is, individuals who would never lie in certain contexts would easily lie in others. Also, my experience with most published tools that seek to measure honesty is that they do so by simply asking the person taking the test if he or she is honest. There are more subtle ways to approach the measurement of honesty, for example, asking an individual how he or she thinks a typical person would act in a certain situation. This ploy, which puts distance between the respondent and the response, will probably evoke a more honest response. An individual responding to a question about how some "average person" would react to a certain situation is most likely telling how he or she would react in that situation, but is spared the awareness that this is so. An evaluator might ask: "Deep down inside, how much do you think the average parent caught up in a custody dispute *really* wants to work out an accommodation with his or her 'ex' regardless of what is said out loud?"

However, having said all this, we do *not* claim we can prove conclusively what dishonesty in a custody evaluation context necessarily means to a given child. Almost all—maybe *really all*—custody disputants lie. Such information must be used interactively, with other data.

Modeling Skills or Competency

The custody evaluator should seek to understand the degree to which a parent congruently offers and models the skills of competency. All sources of data should be used here, as in the following categories.

Empathy and Support

The degree to which a parent can congruently offer and model empathy and support should be an important target for the custody evaluator.

Consistency

The custody evaluator should be interested in the degree to which a parent congruently offers and models appropriate consistency.

Appropriate Role Models

The custody evaluator should be able to identify the degree to which each parent is a good role model for admirable traits and what these traits are.

Source of Assets

The parent who, overall, is a greater source of psychological assets for the child than is the other, should be identified by the custody evaluator.

Desire for Closeness

The degree to which a child seeks to be psychologically close to each parent should be an object of interest for the evaluator.

Child's Conscious Choice

The custody evaluator should make sure he or she knows if the child has a conscious (or verbal) choice, what that choice is, and the source of the choice. Interviews are the prime tool here, although this information can emerge at any time during an evaluation of the child. Other things being equal, I do not favor asking children with whom they would choose to live, or even direct questions about time-distribution aspects of an arrangement. (See Chapter Thirteen for dissenting opinions.) I believe such questioning can be exceedingly guilt inducing for a child, who already, at some deeper level, feels responsible for the situation that exists between the parents.

There are also subtle reasons why it makes no sense to ask a child about his or her conscious choice for PCP, chief among these being that children are not reliable informants about their own inner conditions at conscious or verbal levels. In developing the BPS and PORT, we utilized a rather extensive battery of tools and devices with the children in the various sample groups. We compared a child's conscious or verbal choices for PCP to a variety of choices determined in other ways. Among these were child questionnaires that asked questions of a child like the following: "If you were having a nightmare, who would you like to come to comfort you?" "If you had a question about a homework problem, who would you want to go to for help?" There were 60 items in these questionnaires. PCPs determined from these verbal or conscious data had a much lower correlation with choices arrived at by other sources, including professional sources, *and the child's own unconscious perceptions.* In other words, BPS and PORT choices (essentially, children's less conscious choices) achieved much higher agreement rates with choices arrived at by highly knowledgeable sources than did the children's conscious preferences. BPS and PORT scores (Bricklin, 1984, 1989) were much more accurately predicted by parents, independent mental health professionals and courtroom judges, than by children's conscious choices. Children, in general, are not good verbal reporters of their own conditions even on specifics. If a child, even an older child of, say, 10 or 11, is asked about a favorite TV show, a TV show that has been a favorite for at least a year, a child will typically answer with a program that has been a favorite for one or two weeks. The child may insist this is the case even when the so called "favorite program" was not broadcast during the time period claimed. This same pattern, about favoritism, is found regarding friends and teachers. The same kind of inaccuracy in reporting is found in many areas of a child's life.

It is instructive to note that even with much older children, 12 through 16, things were not much different regarding their ability to choose, with any kind of accuracy, a parent who would act in their own best interests, at least as compared to choices arrived at by parents, mental health professionals, and courtroom judges. Custody evaluators should keep this important piece of information in mind when it comes to evaluating any given child's conscious choice for PCP.

Joint Custody

The evaluator should address the issue of the feasibility of joint legal and physical custody, especially if the relevant jurisdiction presumes it to be best unless proven otherwise. See Chapter Ten.

Independently Reached Parental Agreements

The custody evaluator should make sure he or she has knowledge of any independently-reached agreements between parents. This is not the place to argue the following point at length, but a good case could probably be made for the proposition that the "best" custody arrangement is one that the parents deeply agree about, regardless of whether this jibes with other information or not. The arrangement that will lead to the least hostility and the greatest cooperation is probably the one each participant feels is most fair. Should it occur that an independently reached agreement disagrees with the arrangements the evaluation favors, the evaluator's caveats could be offered to the parents in a nonadversarial way as information the parents might wish to incorporate into their daily living.

If there is extensive disagreement between what the evaluator believes to be in a child's best interests and what the parents believe, the evaluator data can be presented to the ultimate decision-maker along with what the parents believe.

Should the evaluator wish to recommend mediation at the outset (prior to an evaluation), there should be no paper trail of vindictive court hearings and at least some direct observational evidence that the parents can communicate cooperatively.

Collateral Information

The evaluator should make sure all important sources of collateral information have been identified, e.g., pediatricians, neighbors, and relatives.

We have not included a discussion on the importance of ascertaining which parent can better facilitate a religious orientation in the child, because we have not been able to develop any meaningful way to conceptualize this issue. It is likely that if such facilitation were important to a given child, it would influence (via a desirable halo effect) that child's BPS and PORT responses. Rohman, Sales and Lou (1987, p. 80) make the following points. A court *can* seek to determine if a given parent's religious practices are potentially harmful to a child. If a mature child has embraced a faith, the court will consider favorably that parent who can better support this embrace. If a child has not as yet embraced a faith, courts will value that parent who will raise the child in the faith asserted by the natural parents. When a child does not adhere to a particular faith and each parent belongs to a different faith, no particular parental faith carries a higher priority than any other.

GATHERING THE DATA

Suggestions about the tools and sequences with which the custody evaluator might operate are offered for three sets of conditions. One condition is where the custody evaluator has minimal concerns about the quality and integrity of the major participants in the evaluation. This might be the case—rare!—where there is an amiable and cooperative relationship between the parents, and most things are going well for all involved children. (This is not to say such parents do not exist; it *is* to say such folks rarely require an evaluation.) An evaluation that satisfies these conditions typically comes up when well meaning and bright parents are genuinely desirous of finding out what mental health science can recommend to assist them in forging some kind of time-sharing arrangement. In situations we would label as "minimal concern" circumstances, neither parent is suspicious of the qualities and/or motivations of the other. Nothing has emerged in the ongoing life histories of the involved participants that would be a red flag for evaluator concern.

The set of circumstances that we label "average concerns" is the typical situation the evaluator will encounter. Here there is a certain degree of bitterness on both sides, along with a fairly liberal dose of distrust. This is the "average" condition for the simple reason that if these negative conditions did not exist, things would not have progressed to the point where an evaluation was necessary.

The situation we would label "above average concerns," would be the situation that is highly adversarial and involves serious allegations by one party or the other, such as sexual abuse, criminal behavior, etc.

Here is the sequence our various research teams have agreed is the best to use in lining up the procedures to be performed in a custody evaluation of extensive scope. This would fall under the category of ALL-CPE or All-Critical-Participants Evaluation as detailed in Chapter One (or a LIM-CPE, a Limited-Critical-Participants Evaluation, if it was not possible to attain an ALL-CPE).

We are assuming the evaluator has come to understand the involved psychological and legal issues and has clarified his or her role with all critical participants, made sure that whoever initiated the evaluation has the right to do so, and confidentiality issues were resolved explicitly.

The child is typically seen first. It is communicated to the parents that our approach places most emphasis on tools specifically designed to help the evaluator understand issues pertinent to a custody evaluation. It is explained that the heart of the assessment is an attempt to understand the actual impact each parent is having on the involved child. The whole "utilization" or interactive or "congruence" model is explained to the parents. That is, it is emphasized over and over that the "meaning" of parental behavior can be known only by its impact on a child, and that this cannot be accurately judged from parental "intentions." An important corollary of this is that we hardly ever think of a parent as a "bad" or "good" person, but simply are seeking a way to make available to a child the "best" each parent has to offer.

Another important purpose of our approach is to send a loud and clear message to the parents. That message, put bluntly, is that we are not going to be particularly swayed by each parent's list of horror stories about the other parent. Yes, we will listen. We certainly need to know all worries and concerns. It is quite obvious that no parent would follow a custody arrangement if he or she believed the evaluator was not sensitive to all voiced concerns. Nevertheless, we try our best to make sure the parents know that data seeking to assess this interactive dimension will be the most important data when it comes to the evaluator's putting all the information together. We will address, and try to find a solution for, every single worry and concern (whether or not we secretly believe they were voiced with sincerity). We do our very best to get parents off the tack they are wont to follow in the absence of this message, and that is to go out and create greater and greater lists of horror stories in order to prevail in their pursuit of the child.

We try to get *both* parents to bring the child to the first session. This gives the evaluator a chance to assess the way they treat each other (have them discuss some unresolved issue), and reduces the possibility that an attorney will later claim a child's test reactions were biased because of who brought the child to the evaluator's office. If this is not possible, we ask each of the parents to identify a neutral third party each parent knows and trusts to bring the child(ren) to the first visit. (It is true that certain items on the BPS and PORT may vary in accordance with who brings the child to the evaluator's office; however, these items are usually easy to spot and to correct for.)

Next, the critical participants are told to send in all documents they would like us to consider. Documents are also sought from all of the various sources soon to be enumerated. This is done toward the beginning of the evaluation in an attempt to make sure that we are in a position to understand all of the subtleties (as well as "blatancies") in the case, so as to prepare for any special test or tools that may be needed in the evaluation. Remember, that it is imperative to seek information on all prior custody determinations. Interview data are gathered from the parents.

(Although, this is often difficult to implement, if possible, I try to see the involved child with *both* parents present. In fact, nowadays, I am likely to *insist,* saying to the parent who will not cooperate: "Well, it will certainly be interesting information to the judge that you cannot put aside your need to fight for an hour or two.")

Next, parent A is seen with the involved child.

Following this, parent B is seen with the involved child.

Next, parent A is seen alone, followed by parent B alone. Test and (more) interview data are gathered.

Any significant others are seen.

Home visits are utilized when appropriate.

Further configurations of participants may be seen, depending on emergent data. Some evaluators like to see each parent with a child several times. It is vital that the prevailing custody arrangement be amended so that a child spends an equal amount of time with each parent prior to observation or evaluation sessions.

Gathering Data from Child Participants

The following is a "to do" list for a child participant in a custody evaluation. Suggestions are made in three separate categories, which have already been described: where the evaluator has "minimal concerns" about the quality and integrity of the participants; where the evaluator has what might be termed "average concerns" about the participants; and finally, where there are "above average concerns." In each instance, it is our intention to suggest that the items listed under "average" conditions be done *in addition to* those listed under "minimal concerns." With the "above average concerns" category, it is suggested that these items be carried out *along with everything listed in the other two categories*.

I. Psychological Tests

Minimal Concerns: It is suggested that the BPS and/or PORT be used. To our way of thinking, it is impossible to do a good custody evaluation without maximal attempts on the part of the evaluator to understand the actual impacts each parent is having on the involved children.

Average Concerns: If aspects of the child's functioning in school are an issue, but not a major issue, it would be sensible to utilize an intelligence test of the evaluator's choice. Frequently, a technique called "My Parents Would…" (Village Publishing, Inc.) can be used.

Above Average Concerns: Tests such as the *Rorschach, Children's Apperception Test* (CAT) or selected cards from the *Thematic Apperception Test* (TAT) are used only if data emanating from procedures used in the other categories yield data that are equivocal. These tests are not standardized to yield meaningful custody data. I, personally, have not been able to find a helpful way to use the CAT cards. I cannot find a balance of neutral mother and father figures in which the evaluator might wonder about attributions accorded each. I have been able to find a selection of TAT cards where this was possible. Nevertheless, it is an inferential leap to assume that qualities attributed to so-called "mother" or "father" figures on these cards yield data helpful to the custody evaluator. It was striking to us that in the development of the PORT, when we asked children to "draw a person," the results were wildly and significantly different from those yielded when they were instructed to "Draw your mom" or "Draw your dad." Hence, the idea that children identify figures not explicitly designated as their parents in this way (i.e., as their parents) is not proven.

Munsinger and Karlson (1994, p. 8) suggest the following tests as useful in a custody evaluation: the *Personality Inventory for Children* (Wirt, Lachar, Klinedinst, & Seat, 1977) and the *Child Behavior Checklist* (Achenbach & Edelbrock, 1986).

In this category, where there are above average concerns on the part of the evaluator, it may be important to use specific tests designed to identify idiosyncrasies in a child's learning or social or communication skills. Decisions of this type would have to be made on a case-by-case basis. It is always handy for custody evaluators to have available books and catalogues that list existing psychological tests, so as to be able to identify those appropriate in a given, special situation.

II. Documents

Minimal Concerns: When inspecting documents, the evaluator should keep an eye out for any information pertaining to a child's communication style: the possibility of subtle or significant learning disabilities, or *anything* that has to do with the manner in which a child processes information. A child's ability to handle information is at the heart of how he or she will respond to differences in parental styles. Also, the evaluator should be alert for signs of any special needs or problems in the child, e.g., psychological, medical, dental, etc. Where there are minimal concerns, the evaluator might be content to peruse only the records of any prior custody determinations and relevant parent questionnaire forms.

Average Concerns: Here the evaluator would inspect psychological, medical, and dental records, as well as those yielded by involved schools. It goes without saying that special attention would be given to reports from mental health professionals.

Above Average Concerns: In this category, the evaluator might wish to add legal documents of any type, for example, those that would have to do with conditions around adoption, especially where there has been a late adoption or foster home placement. These conditions often bring with them a whole set of special problems.

III. Observations

Minimal Concerns: In this category, the evaluator might be content with observations made in the office. We consider them relatively useless, but it seems evaluators are addicted to performing such observations and reporting them in courtrooms (where I hear them and wonder if they seem as ridiculously useless to the judge as they do to me).

Average Concerns: In this category, the evaluator would want to do much better than free-form observations. Structured interviews of the type described in the chapter on the development of the PORT, *are* useful. We used a one-way mirror, and standardized tasks were used to observe the interactions between parents and their children. Other commercial tools of this type are described in Issue No. 8 of the *Custody Newsletter*. Remember that when observing a child interacting with one parent only, one must be wary of making inferences to other contexts. Without choices, a child will typically cling to and/or play ball with whichever parent happens to be present. Home visits would be advisable. Bricklin and Elliot (1995) offer an observational method aimed at a child's utilization patterns.

Above Average Concerns: When there are above average concerns, home visits are mandatory. Special considerations should be followed if any kind of abuse is suspected. These suggestions have been outlined previously.

IV. Interviews

Minimal Concerns, Average Concerns, Above Average Concerns: We have combined these categories, since the main thing to be wary of under *all* conditions is asking direct, guilt-reducing questions. Pay heed to the fact that interview-generated data from children do not have high correlations with data from other, more meaningful, sources. In line with this, ask *specific* questions (e.g., "What exactly do you do at Mom's house?") rather than "opinion" questions (e.g., "Who do you like more, Mom or Dad?").

Gathering Data from Parents

The following is a "to do" list for involved parents in the custody evaluation. Separate suggestions will be made for significant others. The sequence here is the same as with the child. The idea is to send a message that the more objective test data are what is important, not the interview data, which will consist solely of horror stories, and the observation data, a good bit of which will be insincere.

I. Tests

Minimal Concerns: The devices that yield information most germane to an adequate custody evaluation are the PASS and the PPCP. At the very least, the custody evaluator would want to know something about a parent's awareness of the different facets involved in communicating with children, along with the extent of a parent's genuine interest in a child.

Average Concerns: Here the evaluator would use traditional psychological tests of his or her own choice. I particularly like the *House-Tree-Person* test, especially once I had access to Emanuel Hammer's amazing data base. The HTP is particularly sensitive to any form of psychological conflict. As such, any significant kind of psychopathology is unlikely to be missed. However, lacking knowledge of a specific data base, this might not be the test of choice for others. The evaluator might consider using the Comprehension subtest of the *WAIS-R* as a rough measure of common sense judgment. I really do stress the word "rough" in the last sentence. In evaluating the traditional tests, the evaluator should pay special attention to all areas that could impact a parent's relationship with a child, particularly in the capacity to be distractible (especially for extended periods of time), impulse control, and so-called major impairments, e.g., severe depression, severe thought disorder, etc.

Munsinger and Karlson (1994, p. 8) suggest the following tests as useful in the evaluation of adults: the *Personality Assessment Inventory* (Morey, 1991), the *Minnesota Multiphasic Personality Inventory-2* (Hathaway & McKinley, 1989), the *Beck Depression Inventory* (Beck & Steer, 1987), the *Beck Anxiety Inventory* (Beck & Steer, 1990), the *Parenting Stress Index* (Abidin, 1990), and the *Thematic Apperception Test* (Murray, 1943).

Above Average Concerns: Here, the evaluator might be interested in traditional tests specific to a clearly defined concern. For example, there might be some evidence of adult Attention Deficit Disorder. If this is so, the evaluator might be interested in administering a test with a data base sensitive to this concern.

II. Documents

Minimal Concerns: Where there are minimal concerns, the evaluator might be content to peruse all questionnaire forms.

Average Concerns: Here, there are many documents with which the custody evaluator should be acquainted. Those especially germane to a given case would, of course, be inspected with great care and concern. Any documentation that exists that deals with a parent's developmental history should be inspected. This would also apply to documented records having to do with the parent's employment records and financial history. The parent's educational history is of concern, as is any documentation having to do with the individual's marital and interpersonal history. It is especially important to read anything having to do with each parent's relationships with past husbands and/or wives, significant others, and children with whom the parent has had contact, as well as co-workers, supervisors, friends, and relatives. Of special focus would, of course, be a parent's relationship with children. Medical and psychological records should be perused with special attention paid to anything having to do with problems with illicit drugs or alcohol. Any reports of sexual or physical abuse are of greatest importance.

Above Average Concerns: Where there are above average concerns about the quality, health, or integrity of a given individual, it would make sense to obtain extensive documentation. This might involve any and all possible lawsuits or interactions with the police. The evaluator might wish to obtain records having to do with the individual's driving experience. Some experts claim that financial, psychological and legal integrity might be represented in IRS forms. I would find such an investigation a practice of dubious validity. Extended employment documentation might be especially helpful, such as reports having to do with job performance ratings and the individual's relationship with coworkers. Health issues on the job would also be important. The evaluator might wish to look at extended medical records, which could include histories of hospitalizations, including the reasons for the hospitalizations as well as drug prescriptions involved. The individual's military record might be relevant, as well.

III. Observations

Minimal Concern: Here, the evaluator would again be content with the (relatively useless) observations in the office. (I have often wondered how I would react to a parent who yelled bloody murder at a child in my waiting room. Would I conclude I have finally met an honest custody disputant or was I rather face to face with some truly impaired individual?)

Average Concerns: Here, the evaluator would want to use structured observations. Our team has developed criteria for the following six categories. One deals with a parent's ability to communicate in a way that the child seems to readily find useful. Here we refer to the many parental skills outlined in Chapter Three, e.g., pacing, gauging the importance of getting to main points quickly, etc. On the receiving (positive) end, this could be seen in relatively relaxed facial expressions on the part of the child, as well as in body relaxation. Questions asked by the child would be relevant to what the parent was saying. All child actions would seem to move forward smoothly and easily from such interactions, and the child would engage in risk-taking behaviors (for example, solving problems) without marked hesitations.

The next category would seek to detail the degree to which the parent conveys a sense of warmth to the child. The criteria to look for in the child would involve items such as those enumerated above, plus a ready smile on the part of the child. Remember: These kinds of responses must be observed by several observers, and the data recorded. (Such data, again, are far more meaningful when choices are available to the child.)

Another useful category has to do with whether or not the parent is an adequate role model for the teaching of the skills of competency. All of the above criteria would be utilized, as well as indications that the child is eager to use offered parental suggestions.

Another category would involve a parent's awareness that it is important to understand the child's position on any given issue at any given moment. Here the parent would acknowledge the child's feelings and/or paraphrase how a child may be perceiving a situation in order to constantly upgrade the quality of feedback information.

The next category seeks evidence that when a parent is interacting with the child, the parent is constantly scanning the child's reactions for any signs of emergent needs requiring quick attention. Within this category, the evaluator might consider the ways limits are set and the child's responses to such efforts.

The last category would seek to understand the degree to which a parent's responses engender self-esteem and independence in a child. Here, we look for evidence that the parent allows a child an opportunity to tackle things solo or independently before any type of advice or information is offered. The parental demeanor, including facial relaxation, body relaxation, and tone of voice, all give the child the message that there is no impatient attitude within the parent. The parental facial expression tells the child he or she is valued regardless of the efficiency of the child's behavior.

Structured problem-solving tasks of the type described in the chapter on the PORT are the items most commonly used in association with these criteria.

Above Average Concerns: When there are above average concerns, a home visit is mandatory. Follow the guidelines offered above when any form of abuse is suspected. It is suggested that the materials in *Custody Newsletters* (Issue Nos. 5, 6, and 7), on the detection of sexual abuse be read by all evaluators dealing with evaluations in which abuse is alleged.

IV. Interviews

Minimal Concerns: Here, the evaluator might be content with interviewing the major participants only.

Average Concerns: Here, the evaluator might wish not only to interview all significant others but to seek second-party verification for anything that seems to require such verification. Heed the caveats in Chapter Eight regarding the validity of data obtained from collateral sources.

Above Average Concerns: Here the evaluator might wish to add even third-party verification, selectively, if warranted.

The following is a "to-do" list for significant others. This would refer to live-in companions or persons either parent might intend to marry. Also included in this category would be grandparents, baby-sitters, close friends of either parent, etc.

There are two critical questions to consider with persons who might fall into this category. One question has to do with how much actual contact the significant other might have with an involved child. The second question concerns whether or not anything has turned up that might suggest cause for concern regarding this person's spending time with the involved child or children.

If a significant other is to have a great deal of contact with the child, e.g., a live-in companion, a full-time baby-sitter, etc., then it would be prudent to follow the same guidelines as offered for an involved parent. The same guidelines would be followed regarding the degree of concern.

If a significant other is to have scant contact with the child and there is little cause for concern (e.g, physical or sexual abuse, etc.), then the following guidelines could be followed. If there is very minimum concern about this individual, interviews alone might generate the kind of information the evaluator might wish to consider. If there are "average" concerns, one would proceed on a case-specific basis. If there are above average concerns for any reason whatsoever, we would revert to the prior guidelines offered, and the evaluator would use the same procedure as for an involved parent.

PARENT-CHILD DYADS OR FAMILY "SYSTEMS"?

Some evaluators wonder if assessment emphasis should be on the family systems of which a child may be part, rather than on specific parent-child dyads.

There is merit in this claim, which is why we recommend the evaluator observe as many family configurations as desired. For example, if there are several children, the evaluator would certainly want to know which parent is better able to handle them when they are all together. The PORT can also be helpful. It elicits child-data about several typical family system configurations, e. g., alone with each parent, with both parents simultaneously, within a "whole-family" context, with siblings, and several others.

There are also complexities in a "family systems" approach to assessment. First, the sheer number of "systems" that could be observed, even with a small family, approaches dozens.

Second, most significant parent-child interactions are one-on-one. A parent must get the child up, washed and dressed, help with and supervise homework, enforce chores, administer discipline, etc., all essentially one-on-one interactions.

Third, when one uses a systems approach, it is still important to know the probable range of impacts a given parent will have on a particular child.

Fourth, a systems approach often forces an evaluator into a subjective judge's role. Child A is a much better match for Dad than for Mom. Younger children B and C are much better matches for Mom. Children B and C are exceedingly dependent for emotional and actual support on child A, but child A derives little gain from his relationship with siblings B and C. What is the evaluator to do? It is very hard to generate data to address such issues, which often involve questions as to who should sacrifice what for the sake of whom. Psychoanalyst-physicist Robert Waelder (personal communication) remarked that the Greek search for clarity and the Christian search for charity rarely merge clearly. How true this is in custody evaluations!

Chapter Ten

Creating a Custody Plan: Aggregating and Weighting the Variables

Michael H. Halbert and Barry Bricklin

After the evaluator has scored and assembled data from psychological tests, collected self-report (interview and questionnaire) responses, inspected and abstracted whatever seemed important in selected documents, and learned whatever could be learned from structured and/or unstructured observations and home visits, it becomes time to aggregate this information so that statements useful to a custody decision maker can be made.

Judging from opinions expressed by *Custody Newsletter* readers, and participants at the various workshops we have offered on custody evaluations around the country, this isn't always easy.

Even the authors of *Solomon's Sword,* (Schutz et al., 1989), an outstandingly thorough guide to conducting comprehensive custody evaluations, could offer clear and definite guidelines for weighting assembled data in only two scenarios: One is where all the findings that reach a level they call "reportable" (defined operationally) favor one particular parent, and the other is where one parent "poses a clear and convincing danger to the child" (p. 93).

The rest of the time we all sweat.

Part of the problem is, of course, the number of value judgments that enter into a determination of what is "best" for a child.

We will offer four models that can be used to aggregate the data collected during a custody evaluation, although we do not claim that any of these methods can totally circumvent the "ultimate issue" complexities mentioned in Chapter One. The models are designed to assist in the recommending of a primary caretaking or custodial parent (PCP).

I have chosen not to address the issue of "joint" versus "sole" custody plans in detail. The reader is referred to Chapter Two and to the *Custody Newsletter*, (1990), Issue No. 1, featuring an excellent survey article by Dr. John Call. Dr. Call summarizes the benefits and difficulties of each of the two plans.

I have found that *in actual practice* these terms often have no clear operational referents, in that parents rarely adhere to their custody arrangements in any event, regardless of how any particular "arrangement" was reached (court versus mediation versus self-determined).

Many courts these days order joint *legal* custody routinely (shared decision making regarding important choices), except in exceptional circumstances (e.g., abuse on the part of one parent, physical location/availability difficulties, wildly adversarial attitudes between the parents, etc.). Another way of saying this is that if both parents want joint legal custody (and even when the parents have not reached such an agreement), this is what will often be ordered, unless there are clear reasons to deny it. Very often, the fact that one parent will agree ahead of time *not* to seek primary physical custody in exchange for shared legal custody will be enough for the other side to agree to the arrangement. Often, the parent who does *not* pursue physical custody does not want shared legal custody either. The point here is that when an evaluator is called upon to enter the picture, each parent participant is usually seeking the role of PCP, often from a legal as well as a physical perspective. Hence, the most frequent evaluation-scenario is one in which a judge will be called upon to choose a (physical) PCP; the evaluator will be expected to address this issue.

Where *true* joint custody will work (shared physical as well as legal custody), this is usually obvious *prior* to any evaluation (e.g., there is a high degree of cooperation between the parents, each lives close to the child's school, etc.). It is important, however, for a custody evaluator to be able to recognize the truly flexible child; any plan that has a lot of back-and-forth stuff in it for a child should be reserved for *flexible children* only, children with good multiple-perspective-taking information-processing skills, as well as children highly comfortable not only with change but with *each* parent. *PORT and BPS responses (or similar child-derived data) should reflect this comfort with each parent.*

Summarizing, here are some research and clinically generated suggestions concerning situations where true joint (physical and legal) custody may prove workable: child-derived information should reflect that both parents have mainly positive impacts on the children; the data mirror great flexibility and multiple-perspective-taking skills on the part of the child; there is no lengthy paper trail of (vindictive) legal actions on the part of either or both parents; when the parents *do* argue, it's not about the children; the logistics are favorable; both parents truly want to share custody; the evaluator has physically observed that the parents can talk politely to one another; the parents are reasonably flexible and can cooperate (e.g., about things where cooperation is essential, as in potty training); there are no override factors (e.g., violence). In general, younger children more than older children (who often have a circle of friends near one particular house) desire this type of arrangement. My own feeling is that in cases where an impasse was reached and an evaluation was either requested or ordered, the above conditions will rarely be met.

Hence, again, the problem for an evaluator comes up when there is a need to identify the parent better suited for the PCP role.

CHOOSING A PCP: A DECISION-TREE MODEL USING BPS AND PORT (OR CHILD-DERIVED) DATA

1. Make sure the psychological, legal, and ethical guidelines suggested at the end of Chapter One have been followed, along with the cautions regarding evaluator-bias.

2. Study the test, clinical, life-history, and documented data to identify parental assets and liabilities. Make sure these assets and liabilities are reflected in tests such as the BPS and PORT (i.e., that there is evidence the child's way of perceiving and responding to the world is such that he or she can profit from these parental assets or be hurt by the liabilities).

Make sure all involved children have had enough contact with each parent so that it makes sense to speak of measuring what the interactions with these individuals have been like.

This step is the heart of the evaluation: regardless of who is designated PCP (primary caretaking parent), a good custody plan makes available the "best" each parent has to offer each involved child. It is even possible that a parent who is not the better candidate overall for PCP is the one better suited to address some very compelling need on the part of the child. The plan would have to ensure that this can happen.

3. Consider all of the practical issues which might be involved, e.g., availability and quality of baby-sitters in each household; time availability of each critical participant; the homes and neighborhoods in which the child

would live under competing plans; the quality of interpersonal support readily available to each parent, etc. Consider any legal "override" factor, e.g., abuse. Consider the posttrial plans of each participant, e.g., one may intend to remarry or relocate. A possibly controlling factor could be involved. Other "override" factors might include the possibility that the critical participants could agree on a custody plan on their own or via mediation, and whether it is important to assign greater than usual attention to the stated preferences of the involved children, e.g., advanced age, ultimate disposition by a judge who places great emphasis on a child's conscious preference. This heightened attention does not mean you would necessarily go along with the stated preferences, but that you would address them more fully.

4. Consider whether the child has a special need that must be kept in mind at all times when thinking about the assessed variables, e.g., a physical disability which requires almost constant one-on-one care, a serious psychological or educational problem, etc.

5. In using the BPS and PORT to assist in a recommendation for PCP, keep in mind the conceptual worlds which gave birth to each test. The BPS assumes the parent who can *more* frequently act "in the child's best interests" is the better bet for PCP. The PORT assumes the parent who has been the greater source of assets for the child and with whom the child feels more at ease is the better choice. Hence they yield data and arrive at conclusions from different clinical perspectives. The BPS and PORT will choose the same candidate for PCP in eighty to ninety percent of instances. Exhibit 10.1 summarizes the decision-tree, and indicates what to do when each test yields a different POC. This model asserts that if two tests, both with good validity figures, each of which approaches the measurement task from a different perspective, choose the same POC, which is cross-validated by other tools and tests, the evaluator has sufficient evidence to recommend this POC as PCP. Should the data-based tests each suggest a different POC, there are three possibilities: (1) a NBOAI scenario; (2) the BPS is reflecting recent data; (3) that which is measured by each test constitutes a separate psychological context for the tested child. For possibilities (1) and (2), the PORT U (or unconscious indicators) are used to suggest a PCP. For possibility (3), *all* of the data are used interactively.

THE CONTRIBUTION OF FORMAL MODELS

In a custody case, after the evaluator has collected the evidence in a case, he or she still faces the problem of how to put all these pieces together—how to decide on the probative value of the collection of evidence, taken as a whole, based on the probative values of each piece arrived at separately. (Evidence has "probative value" to the extent that it tends to prove an issue. The relevancy of a piece of evidence refers to its probative value in accordance with the purpose for which it was introduced.) This is especially a problem if one is not using data-based instruments.

In a legal custody decision, there are many different pieces of evidence. This taxes our ability to consider them individually and collectively as we try to come to a single evaluation based on the whole body of evidence.

The utility of having a formal process can be shown with a simple problem.

Think of a triangle and imagine that we are asked to estimate its area. Further imagine that we have no measuring devices at all.

We can tackle the task directly and estimate the area by looking at the triangle, squinting a bit, and doing our best.

But suppose we know the formula for getting the area of a triangle from the length of its three sides. Using this approach, we can estimate the length of each side, and then use a formal process (the formula) to get a derived estimate of the area.

Almost always, an estimate obtained by this formula is more accurate than one obtained by simple estimate. This is because we have confined our estimating process to the easiest aspect of the problem (the length of each of three straight lines), and used a formal process for combining the three estimates to obtain the needed estimate of the area.

When we estimate the area directly, we are allowing error to occur in the total process, and that error will generally be larger than when we can restrict the error inherent in estimation to a single part of the task.

The value of having some explicit, carefully thought-out method is twofold. First, as everywhere else in intellectually supported endeavors, being explicit about our methods permits others (and ourselves, too) to examine, understand, and improve the process. Second, in situations like custody disagreements, where there usually are highly charged emotions, advocacy, preconceptions, and biases, it is vital to avoid letting one aspect of the case, one piece of evidence, overwhelm the others.

The best defense against the latter effect is to have an explicit aggregation process. Each piece of evidence is examined in turn, its credibility, its relevance, and, thus, its value is assessed, and that value is combined with the value of other pieces of evidence that have likewise been evaluated. This orderly process can be explicit without curtailing one's creativity, sensitivity, or responsiveness to the unique character of any particular situation.

Models 2 and 3 create mind-sets that are particularly important when the evaluator is considering target-areas for which there are no published databases. They can also be used to supplement the data-based BPS/PORT decision-tree, i.e., the latter is used to suggest a PCP, and model 2 or 3 is used to consider only those target-areas for which no published databases exist.

Exhibit 10.1

QUICK REFERENCE GUIDE: CHOOSING A PRIMARY CARETAKING PARENT.

Key to Codes: MMU   = mind-made-up
                   PCP   = primary caretaking parent
                   R   = responses
                   PORT U = PORT responses generated from less conscious
                            sources (unconscious sources)
                   PORT C = PORT responses generated from more
                            conscious sources
                   PAS   = parent alienation syndrome

1. *Decision-tree checks for BPS and PORT (or similar data-based information)*
   ☐ Address the psychological, legal, and ethical guidelines suggested in
     Chapter One.
   ☐ Study all data. Address especially the legal criteria of custody dispute reso-
     lution in the relevant jurisdiction and/or those cited in the UMDA.
   ☐ Override (e.g., abuse, neglect, relocation, etc.)?

BPS and PORT each
select same POC

(a) Select this POC as provisional
    PCP.
(b) Is a NBOAI scenario suggested in
    clinical or test data? If so, use
    PORT U to suggest PCP.
(c) Cross-validate (a) or (b) selection
    with PASS, PPCP, and other clin-
    ical information.

BPS and PORT each select
a different POC

(a) Considered NBOAI scenario? If so,
    use PORT U to suggest PCP.
(b) Consider if BPS is reflecting recent
    life-history events (the BPS may
    reflect more recent events than
    PORT U); if so, use PORT U to
    suggest PCP.
(c) If neither (a) nor (b), use all data to
    suggest PCP.
(d) Cross-validate (a), (b), or (c)
    choice with PASS, PPCP, and
    other clinical information.

   ☐ A PCP selected by this approach will agree with external validating criteria in
     about 90 percent of cases.

2. *NBOAI Checks* (See Chapter Eight.)
   (a) Responses sound rehearsed
   (b) Unasked information volunteered
   (c) Responses given too quickly
   (d) No pause between question and response
   (e) BPS choices all for championed parent, and child cannot give real-
       life examples of extreme choices
   (f) No eye contact
   (g) No progressive relaxation
   (h) Verbal R precedes whole-organism R

(i)   PORT C all for championed parent

(j)   PORT U does not match PORT C

(k)   Marked erasures re championed parent

(l)   Distortions re parent "saved"

3. *Four NBOAI and NBOAI-like scenarios*
    (a) The "classic" NBOAI
        (1) MMU
        (2) BPS for championed parent
        (3) Child cannot justify BPS R
        (4) Check BPS unconscious hand movements
        (5) PORT U does not equal PORT C
    (b) An NBOAI or PAS that often goes undetected
        (1) No MMU
        (2) PORT C does not equal PORT U
        (3) BPS for championed parent
        (4) Child cannot justify BPS R
    (c) Looks like PAS but is not
        (1) Mild MMU
        (2) PORT C = PORT U
        (3) BPS for championed parent and child can
             justify BPS R
        (4) No blatant negative remarks
        (5) Other data support choice
    (d) Looks like PAS but is not
        (1) MMU
        (2) PORT C = PORT U
        (3) BPS R can be justified

MODEL NUMBER ONE: MAINLY INTUITION

The first approach, and undoubtedly the most frequently used, is for the evaluator to assemble all the evidence that he or she feels is relevant, examine each piece in turn, and then by some nonexplicit, holistic, intuitive process combine them and come up with a final estimate of probative value for the whole assemblage of evidence. When the evaluator is experienced, competent, careful, bright, unbiased, and thorough, this method can produce excellent results.

But that is asking a lot of any person, experienced or not. There is a tendency to ignore interdependencies among some items, or to base the final estimate of probative value on a small subset of all the evidence.

This is to be expected. Intuitive evaluations seem to do relatively well for tasks that involve simple relations among many variables (TV quiz shows where the contestant has to estimate the market price of a set of goods) and tasks that involve complex relations with few variables (estimating the credibility of a witness's testimony). Intuitive methods do much less well with tasks that involve complex relations among many variables (predicting elections, evaluating financial investments, or predicting earthquakes).

MODEL NUMBER TWO: WEIGHTED AVERAGES

Let us now look at the second approach to aggregating the probative value of the pieces (or packets) of evidence.

In this second approach, the evaluator or expert witness first considers each piece of evidence separately, estimates the two relevances (which yield a probative value for that piece), and then uses an explicit numerical method to combine the separate probative values. (As will be seen, the relevance of a piece of evidence cannot be determined until its chances of appearing are considered from two perspectives. For descriptive convenience, we will refer to each perspective as a "relevance estimate.")

However, before describing the above process, we must address the question of just what constitutes a piece of evidence.

At the limit of disaggregation, a separate piece of evidence is a fact, a datum, an assertion, an observation, or any other information that has two properties. First, it can be stated as a proposition (in the logical sense of "proposition") to which a numerical probability of the proposition being true can be attached. Second, its truth or falsity makes a difference to the matter at issue. That is, the probability of that matter (i.e., the mother could better serve as the primary caregiver for this child) is different if the evidence is true than if the evidence is false.

In actual situations, it is seldom possible, necessary, or desirable to treat evidence at an extreme degree of disaggregation. Packets of related "micro-evidences" are constructed, and are treated as single pieces of evidence. For example, a school counselor's report may contain many separate statements (propositions), but the whole report may be considered as a single piece of evidence. However, it is better to err in the direction of too much disaggregation rather than too much aggregation. (In describing the third method of aggregation, we will offer some suggestions for dealing with "packets" of evidence; they can be used with the "weighted averages" method below, as well.)

The second or "weighted averages" approach to the aggregation of the values of evidence is to consider each separate piece of evidence (or separate evidence packet) and assign three numbers to it. The first number is an estimate of the credibility or "truth" of the evidence. (Avoid the word "credible" in testifying.)

It is convenient to use a 100-point scale for this estimate, because people are used to such a scale, it is easy to describe and explain, and it provides about 18 useful values. (In using rating scales, people often use only the 5's values—5, 10, 15, 20, etc., and they seldom use the 0 or 100. Thus, there are about 18 points on the scale that are actually used.)

A credibility value of 95 assigned to a particular piece of evidence would mean that the rater is virtually certain that the evidence is true, while a value of 5 would mean that the evidence is considered about as likely to be false as it is to be true. Note that the lowest value on our credibility scale means "This evidence has no credibility; the chances are 50/50 that it is true and the same it is false."

It is not frequent in custody evaluations to encounter situations where we would have reason to believe evidence assessed as absolutely and completely false implied the truthfulness of its opposite. A technique for dealing with estimates of credibility in such cases is included here more for logical completeness than because it will need to be invoked often. (We can treat a piece of evidence that we feel is really false by restating it as its negation, and thus the new statement of the evidence will have a credibility in the 0 to 100 range.)

The relation between credibility and probability is a simple one. Credibility goes from 100 (absolute believability) down to 0 (no information or probative value at all). These two credibility values correspond to probabilities ("truth" values) of 1.0 and .50 respectively. To convert from credibility (C) to probability (P) or vice versa:

1) Change probabilities into whole numbers by multiplying by 100 (e.g., .32 becomes 32).

2) $C = 2P - 100$ $\qquad$ $P = C/2 + 50$.

As the example offered below will show, however, even evidence of rather low credibility can be appropriately used in the evaluation process and have some impact.

The second and third numbers required for this aggregation method are each an estimate of the importance, worth, significance, or relevance of the evidence for each of the two particular hypotheses under consideration. The first hypothesis, (that the mother is the better PCP for this child) gets the first relevance estimate, and the second hypothesis (that the mother is not the better PCP) gets the second relevance estimate. In a typical custody evaluation, this second relevance estimate would pertain to the father. These relevance estimates are really estimates of conditional probabilities.

Many people find any discussion of probability (and especially of conditional probability) the perfect example of MEGO (My Eyes Glaze Over). However, the concepts of probability needed for this discussion are quite straightforward.

The probability measure for any statement (hypothesis) is the proportion of "representative" cases in which it is true. For our purposes, a representative case is one where there is contention about the custody of the child, and where evidence has been collected, reviewed, and evaluated to aid the decision maker in choosing a PCP.

In evaluating a particular case, if you feel, based on your professional experience and judgment, that some other conditions (in addition to the general one that a custody dispute exists) could have a major effect on the structure of the custody evaluation, then that should enter into your definition of "reference" cases. Then, we deal with selecting the group to which you wish to compare the evaluated participants. It is important to choose as members of the reference group cases containing the elements you consider salient about the instant case, e.g., custody cases involving a preschool child, an out-of-state parent, a working versus live-full-time-at-home mother, etc.

Suppose you have knowledge of 100 such representative custody cases, and that they are similar to the case under your consideration, and suppose they fall as shown in Table 10.1.

In this table and in the rest of the chapter, assume that the phrase "The mother is PCP" to refer to cases in which a comprehensive appraisal of factors led to the mother being considered the better bet for primary custodial parent, and "The father is PCP" to refer to cases in which the father was so considered.

To make the immediate table more lifelike, assume the evidence is the following statement: "At bedtime, the father reads the child a story more frequently than does the mother." We are seeking to understand the conditions under which we are likely to find this evidence.

The probability (sometimes called the unconditional probability) that the mother is the PCP is .65, the probability that the father is the PCP is .35, the probability that the evidence is present is .60, and the probability that the evidence is not present is .40. These probabilities measure how likely you would be to get a certain kind of case if you picked one at random.

For example, since in 65 out of the 100 cases the mother is the PCP, the unconditional probability of the mother being PCP is .65.

The reader familiar with the Bayesian probability approach will recognize that we are using Bayes in our second and especially in our third approach to aggregation. Other authors have also done so, particularly Schum and Martin (1982). Our approach differs from theirs in several ways, however.

TABLE 10.1   Representative Custody Cases.

	Mother is PCP	Father is PCP	Total
Evidence is present	35	25	60
Evidence is not present	30	10	40
Total	65	35	100

Conditional probability is the same as unconditional probability except that it is applied to a subset of the cases, not to all of them. For example, in our table, the conditional probability of the mother being the PCP, *given that the evidence is present* is .5833 (or 35/60) since in the subset of cases where the evidence is present (60 cases), the mother is the PCP in 35 of them. If you picked cases at random from the subset where the evidence is present, in .5833 of those cases the mother would be the PCP.

Now comes the crucial part! There are two conditional probabilities that sound almost alike, but they are not.

The first is the conditional probability of H given E. The second is the conditional probability of E given H. (While these methods allow the evaluator to reach a conclusion about the probability of H given E, they do so based on the calculated informational value of each piece of evidence.)

In our example, H is "The mother is PCP" and E is "The evidence is present." Thus the prob(H given E) is 35/60 (.5833) as discussed above.

But the other conditional probability, the prob(E given H) is different; it is 35/65 (.5385). The numerator of the fraction stays the same—it is the number of cases where both H and E are true—where the mother is PCP and the evidence is present. But this time the denominator of the fraction, the subset of concern is H, the subset of all the cases where the mother is PCP. There are 65 cases in that subset, so 65 must be used as the denominator.

Now we can go on and talk about "relevance" and define it in terms of conditional probabilities.

The relevance of a piece of evidence (E) for the mother (H) is the conditional probability of E given H. It is the probability of this piece of evidence appearing in a randomly selected case from the subset of cases where the mother is the PCP.

There is a separate relevance of E for the father. Looking back to the table, we see the relevance for the mother is 35/65 (.5385) and for the father it is 25/35 (.7143).

Let us now turn to some additional issues. Again it is convenient to use a 100-point scale for these relevance estimates by multiplying the probabilities by 100. Thus, we will speak of relevances of 23, of 95, etc. and we understand that to mean probabilities of .23 and .95.

It is crucial that the concepts of credibility and relevance be clearly differentiated, and that their estimates not in any way influence or contaminate each other. *Credibility* is the likelihood that the evidence really is true; *relevance* is the extent to which the evidence—if true—supports each of the two basic hypotheses (mother is PCP; father is PCP).

Thus, high relevances (for the mother) means that this piece of evidence very frequently appears in cases where the mother is the better custodial parent. Low relevance (for the mother) means that this evidence almost never appears when the mother is the better custodial parent.

Notice that it is the *difference* between the relevance numbers for each parent that measures the discriminating value of the evidence. If both mother's and father's relevance numbers are high, all we can conclude is that the evidence appears quite often, but that it is as likely to appear when one parent is the better PCP as when the other is. (Note well, then, that one needs *both* conditional probability estimates to be able to speak of the degree of relevance of any particular piece of evidence. As mentioned, for convenience we refer to each estimate as a "relevance" estimate.)

We are now in a position to offer two "model" relevance questions: "In similar custody cases of which I have knowledge where the mothers were found to be the better PCPs, what is the probability I would find this particular piece of evidence?" This would be followed by: "In similar custody cases of which I have knowledge where the fathers were found to be the better PCPs, what is the probability I would find this exact same piece of evidence?" To the degree that there is a difference in the values obtained under the two conditions, the evidence has probative value (or, stated from a slightly different perspective, can differentiate between good and "less good" child-care situations).

In this aggregation method, we multiply, separately for each parent, the two numbers (credibility and relevance) to get a *value* measure for each parent for this piece of evidence.

This process is repeated for each piece of evidence, the values are totaled separately for each parent, and the two totals are compared to see to what extent the total body of evidence supports each of the two hypotheses. The more disparate the two totals, the more discriminating is the total body of evidence.

A convenient way to compare the two totals is to take the sum of the two totals and compute the percentage each total is of that sum.

To illustrate this process, follow this simplified example.

There are five pieces of evidence: *a, b, c, d,* and *e*. They are evaluated as shown in Table 10.2.

This example gives a medium-sized edge to the hypothesis that the

TABLE 10.2   Weighted Averages Method.

Evidence	Credibility	Relevance		Value	
		Mom	Dad	Mom	Dad
a	85	60	20	5,100	1,700
b	75	90	50	6,750	3,750
c	55	35	80	1,925	4,400
d	90	70	10	6,300	900
e	95	65	55	6,175	5,225
Totals				26,250	15,975
Percents (of 42,225—the sum)				62%	38%

mother is the preferred custodial parent (62 percent to 38 percent). It also shows how this procedure dampens the halo effect. Evidence item a has high credibility (85), discriminates 3 to 1 in favor of the mother (relevance ration of 60:20), yet does not overwhelm the final total.

This example also illustrates that a highly credible piece of evidence (*e* at 95 credibility), but with low discriminatory ability (65:55), has little effect on the difference between the two totals. It further illustrates that there is value even in a piece of evidence with low credibility (*c* at only 55); it has a reasonable effect because of its high discriminatory power (35:80).

We can see also how this method discourages an evaluator from concluding that some individual piece of evidence is "really important" in the absence of differential data to support such a belief.

MODEL NUMBER THREE: MODIFIED BAYESIAN

Our third approach to aggregation uses full Bayesian probability calculations and embeds them in a hierarchical procedure. The first step, as with the second approach, is to consider each piece of evidence separately and assign the three numbers to it as was done in the second approach. These three numbers are the credibility (on a 0 to 100 scale), the mom relevance, and the dad relevance.

The relevance values are really estimates of conditional probability and rightly should use a 0 to 1.0 scale, but it is easier to rate on a 0 to 100 scale, and does no harm to the calculations.

We have used the term "probative value" in this chapter quite a bit, and now we can give a clear definition to it in terms of the conditional probabilities or relevances. The probative value of a piece of evidence is the ratio of the two conditional probabilities (the two relevances).

In the section on model number two, we gave an example using five pieces of evidence (*a, b, c, d, e*). The two relevances for evidence *a* are 60 for mom and 20 for dad, giving the ratio or probative value of 3 (60/20). This means that evidence *a* is three times more likely to appear in those cases where the mother is PCP than in cases where the father is PCP.

Notice that this probative value is for mom; the probative value for dad is .3333 (20/60). Probative values less than 1.0 for H reduce the likelihood that H is the PCP; values above 1.0 increase the likelihood.

A probative value of 1.0 means that the evidence has no probative impact or evidential weight. Since the relevance for mom must be the same as the relevancy for dad to get a probative value of 1.0, the evidence is as likely to appear when the mother is PCP as when the father is.

Before we can proceed to combine the individual probative values we need to account for the credibility of the evidence. We adjust the probative value by moving it toward 1.0 as the credibility decreases from 100 toward 0.

TABLE 10.3   Credibility/Probative Value Relationship.

Probative Value	Credibility	Adjusted Probative
5.0	100	5.0
5.0	50	1.67
5.0	0	1.0
0.5	100	0.5
0.5	50	0.75
0.5	0	1.0

Table 10.3 shows the effect of some credibilities on the probative value.

When the credibility is 100, there is no adjustment to the probative value. When the credibility is 0, the probative value is always 1.0 (no information in the evidence at all). When the credibility is between 0 and 100, we adjust the probative value to be closer to 1.0. The size of the adjustment is proportional to both how far above (or below) 1.0 the probative value is and how far the credibility is below 100.

In Table 10.3, the second entry shows a credibility of 50 (or 1/2). The adjustment procedure is slightly different for probative values greater than 1.0 than it is for probative values less than 1.0. If we use C for credibility, V for original probative value, and K for adjusted probative value, then:

If $V > 1$ then $K = V/(V - [C/100] [V - 1])$.
If $V < 1$ then $K = 1 - (C/100)(1 - V)$.

We are now able to proceed to combine probative values over sets of evidence. This is done by simple multiplication. The probative value for a set of evidence (or evidence packets) is the product of their separate probative values. This explains why a probative value of 1.0 adds no information to the evaluation process. Probative values greater than 1.0 increase final probative value, while those less than 1.0 decrease it.

Let us apply this method to the example we used in the discussion of method two (see Table 10.4).

Mom's final probative value is 12.25.

Notice that the probative values are calculated for mom. That is merely a convention that tells us whether to compute the probative values by dividing the mom's relevance by the dad's or the dad's relevance by the mom's. These two probative values are, of course, reciprocals (when they are multiplied together the product is 1.0) and we can get dad's final probative value by taking the reciprocal of mom's final value, which gives us 0.082.

The final step in this process is to convert the final probative value into a probability that we can interpret and use in our evaluation. This comes

TABLE 10.4   Modified Bayesian Method Showing the Adjustment of the Probative Values in Relation to Credibility Ratings.

Evidence	Credibility	Relevance		Mom Probative	
		Mom	Dad	Raw	Adj
a	85	60	20	3.00	2.3077
b	75	90	50	1.80	1.50
c	55	35	80	0.4375	0.6906
d	90	70	10	7.00	4.3750
e	95	65	55	1.1818	1.1712

from the Bayesian formula and is: Probability = Probative Value/(Probative value + 1).

In our example, we get: Probability = (12.25/13.25) or 0.925. (When we use the same formula on the father's probative value of 0.082, we get a probability of 0.075, the complement of the mother's probability of 0.925). The sense of these probabilities is that in about 93 percent of the cases where this package of five pieces of evidence was present, the mother was the PCP. In only seven percent of the cases where this package of evidence was present the father was the PCP.

Notice that this statement is in the form of a conditional probability. It is the probability of H given E, where H is the matter at issue (the mother should be selected as PCP), and E is the evidence packet. In this manner, we may move from the conditional probabilities of E given H to what we may want to offer (*as information*), the conditional probability of H given E.

This statement means that if the evaluator wanted to make a recommendation as to which parent should be selected as PCP, and the recommendation were to be based solely on the specific pieces of evidence that were used in this method of analysis and aggregation, the recommendation would have the degree of assurance of the calculated probability. In our example here, the recommendation would be to select the mother as PCP, and that recommendation would have a 93 percent level of assurance.

So far, the discussion of model number three may have seemed rigorous and mathematical, and except for the estimates of credibility and relevance, to have had no place for the complex and valuable influences of higher mental processes like judgment, reasonableness, pattern analysis, and so on.

Such an impression would be somewhat correct. Remember, the whole thrust of this approach is to use the best of both worlds, the formal and mathematical as well as the intuitive and judgmental. While some of the basic "inputs" are estimates, we can use formal methods to combine and relate those estimates. We now go on to the interplay of formula and judgment in the iterative process of actually working with this model.

All along in this discussion we have talked about pieces of evidence and evidence packets. Let us look at what that really means and how we use it. In a real custody evaluation case, we rarely have all the information we would like, so we need to take account of its relative abundance or sparseness. We do not want the impact of evidence of the mother helping with schoolwork to depend on the number of pieces of evidence that report it, and that is what the arithmetic of this method does. (Redundant information, provided the pieces arise from independent sources, may increase the probability that some fact is *true* but should not affect the value of this fact to the overall decision process.) The probative values keep adding up. We need to have some way to account for the corroborative, the redundant, the contradictory, and the quantity of evidence. And we do have such a method.

Consider the beginning of the aggregation process where we have all these pieces of evidence. We need to sort them into sets of related topics or issues. The criteria that the evaluator will use depend on his or her overall notion as to what should comprise a comprehensive evaluation. (In this sense, there is no total way around "ultimate issue" complexity, since the composition of the sets will reflect judgments about these issues.)

After the evaluator has combined the bits and pieces into reasonable packets of evidence, he or she should employ the techniques of method three and arrive at a final probative value and probability (for the mother being PCP) and then look at it for reasonableness. It may seem too high (perhaps because of many instances of redundant evidence), or it may seem too low (not enough corroboration). In either case, the evaluator should go back and look at the estimates of relevance for each piece of evidence, perhaps reevaluate some, and then recalculate the final probative value and probability, e.g., you may want to reduce the relevances for pieces of evidence all of which bear repetitively on the same issue or, conversely, you may wish to increase the relevances for items that pertain to issues that are underrepresented.

Remember, all this method does (at its best) is to assist, extend, and explicate the way you, a good evaluator, think. But that is no small assist. One way this method helps is by not requiring you to hold everything in your head all at the same time.

The availability of writing and evaluating explicitly gives the same advantage as written history does over oral history. You can think about pieces and sets of evidence, see the impact of your estimates of credibility and relevance, and still give full play to your judgment at lower and higher levels of aggregation.

Of greatest importance, this approach encourages an evaluator to think about data bases rather than about idealisms.

Even though the evaluator could "force" the final result, the method requires him or her to be explicit about how this result is achieved. And that means that the evaluator (and possibly others) can review, modify, adjust, and learn from the entire process. This method gives complete freedom in estimating the credibilities and relevances, but continually displays the logical results of those estimates on the intermediate set values and on the final overall probability arrived at for a recommendation of PCP. That is the meld of intuition and formalism.

We can summarize this method into the following six steps:

1. Sort the evidence into sets according to your concept of custodially relevant factors or areas. Chapter Nine lists about 40 such areas.

2. Select a set and estimate the credibility and the two relevances for each item (or packet) in the set.

3. Compute the summary probative value and probability for that set as a whole.

4. Evaluate the set summary probative value and probability and, if necessary, reexamine and reevaluate the credibilities and relevances of the individual items that make up the set, and recalculate the set summary values. Continue this step until the set summary values seem to most adequately represent all available information.

5. Repeat steps 2 to 4 for each set of evidence.

6. Calculate the final overall probative value for the entire aggregation of evidence by multiplying together all of the summary probative values from the sets. The product of this multiplication is the final probative value for the mother and its reciprocal is the final probative value for the father. These two probative values directly determine the probabilities for each parent being PCP.

The process is now finished.

Notice that in this aggregation method all of the difficulty resides in making the basic estimates, and in thinking about the results of the estimates.

This method locates the embedded hard parts of the complex task and presents them, one at a time, to the evaluator for his or her consideration. (A simple computer program could do away with the tediousness.) The usefulness of this method depends on the skill, insight, judgment, and experience of the evaluator, exactly as it should. It does not depend, exactly as it shouldn't, on the evaluator's ability to understand and do intuitive approximations of lots of complicated arithmetic in his or her head.

Although it may be, and usually is, extremely difficult to give strong support to any particular set of estimates of the probabilities required by this method, it is worth knowing with some exactitude just what it is that we are trying to estimate (even though the estimates themselves may be imprecise). This is far better than allowing the lack of precision of measurement to leak over and cloud the definition of the variable we are trying to examine.

These are fundamental concepts in an effective decision making process:

to use precision in defining the elements that go into the process and in manipulating the components while constraining the area of uncertainty to the actual measurement or estimation part of the process.

A Sample of Evidence, Credibility, and Relevance Estimates

As the last example in this section, consider the following custody case. There are five pieces of evidence, labeled *a* through *e*. The example is in the same format as the previous example in this section.

   a. "The father is in slightly better physical health than the mother."

Because of the sources of this evidence, we give it a credibility of 95; it is highly believable. Since, in our experience and considering the appropriate reference group, the father usually is not in better physical health than the mother, neither of the two relevancy estimates should be more than 50. It is even less likely in cases where the mother had been judged to be the PCP, so we estimate the relevancy for the mother as 30, and the relevancy for the father as 40.

   b. "Most of the child's (age 5) close friends live much nearer to the mother's home than to the father's."

We give this piece of evidence a credibility of 90; there is some slight doubt that all the child's friends have been identified correctly. Since it is common to find this pattern of the location of the child's friends independent of which parent is judged to be the PCP, we estimate both relevances (the mother's and the father's) at the same value, 80.

   c. "The father has as much time availability for the child as does the mother (who does not work outside the house)."

Considering the sources of this evidence, we estimate the credibility at 75. This is a fairly rare situation in our reference group, and thus has low relevances for both parents, but it is twice as often seen in those cases where the father has been the PCP as where the mother is PCP. We therefore estimate the father's relevance at 40 and the mother's at 20.

   d. "The father is not really interested in the child."

This evidence is offered by the mother and is not supported by any other direct or indirect evidence. We estimate its credibility at only 10. However, its relevancy for the mother is 17, since in about 17 percent of the cases in our reference group where the mother is PCP we find that the father is not really interested in the child, but we find that evidence in only two percent of the cases where the father is the PCP. So we estimate the relevancy for the father at two.

   e. "The father earned significantly better scores on the PORT and the BPS than did the mother."

These tests were well administered by a competent and experienced professional, so we estimate the credibility at 95. It is rare to find cases where the mother is the PCP and these scores significantly favor the father; we estimate

TABLE 10.5   An Example of the Modified Bayesian Method.

Evidence	Credibility	Relevance		Mom Probative	
		Mom	Dad	Raw	Adj
a	95	30	40	0.75	0.7625
b	90	80	80	1.00	1.00
c	75	20	40	0.50	0.625
d	10	17	2	8.50	1.097
e	95	10	90	0.111	0.1556
Final probative value:	Mom = 0.0813;	Dad = 12.293			
Final probability:	Mom = 0.075	Dad = 0.925			

the mother's relevance at 10, and the father's at 90. These values are summarized in Table 10.5.

OUR SUGGESTIONS IN ACTUAL USE

We have presented four different approaches with which the custody evaluator can make sense of his or her data. While an evaluation can and should do far more than suggest which parent is the better of the two candidates for PCP, this aspect, the choice of the PCP, is usually the most difficult part of the process.

One approach is in the form of a decision-tree that assigns high priority to BPS and/or PORT (or similar child-derived) data, but offers several important checks that must be carried out before this information can be considered compelling.

Three other models are offered: one is "intuitive," the other two use different degrees of formalism in their analyses.

Chapter Nine suggested many areas the custody evaluator might want to target for assessment. Each evaluator can decide how to group or package the evidence in these areas in accordance with his or her notions of what should go into a thorough custody evaluation. In the language of the present chapter, each evaluator will form "packets of information" in accordance with how that evaluator understands the scope of information that should be in an evaluation mix, and the proportional representation of any piece or grouping of pieces of information in that mix.

It is further likely that every evaluator has personal favorites as to what should enter the mix. A family systems person who does not use tests may pay particular attention to the roles played by each participant within interlocking family systems (e.g., facilitator, mediator, rule-giver, etc.), while the "testers" will rely on favorite tests. (I trust that by this point in the book all of the "naive realists," the simplistic "interviewers" or "observers," have either changed their ways or abandoned us in disgust.)

The suggestions offered in this chapter can be used in a very openly apparent way, or, so to speak, "behind the scenes" such that their use is not detailed in either the final report or in one's testimony.

In all cases, they will assist you in understanding how you make decisions, and further allow you opportunities to fine-tune these decisions in very explicit ways.

In ACCESS (Bricklin & Elliot, 1995), we use an aggregation method that blends the uniform precision of data-based tests with a (formal) way to consider the relevance of the many factors for which there are no published relevance databases. This lacking is largely because of the extreme number of normative or reference groups that would be needed—e.g., children in wheelchairs, large support group available, plans for remarriage and/or relocation, etc.—any of which may have enormous relevance in a given case.

Having now considered both the targets of assessment and ways to aggregate the data collected, we would like to suggest an exact sequence of steps for conducting the evaluation.

THE SEQUENCE OF STEPS IN SETTING UP AND CONDUCTING A COMPREHENSIVE CUSTODY EVALUATION

1. Seek a court order for your involvement, regardless of whether you have access to all or only some of the critical participants. If you lack access to both sides in a dispute, make certain the person seeking your services has a legal right to waive confidentiality requirements for the child and to give consent that the evaluation take place.

2. Make certain there is an explicit (or implicit) database in terms of which the referral question can be addressed. Many complainants want a custody evaluator to help overturn an existing plan on the basis of some highly subjective complaint, e.g., "He lets them go to bed dirty." There are no databases available by means of which an evaluator can address such issues.

3. Consider whether the referral question can be handled in a more circumscribed manner than one requiring a comprehensive evaluation—a procedure that is lengthy, psychologically exhausting, and expensive.

4. Consider whether the change-of-circumstances issue must be addressed.

5. Make certain you understand all of the legal issues in a given case. This would include the "must assess" aspects demanded in your jurisdiction, e.g., whether joint custody is presumed to be the best choice unless proven not to be.

6. When you cannot secure the participation of all critical participants, document efforts to secure such participation. Still seek a court order for your involvement. (Remember to limit your conclusions to those made possible by available databases and to document what should be done further to bring the evaluation to the level of a comprehensive one.)

7. Obtain signed consent forms to waive confidentiality requirements (to share as well as seek relevant information) and to administer tests and

gather interview, observation, and document information in regard to all participants.

8. Mail out requests for relevant documents. Send appropriate consent forms.

9. Arrange to have both parents or a neutral third party bring in the child for psychological testing. If the parents bring the child, have them meet early in the day and spend several pleasant hours with the child prior to the test session (to allow the current noncustodial parent some "fun" access to the child prior to the testing). Have the parents leave the office area while the child is tested. Do not interview a child at this session. Each parent will subtly or openly question the child as to what he or she said, and alienating pressures on the child may needlessly increase.

10. Mail out self-report questionnaire forms or use them for interview guides.

11. Arrange observation schedules that are fair and balanced. Make sure the child spends an equal amount of time with each parent prior to one-on-one observation sessions. Each child should be seen with both parents together and with each alone. It is exceedingly important to see the parents together if you are considering true joint custody; one should document their capacity for cooperative communication. In regard to all observations, pay special attention to how a child *utilizes* parental communications.

12. Test and further interview the parents.

13. Test and interview significant others.

14. Distinguish collateral sources of information that require in-person contact from those that do not.

15. Interview the children.

16. Use the targets of assessment listed in Chapter Nine to organize your data. Use either the BPS/PORT decision-tree model to aggregate the data or one of the others. If you use one of the latter, cast the data into a series of approximately 40 assertions relevant to the referral issues, e.g., "The child's unconscious perceptions of Mom are much more favorable than those of Dad," such that three statements can be made about each assertion. First, rate the credibility of the information. Next, ask yourself: "In custody evaluation cases I have seen that most closely approximate this case and in which the mothers were the better choice for PCP, what is the probability I would find this particular piece of information?" Next, ask this very same question framed so the father can be compared to fathers who were the better choices for PCP. Note important differences in the derived figures and/or use one of the mathematical strategies to aggregate the information. You may use the BPS/PORT model to suggest a PCP and one of the others to consider target-areas for which there are no published databases. Plans based solely on a facet of the child's status, e.g., developmental level, assume an equal "utilizability potential" to the child of each parent and a high degree of cooperation between the parents.

Chapter Eleven

Communicating the Results of a Custody Evaluation

Although there are both legal and psychological reasons (having to do with the maintenance of evaluator objectivity) to view a custody evaluation as an independent endeavor, another perhaps more realistic view would see it as part of an ongoing process in which the members of a divorced family are seeking to establish some new dynamic arrangement among themselves. Most commonly, we are called in as evaluators when the two parents in a given family are caught up in an aggressive competition for certain priorities with the involved children. The motivations to attain these priorities might be genuine love and concern for a child, desires to save (or gain) money, loneliness and conflict, or even hate and revenge factors.

Our job, as mental health professionals, is to offer information helpful in determining parenting arrangements "in the best interests" of the children, and to suggest strategies that can move parents in this direction. But we can do more than this without compromising objectivity and neutrality in the slightest.

We have already suggested that a test-based approach can help deter a parent from the negative-incident model.

We can also use and model a mode of communication with the power

162

and potential to reduce the adversarial bitterness that surrounds the huge majority of custody disputes for which evaluations are requested.

How one can reduce adversarial bitterness *and* communicate "hard data" will occupy much of this chapter.

There are other goals of a custody evaluation as well, and they will be listed presently.

SELECTED GOALS OF A CUSTODY EVALUATION

Perhaps the main goal is to be able to suggest a creative plan that maximizes a child's exposure to the strengths each parent has to offer while, of course, minimizing exposure to weaknesses.

Another main goal is to do whatever is possible (without compromising the objectivity of the evaluation) to encourage the parents toward less adversarial positions. This will help create a climate in which the parents will be able to follow a suggested time-sharing plan. While the greatest part of this reduced adversarial bitterness will come about by our convincing the parents to move away from the negative incident model and to accept a monitoring plan that addresses each of their concerns, another main impetus can come from the evaluator's grasping *and modeling* the nonadversarial system of communication spelled out later in this chapter. Even if one believes that the research evidence (see, e.g., Wolman & Taylor, 1991) suggests that the only way to reduce adversarial bitterness is to provide a forum where each participant feels he or she can have a fair hearing, nonadversarial communication will *still* help, since the focus is on *solutions*. Further, the two notions—perceived procedural fairness and nonadversarial communication—share an important conceptual element: People often feel more strongly about how they are treated than they do about some specific outcome (see Lind & Tyler, 1983).

During an early phase of interaction with the participants, the evaluator should make clear that although all the concerns of a participant will be addressed in any suggested plan of action, the negative incident model is an insufficient basis for significant conclusions.

A third goal is to provide motivation for each parent to be willing to improve or transform himself or herself in any discovered area of weakness. Ways in which suggestions for change should be worded will be given later.

Another related goal is to promote self-healing in each participant in the evaluation. Self-healing would involve the use of terms and phrases that enhance self-esteem.

Another goal is to make sure that the evaluator gains respect from the judge or decision-makers who will be involved in given custody decisions. This can be done by person-to-person meetings or in writing a report that not only *is fair,* but is *obviously and apparently* fair. The evaluator must make sure the resulting report is balanced and shows strengths and weaknesses of all participants.

Keep in mind that scientific caution actually "sells well" in a courtroom, regardless of the impression a witness may gain on the basis of an aggressive cross examination. Judges know expert witnesses are not gods who can predict the future with perfection; any attempt to come across in this manner will only work against whatever useful information the evaluator has to offer. In fact, my experience is that the more honest and evenhanded an expert witness appears on the witness stand, regardless of who did the hiring, the more annoyed the judge will become at any attorney who indulges in overly aggressive, badgering, and/or attacking behavior. (However, most judges do tolerate high levels of the latter.)

Any plan resulting from the evaluation that is offered to highly adversarial parents should provide for a continuing forum to monitor the adequacy of the arrived-at arrangement. This is basically to assure all concerned parties that their worries are being attentively tracked. For example, it is sometimes the case that one parent thinks the opposing parent is mentally unstable. Hence, there is some need to provide continuing feedback on this concern, particularly if the overall evaluation shows that this person, the supposedly "unstable one," is still the parent deemed more frequently able to act in the child's best interests. In such a case, I often suggest that a neutral psychotherapist be hired and paid for by both participants. It is made clear that the purpose of the arrangement is to have a neutral third party available to oversee what is going on as the arrived-at plan unfolds over time.

The "recommendation" section of the evaluation should address, as stated earlier, every concern of each party. *There should be at least one specific recommendation, perhaps more, to address each specific concern.* The point of stating this as a separate goal is to underline the fact that the evaluator should not assume that just because he or she, the evaluator, knows that all important worries and concerns are addressed in the report, that the readers of the report will realize this. The fact that a given recommendation addresses one or several of an interested adult's concerns may go over the heads of the critically interested parties. Each concern, in the concepts and words of the concerned party, should be addressed by a specific recommendation. Here are some examples.

"Mrs. B is concerned that her ex-husband hits the children too much as a method of discipline. Both parents trust Mrs. G, a mutual friend. It will be her job to inspect the child after the visits to insure there are no bruises."

"Mr. A believes his ex-wife does not spend enough time going over their children's homework assignments. It is suggested that they both contact their children's teachers and set up an arrangement whereby adequate feedback can be given to each."

It must be emphasized that there are no "winners" or "losers" in custody cases. The purpose of the evaluation is to make available to the child the important strengths possessed by each parent. Even one strength can be lifesaving to a child. There are several ways to phrase this.

"Even though Mrs. C is the primary caretaking parent of the children, it should be emphasized that Mr. C is excellent in many areas of teaching. He takes the time to make sure his children have the opportunity to understand many things in their lives. It would be wise for Mrs. C to take advantage of this wonderful skill, and to point out to the children when it would make great sense to have their father review their understandings of critical issues."

The report should employ terms that are neither offensive or "clinical." The words and concepts should be congruent with the belief systems of all participants.

Suppose, for example, that Mr. D is harsh and critical in the way he typically communicates with his children. Suppose, further, that the evaluator thinks that Mr. D would profit from psychotherapy designed to reduce this angry and denigrating behavior. The recommendation might be worded as follows:

"Mr. D has a very strong desire to help his children behave in ways he believes would be beneficial to them. The test data suggest he could achieve his fine goals even more so than is true now if he had the opportunity to review the way in which his own past history has influenced his range of choices. Then he could expand his strong desire to be helpful to his children in an even greater variety of ways."

NONADVERSARIAL COMMUNICATION

Nonadversarial communication is a mind-set best acquired through the gradual absorption of a set of propositions, which are then practiced on an everyday basis. It is derived in greatest part from the spirit of Zen Buddhism, particularly the unity between actor and action (there is no "self-image" to protect) and the emphasis on the possibilities of transformation. It draws on applicable sciences that pertain to the use of minimal amounts of energy to create extensive changes. It is based on the fact that great systemic changes can follow from very small beginnings, especially when these small beginnings are chosen wisely. If one thinks of most sciences as involving an "art" aspect in their application, the art aspect of the effective use of nonadversarial communication comes in with an individual's ability to detect critical entry points. This aspect is actually less difficult to apply with nonadversarial communication than with other psychological strategies, since the user can respond to virtually *any* outright hostile or even merely negatively tinged communication of another person with one of its strategies.

The Transformational Power of Nonadversarial Communication in Custody Cases

In one sense intended here, this principle states the custody evaluator can conceptualize any given piece of negative behavior evidenced by a participant in a custody evaluation as something that can be redirected in a positive way. In this way, liabilities can be addressed in ways that are more likely to motivate people to do something positive about them, rather than feeling blamed and condemned for having them. Examples of how this is done, will be given later.

A main advantage in the custody evaluator's absorbing and using these principles is in the evaluator's eventual ability to consciously and, even more important, unconsciously, model such an approach as a mind-set with which to view the enormously intense happenings that surround a divorce and custody decision-making process.

The Misunderstood Catharsis Model

Nonadversarial communication shares with the martial arts and Zen paintings a reliance on minimum uses of energy, along with the proposition that the receiver of a communication is never to receive negative energy or even have his or her own energy used against him or her. Negative energy directed *at* the communicator is most frequently left alone; it is simply not addressed. The closest that a nonadversarial communication actually comes to "martial arts" is in how a communication interchange is seen as a game, a game in which a person being aggressive is left with no moves.

In its application to communication uses, it denies the usefulness of screaming and shouting (negative energies) as favorable forms of "catharsis." Even during the excitement of the late 1960's and early 1970's, with the enormous energy and vibrancy provided by the Beatles, the popularity of "training" groups, the expanded uses of Gestalt therapy, the reemergence of body therapies, which all seem to have led to a variety of "assertiveness training" sessions emphasizing the yelling of one's feelings, I never was sold on the blame-screaming that accompanied these processes as anything very useful. True, screaming and shouting can be "sold" to people as a way of self help; to the extent that an individual buys this as a useful construct, he or she might be helped. In truth, screaming and shouting episodes seen as "healthy" forms of catharsis actually make things worse—not just strategically (i.e., dealing with interpersonal relations) but, more importantly, for the individual doing the yelling. It is my conviction that we operate in complex and nested loops and configurations, such that the motor "output" of any behavior becomes that which is part of a new (emergent) stimulus field. One's own behavior feeds messages back to the unconscious, and these messages directly affect one's self-conception. Aggressive behavior often merely further convinces the person emitting the angry behavior that he or she is truly vulnerable, in trouble, and likely impotent, otherwise some better solution would have received "motor" priority.

Stated from a different perspective, any piece of motor-output behavior is an excellent access code back into the very past experiences that generated the behavior to begin with. Hence, to yell and scream and, as we will show later, to justify one's behavior are access codes into the experiences that made the individual feel helpless and vulnerable and in need of a defense and justification to begin with. The illusion that such behavior is helpful is simply predicated on the fact that sooner or later the person doing the yelling stops. The person attributes the cessation to the yelling. My belief is that future research will show that needlessly (i.e., not directed against any true physical assault) aggressive behavior facilitates more aggressive behavior and not the opposite.

Nonadversarial behavior is exceedingly goal-oriented, but not cynical or directed toward the negative control of other persons. In other words, although it states that the best use of communication is for a person to achieve his or her goals (i.e., achieve goals rather than be "right"), it is not aimed toward creating these conditions in a way that is ignorant of the rights, needs, and desires of others.

Nonadversarial communication becomes much easier to "do" as one practices it. It rarely uses the word "no" or "but." This goes hand in hand with the major idea that the other person's communications are never "resisted."

Despite this, nonadversarial communication is not ass-kissing or caving in, as some learners of these procedures initially assume to be the case. It is *not* a peace-at-any-cost model.

Nonadversarial communication involves not only how one thinks about the world but how one acts in reference to it.

Nonadversarial communication requires an easy and comfortable allowance of penetration of one's body boundaries (since no communication is resisted). All communicative energy is allowed to flow in (or at least, "around"). This is not easy for most people. Achieving this state goes far beyond what might be called being a "good listener." Many good listeners are simply people who have learned to keep quiet while the other person is talking. Advanced "good listeners" may even use Rogerian techniques of acknowledgment. However, the arts and skills and mind-sets of nonadversarial communication involve more than this. When one has achieved the state of allowing easy penetration of the body boundaries, every single aspect of one's muscles and skeletal-framework communicates this state of affairs.

Nonadversarial communication assumes all (or, at least, the huge majority of) people can "do better" if they have more resourceful ways available to them to accomplish important goals.

Another way of saying this is that when one can help an individual to turn off his or her (very limited in possibilities) fight-flight activation and/or emerge from a fight-flight paralysis, far more options are potentially available.

When used in the context of custody evaluations, nonadversarial communication must begin at the very first contact with all participants and must permeate the entire evaluation. This would involve even the setting up of appointments, responding to possibly hostile questions, explanations of ground rules, administration of tests and interviews, setting up observational opportunities, etc.

The Ubiquitous Right/Wrong Mind Set

Nonadversarial communication accepts as a given that there are no psychologically superior positions in a communicative dyad. You might frequently hear things such as: "He's the one who yells; *he* should change." Nonadversarial communication does not make this assumption. This is a very important principle since people seem to either by intuition or by learning come to assume that certain positions, especially in a dispute, carry higher moral priorities than others. Stated simply, if a therapist, for example, deals with a husband who screams and a wife who is terrorized, resolution can be approached through *either* getting the husband to stop screaming or the wife to stop responding in ineffective ways, since movement on either side *compels* movement on the other. Under ideal circumstances, resolution is approached via all avenues.

Expanding on the above, there are no reasons or justifications or entitlements whereby one is "relieved" of the desirability of using nonadversarial communication. I have frequently heard statements such as: "She is so unreasonable; she shuts me off at the drop of a hat," and "He actually says nasty things to other people about me." None of these statements, typically offered as justifications for a continuance of screaming and yelling and battling, carry validity within the nonadversarial approach as I teach it.

These justifications for continuing in the use of adversarial positions are also joined by such as these: "Why should I be the one to do this (i.e., act nonadversarially); he's the one who does all the nasty things." Here, the individual is still trying to find a way to justify an adversarial stance, in this example by asking why one should exert all the energy supposedly needed to adopt a nonadversarial approach, when the other person is more at fault. In this approach, *no one* is at fault, and there is *no* position (save being hit) by means of which one can enter a claim to be adversarial. I usually respond to the last type of complaint ("It's too much trouble") by saying that nonadversarial communication is easier, in any event, than what one is already doing, i.e., "defending." That is, although it takes some time to master this approach, once this has been accomplished, it is much easier to do than is the screaming or yelling the person is championing as a better alternative. It is almost as if one is claiming to be entitled to carry out a piece of behavior that is inherently not only less effective but more subjectively uncomfortable than what is being offered in its place. Unfortunately, this is understandable from an evolutionary perspective. Once angry aggression enters a system, it seems humans are almost instinctually unable to ignore it.

EVOLUTION, LIVING IN THE WILD, THE FIGHT-FLIGHT RESPONSE, AND THE SCIENCE AND SKILLS OF NO-END-POINT NEGOTIATION

It seems evolution has equipped us with two very limited ways of dealing with threat. Typically called the fight-flight reaction, the facts seem to be that when humans feel threatened or even mildly stressed-out, they either want to bite the source of the stress or, if the source has bigger teeth than they, run from it. While these responses occasionally have merit (unfortunately, these days, more so than one would wish), they are relatively useless in most interpersonal disputes. While the energies made available from such reactions may have utility, this is the case only if one can free that energy from the fight-flight context. Once energy is mobilized, it is difficult to escape from a fight or flight reaction, or more typically, the fight-flight paralysis, that attends an angry, yet not outright attacking, individual.

Further, once a fight-flight reaction is mobilized, it is either (nonproductively) used or one remains in a state of mini-paralysis, since additional resources are typically difficult to access in such encapsulated states. The problem is compounded many times over if the individual lacks the skills of nonadversarial negotiation, since there is no broad set of resourceful alternatives to promote and facilitate a person's moving out of the mini-paralysis.

The quickness with which a human being can be ready to attack (or flee) is all too apparent. The ultra-adversarial nature of our legal system, in which the attempt to settle family disputes occurs, is only likely to exacerbate such responses even more so than would otherwise be the case. This is why, even when good folks get caught up in legal disputes, the battle can continue for incredibly long periods of time. *Once the fight-flight response is activated, it is difficult to get away from it; when this mode is operating, other behavioral options are not available.* Another reason why the suggestions made here are important is that, without them, even people who did not mean to fight will end up doing it, regardless of the ameliorating qualities of perceived procedural justice.

Nonadversarial communication is therapeutic for the individual using it. The feedback message sent to the unconscious mind is one of adequacy, not vulnerability. As one uses it, it transforms one's notions of security. Since the

deep inner mind is not bombarded with messages that imply danger and predicted impotence, one can develop an idea of security based on a feeling of
adequacy. Nonadversarial communication, by moving a person out of a fight-
flight paralysis, makes potentially available to that individual a wide range of
resourceful possibilities; it can quickly be seen as an effective way of operating. As this happens, an individual unconsciously makes the mental shift as to
where security is seen as lying, i.e., from fight or flight to the protective qualities offered by the ability to transform an adversary's position.

None of this is to deny that an individual's reaction to perceived threat is
driven by complex, biologically derived processes. In drawing attention to
some very important whole-organism distinctions between predatory ("stalk-
ing") and affective modes of violence, Meloy (1993) reminds us that the
latter type is primarily motivated by an organism's biologically supported
evolutionarily derived desire to remove the source of some perceived threat
(see also Meloy, 1992). The adversarial anger of which we speak is a subset of
such reactions. This approach also makes no assumption about whether aggression is cognitively mediated or more "automatic" (See Wyer, Jr. & Krull,
1993). As will be seen, the only relevant point is that the strategies suggested
be employed, in a heated interchange, as early as possible.

Nor are these ideas meant to deny the possible *therapeutic* uses of ca-
thartic, i.e., "yelling," discharges; here, *the context must be right, and internal
or external resources must be available* when the yelling is occurring (see Rossi,
1993, especially p. 77).

The intervention offered can enter an anger-building sequence at any
point, from the early occurring stage, at which an individual concludes he or
she is threatened, to any time subsequent to this. The sooner these cognitively originating processes enter a dyadic system the better. Biological support for angry forms of aggression build quickly. Unfortunately, when one
organism perceives even tiny amounts of aggression in another organism,
"threat" is typically perceived.

Hence, optimal results come by the continual shrinkage of behaviors
defined as "threat." In an ideal world, perhaps unattainable with our current
biology, "threat" as a category would be reserved for behaviors leading to
imminent physical harm. Nonadversarial communication, if practiced, will
lead *automatically* to a shift in one's definition of threat, since it brings with it
a different definition of security, i.e., "safety" is the *power to transform* the
behaviors and intentions of one's "adversary."

With its emphasis on communicative efficiency, and its ability to keep
people away from psychological access codes that activate behaviors born
amidst mind-body sets in which they felt vulnerable and perceived the world
as dangerous, nonadversarial communication makes it possible for individuals to redefine security. The phrase "no-end-point negotiation" in the heading

of this section is meant as a reminder to the user of nonadversarial communication *not* to keep an internal scorecard of how many interchanges are needed to get a good result. One uses as many interchanges as are required.

Selected Strategies in Nonadversarial Communication

1. In any dispute, even "mild" ones, one should focus on solutions; suggestions should be offered as alternatives. These suggestions should not be framed in such a way that they will be perceived as things the individual must do, or even as things to do *instead of* what the person is already doing. They should be experienced by the receiver of the communication as alternatives that exist *in addition to* the alternative currently chosen. This approach frees the individual from having to defend what is being done currently.

In this we see also a similarity between nonadversarial communication and what might be called an "irresistible communication." It is very difficult to resist suggestions made as alternatives; it is very *easy* to resist alternatives that are offered in any other way, since they instinctively mobilize counter-energy. It might be said that all communications are irresistible in the sense that the human central nervous system and whole organism will process whatever is offered. However, it is also true that certain communications will trigger more conflicts and blockades within an individual than will others.

An operational example of this principle might be seen in a situation where a custody evaluator is concerned that a given parent too frequently yells at his children. It is *not* nonadversarial communication to say something like the following: "Mr. H should try his very best not to yell at his children. He may mean well, but he is hurting them." While we will show below that it is often the best strategy to precede any recommendation with an identification of a positive purpose, the operative part of this suggestion would be something like the following: "Here are some additional ways Mr. H can communicate with his children." It is not necessary even to mention that these are alternatives to yelling; that will (at least, mostly) be obvious enough. When combined with the aforementioned point of identifying a positive purpose, the entire recommendation might read something like this: "Mr. H shows that he has great concerns with getting through to his children by the intensity with which he yells at them. Here are some additional ways Mr. H can communicate with his children, and he can then see if he is satisfied with the results."

2. In nonadversarial communication, the receiver of a communication is never blamed or made to feel wrong, even slightly so. Here is an example of this principle: "Mr. D shows his fear that the children's mother will turn the children against him by the manner in which he finds fault with her in front of the children. He can be helped to discover additional ways, ways that are safe

and effective, to maintain the love of his children." It can be seen that this approach is in contrast to some of the suggestions offered by Ward and Harvey (1993) in their (sometimes quite harsh) recommendations for dealing with parents who are alienating the other parent.

I do not claim that there are *no* cases in which "adversary" communication might be warranted by the psychological system; however, I would reserve such behaviors as a very last resort. It is important to keep in mind that most aggressive behaviors are launched on the basis of inner fears or hurts. Aggression is the psychobiologically, seemingly "natural," response to real or imagined threat. (For a much more refined analysis of the differences between aggression and anger, and forms of violence, see Berkowitz, 1993.) None of this is to say that anger is "wrong," or that an angry person must be self-condemning. It *is* to say that humans seem "wired" to be unable to turn away from, or get beyond anger or aggression— no matter how slight its manifestation— once it enters into some interactions.

Anger and interpersonally aggressive feelings and actions contain energy and information; the individuals experiencing the latter can learn to take what's good from them and *move on.*

One paramount purpose of nonadversarial communication is to help both the launcher of angry behavior and the recipient *to move as rapidly as possible ahead into resourceful, problem-solving behavior.*

3. In nonadversarial communication it is important to distinguish between explanations and justifications. Defined simply, an explanation is the information that forms the foundation for some act or belief; it is often given in response to what someone else requests or demands. It is frequently given also in response to a challenge. Strictly speaking, an explanation is information. A justification, on the other hand, is an attempt to get another person to "buy" one's explanation. My clients are taught never to allow themselves to be put in a position where they engage in justifying past or present behavior. To do so will just make the "justifying" person feel more defensive, more hurt, more vulnerable, and hence more angry.

One must keep in mind that behavior accesses its emotional precedents. Justifications—in actuality, a pleading that the other person accept one's reasons for doing or thinking certain things—were born amidst feelings of nonacceptance and vulnerability. They were mobilized during times in which the person felt misunderstood and not listened to. To use them simply reinforces a very vulnerable and weakened self-image, one that essentially says: "I am safe in the world only if this other person accepts my reasons." I explain to all my patients and clients that I do not want them to live in psychological worlds in which their safety and security depend upon an external person's "buying" their versions of the world.

Here is a way to see the difference between explanations and justifications and the role of value systems.

My daughter, Alisa, at age 11, asked if she could go to a certain combination rap, thrash, grunge, heavy metal concert.

I responded: "No, there were six stabbings at the last concert of that type."

She answered: "Oh, six stabbings per twenty thousand people isn't that bad."

At this point, my child was not questioning my explanation; she was challenging my (statistical) value system. There is no way to justify one's values, whether backed by statistics or not.

4. In using nonadversarial communication, when commenting on someone's behavior or position, always begin by seeking to identify at least one positive purpose behind this behavior, even though the type of behavior in question might be of a character typically seen as negative. Follow this with alternative ways of achieving the same goal. We have already given an example above where "yelling behavior" is positioned as one way of showing concern for a child; this is followed by suggesting a list of other ways to achieve this same purpose.

5. No communication offered by the other person is resisted. This is a most critical aspect of nonadversarial communication. It is not so much that it is difficult to grasp the concept, rather, it is difficult to recognize the myriad forms resistance can take. Even the very use of the word "but" sets up a very definite resistance in an individual who hears the word.

Consider the following conversation between a well meaning counselor and a mother client. "I know you mean well, but you hit the child too much."

"He keeps putting his fingers into the ashtray."

"I know that, but there's still no need to hit him. You can simply take his hand and give him a firm 'no.'"

"I didn't want him to get his hands all dirty."

"But all I'm trying to tell you..."

The use of the word "but" here (or anywhere) will make it harder for the recipient of the advice to hear it.

It would be far smarter to say something like the following: "I know you are concerned that the child will get his hands dirty and you may even be concerned that he can burn himself. Here are some other ways you can try out, to see if you get the results you are looking for."

As soon as a person hears a word like "but," an unconscious wall goes up and resistance is created. The word "but" means one is resisting what the other person is trying to say.

Summarizing, some basic strategies of nonadversarial communication involve focusing on solutions, never blaming or making the other person feel wrong, differentiating explanations from justifications and avoiding the latter, identifying positive purposes behind another person's seemingly negative behaviors and never setting up resistance to the other person's communications.

Objections to a Nonadversarial Stance

In one way or another, most objections individuals voice to adapting a non-adversarial stance have to do with wrongly equating a nonadversarial attitude with being defenseless or vulnerable, and, ultimately, with being taken advantage of. When one has the advantage of teaching nonadversarial communication directly, this can be addressed. In custody evaluations, the nonadversarial approach is both used and modeled; one might say, the "teaching" of it is indirect and largely unconscious. Here, one might not have the option of making sure that the person being taught nonadversarial communication skills understands that being nonadversarial is not to be equated with vulnerability, giving in and/or being a patsy.

In the midst of a custody evaluation, I have heard the objection: "If I treat him nicely, he'll make the children hate me even more."

I go to great lengths to convince people that the best way to have a good relationship with one's children is to be a good parent. The more a parent understands this, the more protection one actually has against another parent's being an alienating force. This is sometimes a hard sell, and I go to great lengths to show parents how this can operate over time.

This is not to say I would refrain from direct action against an alienating parent in extreme cases. I try to reassure parents who worry about the other parent being an alienator by setting up monitoring processes (in the recommendation section of the evaluation) that very directly address these issues.

The real problem is that in any negatively tinged interchange, each participant chooses his or her responses by trying first to figure out who is on the moral high ground, who has the "most right" to feel slighted or to be annoyed and hurt. After this rapid inner calculation, during which each participant concludes that he or she is obviously the one in this morally superior, "justified" position, each participant launches his or her attack and justifications. Part of nonadversarial communication involves a gradual shift from running one's life from this "right versus wrong" orientation to one that says: "Regardless of how right or wrong the other person is, if I do things in this nonadversarial way, I have the power to transform the outcome to a positive one."

Notice that without this gradual inner shift in which each individual redefines where "power" lies, it is unlikely that any individual would feel strong enough to use nonadversarial principles with any consistency. The perception of power is shifted away from proving one is "right" to one's ability to transform bad things into good things, i.e., to be effective in one's communications while sending feedback messages of competence to one's unconscious self-perception rather than information that reflects powerlessness, vulnerability, and nonacceptance. Once one stops needing to run one's life from the perspective of getting other people to buy one's "reasons" and "justifications" in order to feel safe, powerful new feelings of adequacy can be created.

Redirecting Aggressive Responses

It is obvious that a number of things can trigger a highly aggressive response in human beings. Stated simply, it doesn't take much to get people riled.

Those who learn the nonadversarial approach must be willing at first to operate in a fairly calm way, *while not necessarily feeling that way internally*. It is vital to do this, because once one is engaged in a battle, even a small one, things tend to progress quickly in a negative direction.

Every day we see a failure to use such tools in custody cases where even well-meaning people who try initially for amicable settlements get rapidly caught up in the terrors and intricacies of basically adversarial situations. Once this happens, once the fight-flight mechanism is engaged, it is exceedingly difficult to back away from it.

The practice of nonadversarial skills makes it easier and easier to continue using them, for in their use the individual gradually redefines safety and security to reside in negotiating skills rather than in the use of attacking, defending, and justifying maneuvers. This ease of use can be achieved only by practice. *It cannot be achieved by insight alone.* At very basic levels, the individual is learning to substitute resourceful responses for less resourceful responses.

I am not, however, blind to the enormous animosity and hatred that attend many custody disputes. I certainly do not mean to suggest that the employment of nonadversarial skills will help resolve every single situation. Further, those involved in custody disputes, in my opinion, have poor multiple-perspective-taking skills to begin with. Hence, you may at this point be thinking, "Are you kidding!? These people usually *hate* each other. Each thinks the other is a real jerk! Will they really be able to change such deep-set patterns with nonadversarial communication?"

The secret is in whether by practicing nonadversarial communication one or both parents can build up an internal "critical mass" sufficient to create a subtle but overwhelmingly useful mind-set shift: the ability to see safety and security as residing in one's own ability to create transformations rather than in launching attacks and counterattacks.

The principle of how *de-* then *re*contextualizing a behavioral pattern can have enormous transformational power has been around a long time. Aeschylus (in *Oresteia*) details how the absence of these skills would lead to endless bloodshed. Athena turns around the Furies, the ancient goddesses of revenge, by offering them an opportunity *to redirect their powers by becoming the protective spirits of Athens*; thus, the shift to their becoming the Eumenides (the "well-intentioned" ones), starts by de- and then recontextualizing their behaviors. (See Waelder, 1967, pp. 6–7.)

THE CUSTODY EVALUATION REPORT

As chair of the Executive Operating Committee of the Professional Academy of Custody Evaluators (PACE), and as Editor of the *Custody Newsletter*, I get to see hundreds of custody reports written by persons around the entire country.

I would like to share some general comments based on the many reports I have reviewed.

While most are exellent, I think many are needlessly long. This is especially problematic when a tremendous number of details are listed without any attempt to delineate the relevance of this huge array of details to the issues at hand. Why list so many details if one cannot pinpoint their relevance? It is especially important in psycholegal matters that the issue of relevance be given greater due than might be the case clinically. My suggestion is that when one lists facts of life history, mention should be made of whether or not some particular item is being used to come to a conclusion and, if so, the assumed relevance of the evidence to the arrived-at conclusion. (See Chapter Ten.)

A main reservation about many of the reports I have seen (and the reason why we initially developed the BPS and PORT) is the "leap" I often see from the information collected, whether this be of a clinical nature or from traditional tests like the MMPI or *Rorschach*, to assumptions about the adequacy of a given parent for a given child at a particular time in that child's development. There is often a rather naive assumption that things taught to us as having a negative nature from a clinical standpoint can be automatically assumed to have negative consequences in a parenting context. While this may be true a certain percentage of the time, one should not make such assumptions in the absence of relevant data.

Also distressing is the degree of subjectivity I see in many of these reports surrounding life-circumstance issues. I refer here to items like sloppy housekeeping. (Keep in mind, also, that a parent who gets nailed for sloppy housekeeping on a home visit probably did not take the time to do the extra cleanup that the other parent might have done.) Home visits must be done in a fairly sophisticated way or they are useless. Giving "high grades" to a spotless house constitutes for me a shaky assumption about the relationship between such housekeeping skills and parental adequacy. (Of course, one could argue that the high grade is being awarded to the *knowledge that one ought to make one's home spotless*, not the "spotlessness.")

Another item that I think comes up all too often is where the evaluator comments negatively about a certain shrill and defensive tone on the part of a mother. I think many evaluators are insensitive to the chauvinistic pressures such women may have lived with, and the degree to which these women could have been manipulated and controlled by forces beyond their control, such as the economic. I have seen many lunkhead aggressive husbands come across oh-so amiably and easygoing during interviews while there is a shrill and defensive tone to the mother's presentation, where, from my vantage point, the mother's stance was quite understandable in terms of what she had endured throughout the marriage and her subsequent expectation that she will be treated abusively. I believe an insensitivity to the degree to which male power (physical and economic) plays a part in American family life is a serious liability to a fair and objective custody evaluation.

Subjective conclusions are particularly distressing, especially in the absence of data coming from suitable tests, since they may become the controlling factor in the evaluator's conclusions about who would constitute the better primary caretaking parent.

Along these same lines, I am continuously amazed at how some evaluators (who rely predominantly on interviews) are so easily conned by a good presentation. When I am interviewing people with a good presentation, I remind myself of my early experiences working in a maximum security prison, where convicted murderers and armed robbers could be as amiable and friendly as you would like to see. Such factors work particularly strongly against women, as it is often the man who has been out in the business world learning to make a very persuasive presentation. Men who have been in sales positions have had years to practice pulling off flawless snow jobs. (Contrarily, there is the assumption, especially among older people, that women are "just naturally" better parents than men.)

The Mind-Set for Preparing a Custody Evaluation Report

Here, we are talking about the *mind-set* to prepare the custody evaluation report. Elsewhere in this book we have mentioned the ingredients that one might want to consider for inclusion in the evaluation itself.

First and foremost, the heart of the report should attempt to delineate the range of impacts each parent is having on each involved child. This should always be done in positive terms. We label all forms in the Bricklin Associates group that have to do with custody: "Child's access to parental strengths." There is a constant attempt to show that we are not looking for winners and losers, but rather attempting to make available to the children the best of what each parent has to offer. By implication, of course, we are seeking to protect children from the "worst" of what each parent has to offer. This is often handled, however, in an indirect way by having the suggested arrangement be one that simply downplays or does not allow the operation of the negative aspects. When we mention negatives, we do so in a nonadversarial way, by attempting to show the positive purpose behind the negative behavior.

The second thing to keep in mind is the need to reduce adversarial bitterness. One does this by gently nudging the participating people throughout the evaluation process away from the negative incident model mentioned earlier. The adversarial attitude is further reduced by the continuous modeling of nonadversarial communication strategies, by the assurance that all of the concerns of each parent are addressed with a positive plan for action in the report, and by the setting up of a continuing nonadversarial forum in which fears and complaints can be voiced and addressed after the evaluation.

The judicious use of compliments along with nonadversarial communication is used to encourage parent willingness to move toward improved parental skills. At all times, regardless of how the evaluator entered a case, the use of an evenhanded approach furthers this same goal.

Critical Issues in Formulating the Report

Here is how I worded certain critical issues in a recent report. The evaluation itself involved four people, all of whom lived in a western state. The father, John, owned and operated a ranch. The mother, Mary, was a schoolteacher. There were two children, Edward, age 5, and Donna, age 4. Both children were too young to attend school, and there was no indication of a need to do educational or intellectual testing of the children.

Each parent wanted to be the primary caretaking parent; both wished to share jointly in legal custodial rights. The mother's main concerns were that the father became angry too easily and was too controlling, although she did not believe that he was ever abusive toward the children. She also worried that he worked so hard that he was not a very attentive parent; she recognized that running a ranch was an enormous endeavor.

He basically believed she was too timid and fearful to be as effective a parent as he could be.

These are not really heavy-duty issues as custody disputes sometimes go, but each was firm about desiring to be primary caretaking parent.

The following tests and tools were used in this evaluation: a parent questionnaire called *Child's Access to Parental Strength Data*; another parent questionnaire called the *Self-Report Data Form*; the *Rorschach* test; the *House-Tree-Person* test; the *Parent Awareness Skills Survey* (PASS); selected parts of the *Wechsler's Adult Intelligence Scale*, primarily the Comprehension subtest to get some idea of so-called commonsense thinking; the *Parent Perception of Child Profile* (PPCP); and the *Perception-of-Relationships Test* (PORT) (both children were too young for the BPS).

It has always been my contention that the typical custody evaluator gathers more information than he or she knows how to prioritize and/or even how to formulate into meaningful chunks of information (so that the decision-maker can absorb them). That is why I summarize all self-report data under certain main headings. A bit later I will suggest an outline for a comprehensive custody evaluation report, where these headings will be outlined.

In the present case, the *Rorschach* test, the *House-Tree-Person* test, the PASS, and the PORT all indicated some rather significant flaws in both parents. The main purpose of this section is not to give a comprehensive report, but rather to highlight how such concerns can be addressed in a way that honors the other recommendations made in this chapter—a nonadversarial approach to promote healing and an approach that encourages each parent to be interested in upgrading his or her skills.

I would like to go through the data and select certain pieces of clinical information of a problematic nature, presenting this piece of information as it would be expressed from a clinical perspective. Next, I will offer what I would consider a nonadversarial "translation" of this information into something I might put in the report. Remember, it is *much* easier to do this if one has thoroughly absorbed the nonadversarial communication points mentioned throughout this chapter, such that one does not see "pathology" out there among parents and children, but rather pieces of behavior that happen to have certain kinds of consequences and which can be transformed. Nevertheless, I will list these points first more as a typical clinician not educated in the nonadversarial mode would think of them and *then* translate the finding into information as it would be put forth within a nonadversarial context.

Both the *Rorschach* and the H-T-P showed that it was difficult for the father to maintain stable perspectives (there were near-contaminations and DW *Rorschach* responses as well as transparencies on the H-T-P), and as a reflection of this, a strong tendency to come up with sweeping generalizations. (This was clear on his PASS performance.) In my report on this, I spoke of the difficulty he had with maintaining stable structures as is "frequently manifested in the lives of highly creative people," going on to talk about how the ability to see things from several different perspectives at the same time (instead of sequentially) often will bring a very unique and creative aspect to one's life. I then pointed out how this could be confusing to children who do not understand the potentially creative value of such processes. I next pointed out that the ability to make sweeping generalizations might be occasionally helpful from an entrepreneurial perspective in the running of a very big business, while this same trait could be experienced as intimidating and/or stifling to others who do not understand the need to come to such sweepingly assertive conclusions.

By these few examples, I hope I have conveyed how one always seeks to find some positive purpose behind any piece of behavior. One can then follow this with how such behavior may be possibly viewed by other people so as to become a source of confusion or difficulty in communication, when viewed from this other perspective.

A strong tendency to become easily angry showed up in both of the projective tests; it was described in the written report under the rubric of the father's having learned to depend on anger as a source of motivation to get things done. It was then suggested that he could learn to use alternative ways of achieving these important purposes.

Mary's timidity and lack of assertiveness did indeed show up, as the father had claimed, in the projective tests. This was framed in terms of her keen sensitivity to the needs of others and the nuances of a given external situation. It was then suggested that she could learn to more appropriately prioritize such concerns, that is, to more accurately set the level of concern about the evaluating opinions of others and the demands of others in any given situation, and hence learn to do a better job of weighing the risks of making an error.

Each parent performed adequately on the PPCP and the PASS, except that the father had the sweeping-generalization, authoritarian attitudes mentioned before. His way of communicating with children is to tell them what to do. Again, this was contextualized as being within the patterns he has come to depend upon in running his ranch. It was then pointed out that he could use this same skill in a more flexible manner, which would then have the additional benefit of encouraging the children to do more thinking for themselves.

Of greatest importance was the fact that on the PORT drawings of both children there were serious flaws in connection with self-figures in relation to the father-figure. This would mean his set of styles in relating to them were having some important negative effects.

This is a real challenge; when a parent, so to speak, does "poorly" on the PORT (in the psychological eyes of a child) by virtue of flawed drawings, we deal with something of a more negative nature than would be the case had the poor score occurred as a result of "closeness" aspects. (A typical scenario in which a father shows up poorly on the PORT in "closeness" factors, would be the father, who though otherwise "good," has simply been too busy to be attentive and nurturant to a child. Not that this is "good" insofar as being a truly adequate father is concerned; it's simply that this is not as serious a scenario as when the negative aspects of a PORT have to do with distorted images. In the latter case, where there is a distortion, we deal with something that is causing conflict and inner turmoil within the child.)

The ameliorating phrase used to contextualize this information in the report had to do with "the father's failure to realize the forcefulness of his own personality."

A significant part of the "recommendations" section of the report suggested how each parent could take his or her behavioral patterns, those a clinician would view as negative, and flexibly vary them so that they could become useful to the children.

For example, it was recommended that the father take the children out on the ranch with him when he works, to show them how having a forceful personality can be sometimes useful in that kind of setting. They could then be shown (or it could be talked about) how no particular behavior is universally good or bad; everything has some use some place.

AN OUTLINE FOR A COMPREHENSIVE CUSTODY EVALUATION

The remaining headings in this chapter will show the categories I have found convenient to organize the information our teams typically gather during a comprehensive evaluation. Here is a summary list of these headings

1. Brief statement of purpose
2. Factors leading up to the current evaluation
3. Prevailing living/custody arrangement
4. Current preferences of adult participants
5. Purposes of evaluation and sources of information
6. Self-report data and information from selected documents
7. Family interaction observation data
8. Parent awareness skills
9. Parent knowledge of child(ren)
10. Results of traditional psychological tests (by name)
11. PORT and/or BPS results (i.e., child-directed tests, measuring parental impact, if used)
12. Summary and suggestions

1. Brief Statement of Purpose

Since I like to use the main "purpose" section (positioned later) to explain the relationship between the concepts we have developed with which to think about custody decision making and the tests and tools designed to measure these concepts, more space is required than one might usually use to begin a report.

As a "brief statement of purpose," I might typically write: "The overall purpose of this evaluation is to help create a plan that makes available to all involved children the best each parent has to offer."

I do not even, these days, use the phrase "time-sharing" plan, since it is conceptually closer to the world of "winners" and "losers."

2. Factors Leading Up to the Current Evaluation

Here is where one would report all previous attempts to find a plan in the child's best interests. The chances of discovering all hidden, as well as open, agendas (not that the evaluator would necessarily comment on the former), will have depended upon the thoroughness with which all data were considered (court transcripts, prior reports, interviews with all major participants, attorneys, judges, etc.).

The evaluator might want to note the concerns or worries of each participant as they appear in these data, and delineate those that have not as yet found a comfortable resolution for one or both of the disputants.

Some evaluators like to use this section to offer long, detailed personal and marital histories of the main participants. We are much more selective.

3. Prevailing Living/Custody Arrangement

One piece of information here is the amount of time each child has spent, and is spending, with each parent. If one is going to talk about a child's relationship with a given parent, it is necessary that they spend sufficient time actually interacting. It might also be noted how the current arrangement was altered in order to achieve counterbalanced child-evaluation sessions.

4. Current Preferences of Adult Participants

In this section, the evaluator would state what each parent desires vis-à-vis the involved children. I usually give a brief summary of each parent's major concerns and worries here, and a much expanded version of these items in the Self-Report Data section, since these concerns usually permeate questionnaire responses.

5. Purposes of Evaluation and Sources of Information

Here is where the evaluator synthesizes the major issues and/or concerns and lists them, along with the sources of information chosen to yield data pertinent to their resolution. (List dates to go with all entries in the "sources of information" category, even as pertains to documents reviewed, and arrange materials in your case folder in the same order as each item is listed in your report. This will make courtroom testimony on these issues much easier should you choose to bring such data to court.)

I often use this section to educate readers on the importance of the utilization model upon which our custody decision-making concepts are based. Here is a sample of this section as it was written for a case in which adversarial bitterness ran deep, and each side was enmeshed in the negative incident model. In making a strong case for test data (which I, of course, believe in anyway), I am also attempting to move each disputant away from the need to create more horror stories about the hated other family to add to each respective list. (The recipients of the following were bright and college-educated. The language used should be adjusted on a case-by-case basis.)

A major purpose of this evaluation is to measure the impact each parent is having on the child in a wide variety of situations that are vital for the lad's healthy psychological development.

The main test used, the *Perception-of-Relationships Test* (PORT) (or whatever child-directed test the evaluator might consider "main") measures the degree to which the child feels relaxed and confident when dealing with each parent, plus the extent to which he actively *seeks* psychological interactions with a particular parent.

At no time were direct, guilt-inducing "choice" questions that pit one parent against the other ever asked. In fact, a child rarely understands at a conscious level the full implications of any particular test task.

The child's responses to the test items are mostly deep, unconscious, gut-level reactions. An unconscious response is based on thousands of observations and interactions filtered and "weighted" by each child's unique set of needs, assets, and liabilities. In other words, when a child responds to a test item, that response is the result of countless interactions with the "measured" parent, weighted and filtered through the child's unique personality system. This brings us to the complexity of custody decision-making.

In contradistinction to what one might think, the most critical data in custody decisions are not, strictly speaking, what a parent may do, but *how a child reacts to what a parent does.*

Hence, the major thrust of an evaluation is not only to measure things about parents, but more importantly, to gather in-depth information about *how well a child is able to use or profit from a particular parent's way of doing things.*

6. *Self-Report Data and Information from Selected Documents*

I group these two sources of information into one category, i.e., what people have to tell me either via interview or structured questionnaires, along with information from documents, because I consider much of such data to be of unknown credibility and validity. Obviously, interview and questionnaire data are difficult to assess in these latter regards, but it is similarly difficult to assess interview data, affidavits and letters from friends, relatives, pediatricians, teachers, principals, etc. Likewise, the meaning and utility of medical documents, reports from teachers, etc. are also difficult to discern in given cases. This said, however, the evaluator *should* interview *anyone* a main participant believes to have important information.

Nevertheless, this is an exceedingly important section of the evaluation report, for if the evaluator fails to convey that he or she has fully grasped all important concerns and/or worries—or has accorded short shrift to any of the latter—the overall effectiveness of the evaluation will have been greatly diminished or even destroyed.

Here is how I began one such section to show that although what I would learn from interviews and questionnaires was very important, it was certainly not as important as how a parent was actually impacting a child, information discernible from some of our test data.

The Bricklin Associates team's primary interest in questionnaire data is whether an adult participant manifests the strength first called for by King Solomon. His wisdom may be summarized in the following question he posed to parents: "What sacrifices are you willing to offer your child if indeed a sacrifice is what your child most needs?" In today's language, this same question would be: "Are you willing to put your child's need for you to find solutions ahead of your own need to fight?" This willingness to find solutions is far more important for a child's eventual well-being than many of the other kinds of information questionnaires typically ask for, such as methods of discipline, etc.

But keep the following *solidly* in mind: Both interview and questionnaire data can reveal only whether or not a participant *has* certain knowledge; it *cannot reveal the extent to which a person chooses to use these skills* when interacting with a child. Only tests such as the PORT attempt to do this for they seek to measure the *actual effect* a parent's behavior has on a child.

This same warning applies to observations made in a doctor's office. When people know they are being evaluated, they are certainly going to put their best foot forward. Hence they show what they are *capable* of doing. There is absolutely no guarantee that what people do in a doctor's office or even in their own homes when they are being watched is what they will actually do in real situations.

Nevertheless, this information *is* very important. It is of the utmost urgency that we learn about every single worry and concern each participant may have, so we can address each and every one of them.

Remember: it is imperative in the "recommendation" section of any report that each and every parental worry and concern be addressed, along with some (hopefully, creative and doable) positive suggestions. Remember, also, that parental concerns should all be listed as separate entries, in separate paragraphs. An evaluator may realize that one suggestion can address several concerns, but the readers of the evaluation may not realize this.

Since interview and questionnaire data usually result in a welter of disparate statements, many of which are versions of naive or sophisticated name-calling, I often summarize all of this information with ratings assigned to several different categories I consider relevant in custody decision-making.

The ratings are usually the result of my asking one or more members of Bricklin Associates to review and rate the data independently. (You may choose trusted colleagues of your own.)

Reported ratings are the means (averages) of these independent assessments of the self-report data.

Several of our questionnaire items yield information about honesty, flexibility, and degree of adversarial bitterness. We consider these areas very carefully since the attitudes they reflect can be very helpful to the involved children.

Here is an updated version (Bricklin, 1993) of the categories we currently use to summarize self-report data. One purpose is clearly to demonstrate some of the attitudes that really "matter" to the children involved in a custody dispute.

1. Solution-oriented versus adversarial attitudes expressed
2. Flexible versus closed-minded
3. Honesty
4. Awareness of involved children's needs
5. Number (actual) of constructive ideas proposed

Our teams look for any "openings" whatsoever, on either side of the dispute, to get things moving in a positive way. No matter how slight such a window may be, it can be a beginning point toward improved relations.

To search for such opportunities in no way clashes with the evaluator's neutral stance.

7. *Family Interaction Observation Data*

Keep in mind that the best way to use structured observations is in situations where the child can interact *simultaneously* with both parents.

However, aside from being difficult and awkward to arrange, even this situation is not foolproof. Some children are more frightened of one particular parent's reactions (either because of physical fear, or the need to protect), and hence may not, even with both parents present, act, so to speak, from the heart.

However, structured observation sessions can be valuable, especially if the evaluator keeps an eye out for how each parent takes into consideration a given child's unique symbol systems and information-processing strategies. In ACCESS (Bricklin & Elliot, 1995) we have developed two separate forms, one for parents and the other for children. We consider the latter to yield the more important information.

What comes out of these observations, or the *results* of these observations, are expressed by ratings in the following categories.

1. The parent's ability to *meaningfully* communicate a sense of warmth, love, and acceptance.

2. The parent's ability to communicate clearly. This, in turn, is based upon a parent's choice of words, the amount spoken at any time, and the extent to which a parent's communications are based on accurately perceived feedback from the child. Here is where we watch carefully for the many skills outlined in detail in Chapter Three, such as the parent's skill in knowing when it is important to get to main points quickly, if a particular child is good at planning self-initiated sequences, when it is important to let the child speak first, how to regulate the flow of information, when it is especially important to encourage or discourage interruptions, and similar skills.

3. The parent's ability to teach and be a role model for competent problem-solving.

4. The extent to which the parent conveys a sense that he or she (the parent) understands (even though not necessarily agreeing with) the child's views and feelings. This ability to make a child feel listened-to and understood is a main ingredient of a child's growing sense of self-esteem.

5. The extent to which the parent accurately gauges any emergent needs on the part of the child and how limits are set and reacted to by the child.

6. The extent to which the parental response engenders independence and a sense of self-sufficiency in the child.

Observations are made under two sets of conditions, spontaneous and structured. One set involves the waiting room prior to formal introductions (or, in a home visit, the living room), playing games of the parent's choice and playing games of the child's choice.

The other set involves the teaching of competency skills (simple and complex), the parent's ability to be a valuable source of information, and co-operative problem-solving.

Following the above, the results are reported.

Here, in amended form, is part of what I add to the appendices of my written reports, to further explain the structured observation data.

We are much less interested in whether a parent does things "by the book" or in accordance with what experts might say, than in whether the parent chooses his or her words and actions in a way that is based on the child's ability to profit from these words and actions. This means that we place a high value on the parent who is a consistent and accurate listener to, and observer of, what is going on in the child. It is only with this information that a parent can choose what the best words and actions at any given moment happen to be. This underscores the fact that excellent observation and listening skills, coupled with a high degree of flexibility, are far more important tools for a parent to have than "book learning."

The following outline will remind you of the formats in which we carried out our observations:

I. Spontaneous Response Data
 1. Waiting room, prior to formal introductions
 2. Playing games of parent's choice
 3. Playing games of child's choice
II. Structured Response Data
 1. Teaching competency skills
  a. Simple tasks
  b. Complex tasks
 2. Ability to be valuable source of information
  a. Child asked to solve simple task, utilizing parent help at child's initiative
  b. Child asked to solve complex task, utilizing parent help at child's initiative
 3. Cooperative problem-solving
  a. Simple
  b. Complex

8. Parent Awareness Skills

In this section I report the results of the *Parent Awareness Skills Survey* or PASS.

Here is how I introduce the results of this section.

The *Parent Awareness Skills Survey* (PASS) yields scores which reflect the degree to which a parent is aware of certain important elements in interacting with children. The first has to do with a parent's ability to be aware of, to identify, so to speak, the critical issues involved in given situations. For example, a question asks about a three-year-old who grabs toys away from an eight-year-old. There are a variety of issues one could choose to address in this situation. One might, for example, simply hit the three-year-old or yell at him not to grab. This may even be effective, at least in the short run, in stopping the grabbing. However, the savvy parent is aware of several other critical issues in a situation like this—for example, that it is not all that unusual for three-year-olds to "grab." Secondly, there would be an awareness that *both* children need help in coping with the described situation. This is what is meant by an *awareness of critical issues* involved. It is an awareness of just what it is that needs to be addressed in creating a good solution.

Other areas measured by the PASS include the parent's awareness of solutions that are adequate to a particular situation, an awareness that it is important to communicate in words that are understandable to the child, an awareness that one should address the child's emotional feelings aroused in the various situations, and an awareness that it is often important to take into consideration the child's past history. For example, suppose a parent notices that his or her child cannot take in too much information by the spoken word all at one time. A parent noticing this would give directions in short spurts rather than in long sentences.

The final area measured by the PASS reflects the degree to which a parent pays attention to whether or not what he or she is communicating is "working." We call this an awareness of feedback data. This means that the parent fine-tunes his or her response as things go along, based on how the child is responding, and modifies what is being done so as to ensure comfortable results.

In giving results, remember to make recommendations that will make things better for the children, such as, "Mr. A could demonstrate his obvious concern for his children even more effectively if he lets them know, from time to time, based on his observations, that he understands how they are feeling."

9. *Parent Knowledge of Children*

In this section, I summarize the results of the *Parent Perception of Child Profile* or PPCP (or any similar tool). Here is how one might introduce this section in the report. (Remember that in some prevailing living/custody arrangements one—or even both—of the competing parents may have, or have had, limited opportunities for contact with a given child. It is important for the evaluator to indicate awareness of such facts in the report, along with reassurance that these factors were taken into account in interpreting PPCP data.)

The *Parent Perception of Child Profile* (PPCP) allowed each parent to express what he or she knows about (child's name) in a wide variety of important life areas. These areas include the child's: interpersonal relationships, daily routine, health history, developmental milestones, school history, fears, personal hygiene habits, and communication style.

It also helps us to understand each parent's accuracy of perception and depth of knowledge in any particular area, and the overall scope of knowledge displayed.

While we rarely wonder about a parent's "emotional interest" in a child (the feelings a parent gets deep inside when with, or thinking about, a child), it *is* important to understand how many actual facts a parent has had the interest to learn about the child.

10. *Traditional Psychological Test Data (by name)*

In this section, the evaluator has the opportunity to detail what the specific tests he or she has chosen to use (such as intelligence, personality, etc.) can contribute to the decisions that must be made. Mention could be made of special developmental and/or other needs of the child.

In a preceding section of this chapter, examples were offered about how such materials might be used. Our teams absolutely avoid clinical jargon. Further, there is always an attempt, when describing behavior (whether seen as positive or negative) to offer these descriptions along several dimensions, i.e., the *context* or psychological "setting" in which the behavior appears, its *frequency of appearance*, the *duration of time involved*, and the *intensity* of any given manifestation. If negative, the latter information is offered along with suggestions for improvement. Here is an example. Let us suppose test, as well as clinical and life-history data, point to depressive episodes. Let us even suppose the parent has been in psychotherapy and is on antidepressant medication, with only moderately successful results.

The evaluator might summarize this as follows:

The test data, as well as clinical and life history data, suggest Mr. B must occasionally take a time-out in his activities due to blue moods for which he has taken appropriate action. These moods occur once every two to three days, last about an hour, are of moderate intensity, and do not seem related to any particular outside stressors or triggers. Currently, therefore, he may require one time-out every two to three days. It is suggested that a plan be worked out so the children simply see these episodes as time-outs-to-recuperate sessions, and that Mr. B. reassures the children's mother that appropriate help is available to the children during such episodes. The details of such a plan can be worked out—and monitored—by a neutral psychotherapist.

Note once again, it is not wise from a communications standpoint—nor from an evaluator perspective—to see any given piece of the parental picture as inherently good or bad, regardless of what one learned in graduate school.

For test or clinical data to be useful in a custody evaluation report, one must first "translate" it by use of the following questions.

If I were in so-and-so's home, what would I actually witness? What would trigger this behavior? How frequently would this occur? How long would it last? How intense would it be?

And especially, given everything I know about (a particular child), what actual impact would this have?

Finally, how can I express this information in a way that does not cause denial or defensiveness?

Related to the above, with some modification, can such behaviors be made to work *for*, not against, any involved child?

11. *Bricklin Perceptual Scales (BPS) and/or Perception-of-Relationships Test (PORT) Data*

Since both the PORT and BPS are data-based, I give their results a good bit of weight when attempting to create a plan that maximizes a child's exposure to behaviors that will be helpful.

Here are questions I ask myself in regard to BPS data (in addition to the more formal ones detailed in Chapter Ten). These particular questions will show the categories I use in my written reports to communicate what the BPS has had to contribute.

First, I always ask myself if the child responded spontaneously. The BPS is more susceptible to MMU strategies than is the PORT. Who does the better job of helping the child acquire the skills of competency? Is this across-the-board, or limited to certain areas? Are there any particularly positive or negative situations to be aware of?

Who seems to do better at helping the child feel loved and appreciated? Is there any way to tell *specifically* how this is happening?

Who seems to demand more consistency? Does the child see this as good or as a drag? If the latter is true, does this make sense, or is it the usual case of a child who wants more freedom, but does not really act responsibly enough to warrant this freedom?

Who seems to do the better job modeling admirable traits for the child? Again, is this across-the-board or limited to certain areas?

Were the child's choices rather consistently in favor of one parent or highly contextualized (spread out, with less apparent internal consistency)? Did a POC emerge by virtue of small or large differences on the various items that comprise the test?

If the child attributed low degrees of "wellness" to *both* parents, is there evidence of severe depression or schizophrenia anywhere in the picture (in the child and/or either or both of the parents)?

Here are some questions I ask myself about PORT data. The answers to these questions reflect the kinds of information I might include in a written report.

What kinds of assets (confidence, assertiveness, etc.) is the child acquiring by virtue of interaction with each parent? What kinds of liabilities (fearfulness, confusion, and/or ambivalence)?

In which contexts does the child desire to be close to each parent (alone, within a "family," or in wishful fantasy)?

Very importantly, are these desires for closeness based on positive factors (such as feelings of security and/or exuberance) or on negative factors (fearfulness, desire to protect)? In the latter regard, is the child paying a frightful price (greatly distorted figures) in order to accommodate the closeness?

Very importantly, do the PORT indicators that reflect conscious sources tell the same story as do those emanating from less conscious sources? Do we have a NBOAI scenario?

If one likes to think in more global terms, the PORT and BPS can answer for a child, what Freud thought of as the two critical variables one would use to reflect upon an adult's mental health: the ability to love (for a child, the ability to sustain healthy interpersonal relationships), and to work (for a child, to be productive and secure in school). The BPS and PORT can reflect the degrees to which a child, in relation to each parent: feels loved and worthwhile, feels protected and safe, is willing to take risks, has a sense of exuberance, feels comfortable relating to others, is picking up worthwhile traits. These data can also help discern the degree to which each parent is sensitive to the child's symbol systems and ways of using information.

12. *Summary and Recommendations*

Basically, one has to decide the format one will use in the "summary and recommendations" section—for example, long and detailed versus short and to the point.

Regardless of the length and amount of detail, here is a suggested outline of the areas one would want to cover. The custody evaluator should:

- clearly delineate all purposes of the evaluation, including a consideration of the role being assumed by the evaluator (e.g., ALL-CPE, LIM-CPE, researcher, etc.) and any limitations following from this role;
- provide a summary of previous custody evaluations and/or legal determinations, as well as noting areas of continuing concern;
- carefully identify parental assets and liabilities (both personally, "within" each parent, and externally, in what each can provide for a child, such as extended family members) in terms of the importance of these variables for a particular child's needs, being careful to use nonadversarial, and health-inspiring concepts and wording in the report;

- delineate any "override" factors that may have a controlling influence on an eventual decision, such as abuse, a decision to switch to the use of mediation, some very special need on the part of the child, an "extreme" in terms of the time availability of one particular parent;
- suggest what remains to be done to produce an optimal evaluation if a LIM-CPE was all that was possible to do in the present circumstances;
- (perhaps) delineate the model used (see Chapter Ten) to aggregate the data, if one is going to suggest a PCP (and offer this as *information*);
- suggest a monitoring plan if it is obvious that the adult participants continue to have worries and concerns about a child's safety or well-being (see Chapter Thirteen).

If a particular case is adversarial, one may choose to conclude one's report with a rather brief "summary and recommendations" section, highlighting critical strengths rather than providing a mountain of supporting details, that have already been documented in the rest of the report. A purpose is to take advantage of a principle often stressed in Ericksonian communication strategies: Once you get a ball rolling in a positive direction, even if it rolls only a short distance, the possibility of greater rolling in the future is more likely since the system is now more open to extensive beneficial changes. The principle is sometimes stated from the opposite direction: Once you start to dismantle any negative sequence, no matter how "little" the dismantling, the sequence can never again reconstitute in exactly the same way (O'Hanlon & Wilk, 1987). Of course, time may have to pass for the beneficial changes to become evident, since every piece of behavior is part of some system, and this system itself interacts with other systems. Hence, the initially small change must find an accommodation within several other interacting and overlapping systems.

Stated succinctly, it is better to start with changing some small piece of a system and procure *some* movement rather than attempting to change an entire system and end up changing nothing.

Chapter Twelve

Validity and Reliability Issues

The degree of validity for some particular test shows the extent to which any measurement made with that test really reflects the value of the variable that the test purports to be measuring.

A good illustration of this issue is shown in some of the controversies associated with the measurement of intelligence. One approach asks of the IQ test: "How well does this test measure what we really believe intelligence to be?" The other approach begs the validity question by defining intelligence as "that which this IQ test measures."

The degree of reliability of a test is the extent to which the test gives the same measurement results when applied repeatedly in exactly the same situation. Suppose I measure the length of an iron bar with an elastic ruler. Repeated measures would not give identical results, even though the "true" length of the bar would not have changed.

But even in this sample example, we cannot be sure the length of the bar has not changed. Maybe the temperature is different or we are holding the bar vertically (thus gravity will have a slightly different effect).

In a conceptual sense, both validity and reliability depend on the idea of a criterion measure or a detailed, explicit model. The criterion measure of the length of our iron bar is probably some laser measuring device whose results can be used as the standard against which we may compare the results from our elastic ruler. Or we can use a model that lets us calculate the effect of gravity or temperature on the length.

193

In the case of custody evaluations and the measurement properties of the PORT and the BPS or any such test, there are no universally agreed-upon standards against which they can be calibrated. There is no agreement, even conceptually, as to what constitutes a "best" custodial arrangement, and for any custodial arrangement, there are difficulties in measuring the effects on the child.

But the lack of a standard for calibration does not mean that nothing can be said about how valid and reliable such tests are. The rest of this chapter discusses these issues in more detail.

Two research points of departure have been taken in the custody evaluation field.

One seeks to understand the relationships between the adequacies of the outcomes associated with various custodial dispositions (e.g., joint versus sole custody, same-sex custody) and other actuarial parent and/or child variables such as age, gender, presence or absence of stepparents, etc. Those interested in custody research attempt to use the actuarial variables thus identified in a predictive sense, to fashion optimal custody arrangements.

The other approach seeks to predict which of two competing parties could more frequently serve in a given child's best interests by obtaining more finely-tuned measurements directly from the involved participants. The methods outlined in this book exemplify the second approach. (See also Gordon & Peek, 1988, and Ackerman & Schoendorf, 1992). Interestingly, this second approach receives strong support from a study by Stolberg and Bush (1985). They had 82 mother-child pairs from divorced homes complete measures assessing life-change events, marital hostility, parent skills and adjustment, and child behavior and adjustment. "Parenting skills was found to be the single most important influence on children's postdivorce adjustment" (p. 53). They discovered that even a mother's having achieved a healthy post-divorce adjustment "was not...of any value (to an involved child)...unless this adjustment was reflected in improved parenting practices" (p. 53).

It should be noted that validation is difficult within either approach. (See Chapter Two for a discussion of the validational difficulties regarding the first approach).

Let us set aside, for the moment, the types of complexities brought up by so called "ultimate issue" value assignments. By this I mean there is no way to decide "objectively" what constitutes an optimal outcome regarding psychological "health," e.g., does one value competence over subjective comfort? Indeed, a judge who has the job of deciding what is in a child's best interests need not follow research evidence, anyway. If a judge assigns a high priority to the importance of religious upbringing, he or she may give custody to the particular parent who more rigorously insists the child attend a religious school. This is a legitimate judicial option, and need have nothing to do with the presence or absence of empirical data that might support such a priority.

In some ways, one might be able to get around "ultimate issue" complexities in the sense that one could specify, within a predictive framework, that if a certain future outcome were desired, then such-and-such are the traits one would look for among existing parent and child variables. In other words, we could say that given the desirability of future outcome X, these are the markers to look for in the current parent-child situation. Here "X" stands for some "best" outcome. Note that one would require evidence (or an exceptionally detailed model) to relate the markers to X.

Other difficulties shared by both approaches have to do with time-frame issues. By this we mean that if a custody disposition was made on some basis, and then one decided to do follow up research to evaluate how the arrangement is working, the first question one faces is to identify the time-frame within which to make these measurements or observations. It seems rather clear that maximum chaos prevails in the immediate aftermath of divorce, and no matter what the disposition, things are fairly grim for at least several months while everyone is trying to find his or her footing within some new dynamic arrangement.

The second major factor in doing follow-up research has to do with the confounding variables that enter the picture over a longer time frame, such as remarriage, new stepparents, new schools, etc.—the multitude of other influences that enter the picture. First of all, most individuals do not exactly follow whatever the custody decree is in any event. Parents make loads of adjustments on their own, so a researcher cannot assume that the individuals involved in any given plan are necessarily following what was either ordered or agreed upon.

Far more important, are the often overwhelming influences of the variety of other institutions and individuals that enter into the picture in any given arrangement and, to put it mildly, muddy the waters. Here we speak of remarriages, live-in companions, and especially the degree to which a child finds himself or herself in a supportive social environment and/or a supportive school setup. Within the school, one particular child, living in one arrangement, may find a supportive teacher, a supportive counselor, a supportive set of friends, while another child, living under the same (or a different) disposition, may encounter the exact opposite. This makes it difficult to come to clear conclusions about the relationship between a child's mental health and any particular custody disposition. Further, it is well known that "damage" to a child has a lot to do with the kinds of conflicts that exist between the child's parents. To the extent that these conflicts are directly child- or custody-related, that child is likely to suffer.

Another substantial problem involves the difficulties in measuring a child's "quality of life" at *any* time. This goes beyond ultimate-issue questions. Many PORT and BPS users have phoned me over the years claiming to be highly motivated to conduct validity research on these tools. A common desire was to locate ways to tell how well a child was doing at some point in time without depending on human "subjective" opinion. Once they discovered what a complex issue this really is, enthusiasm for the validity research lessened quite a bit. I remember one conversation vividly. The caller, a respected researcher/clinician, warmed rapidly to the challenge of discovering "objective" quality-of-life indicators. "We can use school grades and attendance," he began, "and number of trips to the pediatrician, and the number of friends the child has, and.…" His voice trailed off. He was either realizing that there aren't many of such items or that almost all of the mentioned ones (whether or not a child should visit a physician or "tough-it-out," whether a child should go to school or stay home "sick," even school grades) *all* involve human "subjective" opinions. It would be hard even to get a consensus about the value of the number of a child's friends (Is one *good* friend better or worse than *lots* of superficial friends?). This illustrates not only the difficulties involved in *measuring* a child's quality of life, but also in *defining* it to begin with.

Another thorny validational issue is whether or not it is legitimate to use the decisions of courtroom judges as independent criteria to which predictive measures can be compared. One should note that a judge's decision, in a very real sense, is indeed what a forensic expert is *attempting* to predict.

One could point out some problems with judges' opinions. Their actual decisions, the memories of which may constitute their "internal" databases, were influenced not so much by behavioral data, but rather by what they have been told by other experts (as well as by their own actions; in this sense, the longer a judge uses some decision rule, the more he or she tends to believe in it, regardless of its true merits).

For a further discussion of the what-is-validating-what issue, as well as related ones, see Golding, Roesch, and Schreiber (1984). Heilbrun (1992, pp. 262–263) discusses this same issue, as well as some of the problems in using so-called "base rate" information or, indeed, any statistics at all. Tribe (1971) is the most frequently quoted "anti-numbers" writer in forensic books and articles. Einstein's protestations notwithstanding (in a 1936 piece entitled *Physics and Reality* he assumed any theory that needs "statistics" is incomplete), statistics will probably remain a major voice of science for many years to come.

The biggest problem is in that we can never carry out a truly ideal validation study. Here is what I believe the ideal research situation would be for a study relating to the approach advocated in this book.

One would administer the tests and decide which parent could more frequently act in a child's best interests in the widest variety of situations. The custody dispositions would be determined by these match-ups. Measurements of mental health would be made. One would then allow time to pass, following which one would come in and measure the same variables to ascertain the degree of mental health, comfort, achievement, etc. among the evaluation participants.

One would next roll back the hands of time to the starting point and now give the child to the opposite parent and repeat the procedure.

Regardless of the theories of physics to which one subscribes, this would be a very difficult experiment to implement.

There are ways around the dilemmas posed in conducting an ideal follow-up study. One could track cases where the custody disposition followed was counter to the PCPs as determined by a test, and compare them to test-chosen PCP situations. Here, one would select a reasonably large and representative group of custody cases where neither the PORT nor the BPS (or a similar prediction test) was being used. The child-directed test could be given for research purposes only, the results sealed and in no way used in the deliberations, and "outcome" measures of the mental health of the children made at a later date. (All of the difficulties just discussed apply to selecting an appropriate time-frame.)

The degree of mental health of the children could be compared for two groups: those where the court's decision agreed with the test results, and those where it disagreed. If there was a higher level of mental health in those children who had been given to the parent chosen by the test, then an additional way would have been found to demonstrate validity. All such studies are difficult to implement—and none can escape the number of confounding influences that rapidly mount up as time passes, any combination of which could affect a given parent's range of parenting styles as well as a child directly.

A reduced requirement for the outcome measure might be framed as follows: At least the child is not worse than he/she was when the parent-child match-up was created.

In such a scenario, the hypothesis to be checked would be that a "correct" parent and child match-up would be one in which, upon follow-up, the child's health was at least as good as it measured when the experiment began.

Given the variety of complicating factors encountered in designing validational studies that can yield data useful to a custody decision-maker, we believe the approach we used is reasonable. Even though this approach depends on human opinion, the opinion at the heart of the proffered independent criteria designations at least was formed by people most qualified to do so: mental health professionals with access to enormous time-samples of data generated in a maximally honest forum, family therapy sessions. Reviewing data about family interactions from time samples of never less than two years, and up to seven years, these mental health professionals were in a fairly comfortable position to make a judgment about which of the two parents in a given family was functioning in a more nurturant and useful way to a given child.

All of the other manual-reported data (such as from questionnaire forms or the opinions of courtroom judges, etc.) are helpful to a validational enterprise (especially in establishing construct validity), but none so much as the family therapy data.

Reliability matters are also complex. The issue of the reliability of the PORT and the BPS (or any such test) is not completely separate from the issue of validity. If one picks measures that have high reliability, it may be because they do not change much and are not sensitive to changes in the actual situation. But we do not want to choose variables that we can measure well (high reliability), but that change so rapidly or so easily that they have little use as predictors of important outcomes (low validity). Thus the discussion of reliability must consider both the extent to which the underlying factors being measured change with time or circumstance, and the accuracy with which the test can measure the factors. In the field of custody decision-making, we would want to formulate concepts whose empirical referents—in our approach, this would be test measurements—reflect processes that are fairly stable over time, but able to mirror the psychological equivalent of a "change of circumstances." In other words, tests that have utility in custody cases should be sensitive to a child's changing perceptions of his of her parents—but this sensitivity should mirror important, not trivial, changes.

Chapter Thirteen

Dilemmas in Child Custody Evaluations

HOW IMPORTANT ARE GRANDPARENTS?

It is usually assumed that the more a child has access to his or her grandparents, the better. In fact, as editor of the *Custody Newsletter*, I frequently get letters saying that custody evaluators should pay more attention to intergenerational issues in determining what is in the best interests of a child.

The reasoning goes that if there is no obvious reason (for example, abuse) to deny a grandparent visitation, then the more visitation that can be facilitated, the better. I am not personally aware of any empirical data that support this view, although common sense and extrapolation from other research suggest merit in a child's having relationships with *any* human beings characterized by special warmth and love on both sides.

Grandparents only rarely will have (or need) standing to seek legally enforced visitation with a grandchild unless something has happened to the natural stability of the child's family, such as divorce or death of a parent.

In a custody context, grandparents who have a good relation with their child will rarely encounter difficulty in seeing their grandchild regardless of what the grandchild's other parent may think of them, since such visitation will take place when the involved child is with their own child.

Visitation disputes typically arise within custody evaluation scenarios when the grandparent's own child, one of the parents of the involved youngster, has died, moved away, or is indifferent about using his or her own visitation opportunities. This leaves the grandparents at the mercy of the youngster's other parent.

Another type of dispute arises when a member of one "camp" believes the grandparents from the other "camp" are alienators.

The most bitter disputes, however, arise when it is the grandparents' *own* child who wants to deny them access to their grandchild.

On a more "peaceful" level, the custody evaluator must often, in the course of a standard evaluation, decide two things relevant to grandparents. One is whether a particular parent can provide a child with greater access to an extended family than can the other. If so, the second task becomes deciding the degree of importance to assign to this expanded access.

Here are some points of perspective for a custody evaluator to keep in mind regarding all such issues. Almost all states have passed some kind of statute making it "legal" (i.e., provide standing) for a grandparent to pursue visitation rights with a child over the objection of the parents. In this legal presumption, one deals with a situation that reflects empirical findings along with aspirational idealisms—these laws reflect not necessarily what *can* work, but what someone thinks *ought* to work. Many times, in regard to such "social policy" laws, the mix is high on the latter (idealism) and low on the former (empirical findings).

These grandparent visitation laws presume the good accruing to a child from the visits with the grandparents will outweigh what this enforced access will cause negatively to the mental health (let alone authority and pocketbook) of the parent caught up in the conflict.

The very fact that many states have given grandparents the power to use the court to gain access to children against the will of one or both parents shifts the balances of power that exist in pretrial negotiations, since the mere threat to launch a lawsuit is coercive.

Whether this new power in the hands of grandparents will always be used wisely is hard to assess. In many situations, lawsuits thus launched may only raise the amount of conflict to which the involved children are already exposed.

A custody evaluator who gets called into a case that involves a grandparent issue should read an article by Thompson, Tinsley, Scalora, and Parke (1989) arguing that the fallout for family functioning of the laws that give grandparents standing to pursue visitation in spite of parental objection would be a lot more "... acceptable in the face of additional evidence that grandchildren always benefit from ongoing contact with their grandparents, *despite parental objections*" (p. 1221). They reason that in the absence of this evidence, the consequences might bring about much greater multigenerational involvement in child-related situations than courts have typically tolerated under the presumption of the merits of parental autonomy.

Child-derived data can go a long way in helping to answer the questions arising in these kinds of situations. For example, both the BPS and PORT can be adapted so that any person can be compared to any other person. This may be a parent with a grandparent, or a grandparent with any other person chosen to represent some standard. (This might be an adult with whom the child is known factually to have had a loving and warm relationship. Such a comparison could help delineate the psychological role a particular grandparent is playing in a child's life.)

The PORT especially can show if there are exceptional signs of closeness, warmth, and stability as opposed to signs of distance and/or anything else bespeaking negativity or conflict.

Having had wonderful grandparents myself, and having grown up in an 11-person multigenerational household (with one bathroom—unthinkable in middle-class America these days), and having witnessed how a grandfather's love and wisdom was able to permeate and set the standard for this household, I am personally biased in favor of large, extended families. However, data from the household in which I grew up are not necessarily comparable to situations where grandparent visitation could cause parental strife.

WHY NOT MEDIATION INSTEAD OF EVALUATION?

I have met a number of professional colleagues who believe those of us who perform custody evaluations are part of the problem, not the solution. These individuals believe postdivorce controversies should be routinely settled through mediation. Some of the less committed of these individuals do realize that mediation might not work for all those involved in postdivorce disputes, those who are simply too bitter and enmeshed in adversarial attitudes.

There are several forms of dispute negotiation. The main groupings would involve pure mediation, arbitration, and a category composed of elements of both. The difference between arbitration and mediation is that the decision by the arbitrator in an arbitration procedure is generally considered binding upon both sides. This assumption is not made in pure mediation; there, the skills of the mediator are to bring the two or more disputants to a position where they can agree on all (or most) of the elements in a particular postdivorce plan, including those aspects that have to do with custody. (See Strochak, 1991, for an interesting approach that blends evaluation and conciliation components.)

Melton et al. (1987) have several important points to make about mediation (pp. 331–333). First, they make the general point that the fact that a mental health professional may be a good evaluator is absolutely no reason to assume this individual would be a good mediator. Not only is dispute resolution a skill that has very little to do with evaluation, there is also the problem that far more issues will come into a divorce mediation (e.g., financial matters) than the typical evaluator would be familiar with. They reaffirm the importance of not trying to combine the role of evaluator with that of mediator.

Melton et al. (1987) also cite the same evidence as others arguing for some (limited, but important) benefits of a well maintained adversarial procedure (Thibaut & Walker, 1975). What research there is regarding adversarial procedure seems to suggest that "success" in such a process is related to the degree to which each participant feels he or she has taken part in a fair and thorough hearing. Wolman and Taylor (1991) indicate that even the children involved in an adversarial process may profit from having indirectly taken part in it (although they believe more research needs to be done to tease out just what is harmful and what could be helpful to children about going through contested versus uncontested processes).

The most recent and thorough study on the success of mediation as of the time this was written is that of Pruitt, Peirce, McGillicuddy, Welton, and Castrianno (1993). These authors attempted to discover the variables that could predict long-term success in mediation processes. Seventy-three mediation sessions were recorded and their content analyzed. Persons who participated were interviewed twice: just after mediation and about four to eight months later. The researchers could find no clear relationship between the quality of the agreements reached in mediation, that is, the extent to which they helped to solve then current problems, and the long term success of the endeavor as measured by "compliance, improved relations between the parents, and the absence of new problems" (p. 313). They did, however, find that the ability to engage in the mediational process, that is, to solve problems jointly, was related to the participant's perceptions of improved relations with the other party.

ALLEGATIONS OF SEXUAL ABUSE

One of the most troubling aspects of a custody investigation occurs when one or both of the participants bring up a sexual abuse allegation in the midst of the proceedings. This area is particularly vexing because it seems to me that the professionals involved in the process take polarized positions—they are "for" either the supposed victim *or* the alleged perpetrator. It further seems to me that the pendulum has swung so far in this area as to resemble what has happened in regard to the parent alienation syndrome. If a parent, these days, raises an allegation of sexual abuse during a custody dispute, he or she is automatically assumed to be lying. I think this is regrettable. Any pendulum swing "extreme" is as bad as any other.

The aspects of this situation with which the custody evaluator will have to deal fall generally into two categories. One has to do with the ethical and/or scientific "positioning" assumed by the involved mental health professional toward the investigation or the resolution of the abuse charges, and the other with the technical difficulties that come up in the attempt to discern true from false instances of sexual abuse.

Regarding the former, it would be wise for any involved mental health professional to read an article by Melton and Limber (1989) entitled "Psychologists' Involvement in Cases of Child Maltreatment: Limits of Role and Expertise."

This is as good a place as any to pass along a suggestion to forensic mental health professionals. If you wish to "locate" your own psycholegal position on some matter, it is usually a good idea to see if Gary Melton has written anything on the involved subject. A reading of any of Melton's materials typically offers a thoughtful, thorough yet concise, *extremely conservative* interpretation of whatever the area happens to be. A mental health professional may then measure his or her position on the issue against this standard. To the degree that one inches to the left of Melton's position, is one probably moving into less sensible (and less defensible) territory. (This is not to say I agree with all of the points he and his various coauthors assert in the name of this conservative position.)

Regarding one's ethical and scientific positioning in a case where sexual abuse allegations arise, it is wise to pay heed to the important difference between a mental health professional's serving in the adjudicatory phase of a case, as opposed to the sentencing or dispositional phase. As Melton and Limber (1989) point out of the latter category: "Because the event has not yet occurred, no better, more case-specific evidence is available in determining the relative merits of various possible dispositions" (p. 1225).

In contrast to adjudication issues (the "Who done it?" phase), dispositional and sentencing issues are inherently probabilistic, meaning that they legitimately permit the use of predictions (involving probability data) that are taken into account in deciding the various merits of possible outcomes. The adjudicatory phase, in seeking to determine whether some act did or did not occur, often forces an expert witness to depend upon group data relating to abusers and/or abused children, a use of probability data in a way that is (arguably) not "legitimate."

Among the many important points made in the Melton and Limber (1989) article are the following. It is very important that mental health professionals not do anything that violates or decreases the legal and civil rights of people who may be affected by their actions. The example given is in criminal cases where mental health professionals are called upon to evaluate defendants before the latter have had an opportunity to consult with their attorneys and are used, unwittingly, to gather materials that the prosecution will then use against the defendants. On the other side of the fence, mental health professionals should realize that to do, for example, all of the many tests, interviews, and observations necessary to see if a child fits the "abused victim" profile is amazingly lengthy and intrusive. This would also be an example of a mental health professional *possibly* violating or diminishing the civil rights of a person involved in such a troublesome and tragic case.

They make the important point that the mental health professional should help the involved participants to look with respect on the judicial process. This follows from other materials cited in this book that show satisfaction with the legal process in general is often dependent on what is called "perceived procedural justice."

Another very interesting point that Melton and Limber bring up is the importance of keeping the participants informed of what is going on. This is wise to keep in mind since mental health professionals carrying out comprehensive evaluations generally get caught up in gathering tremendous amounts of materials, which takes a long time to do. They bring this up especially in relation to children. When children are part of an evaluation and are not kept appropriately informed, there is evidence to suggest their anxiety will increase. They cite the evidence that "...studies of the effects of testimony on children suggest that the experience of being in limbo while proceedings are pending has far more deleterious effects than testifying itself..." (p. 1227).

The beneficial effects of being kept informed accrue from the fact that "informed people" feel more in control of their personal destinies. Of course, this reminder leaves unanswered the complex question of just what "keeping a child informed" would mean amidst an investigation into sexual abuse. Nevertheless, the point is an important one, and must be thought through on an individual basis. That would require that the mental health professional find just the right words to allay anxieties that could accumulate by virtue of children being kept in an ambiguous situation. Children feel guilty enough, as we all know, when they take part in *any* kind of family evaluation, and this is doubled and tripled when there are perceived "winners" and "losers." And the "loser" in an investigation of sexual abuse could turn out to be a mighty big "loser." The truth, of course, is that *everyone* suffers in such cases, regardless of which side prevails.

Under the heading of "The fulfillment of promises," Melton and Limber (1989) remind us to be honest about the limits of our roles and expertise. Where children have been abused, ethical violations are apt to occur because of all of the different roles the involved adult professionals are required to take during the investigatory process.

Any mental health professional who practices in the forensic field is well advised to understand evidentiary rules. Here we refer to the issues covered in Chapters One and Ten, which pertain to the roles and limits of expert testimony and useful ways to offer evidence.

The other major category of complexity for the mental health professional has to do with all of the technical difficulties involved in assessing whether or not sexual abuse has in fact taken place. In the absence of physical evidence or meaningful confession, one is basically relying on probabilistic data and hence any investigative conclusion is already on thin ice, given the seriousness of the charge.

As the body of this book has hopefully demonstrated, interviews are not really terrific ways to gather meaningful data. And most evidence in sex abuse cases is gathered via interviews.

Compounding the difficulties with the interview, is the sheer number of people who do them in sex abuse investigations. Many are not well trained. Difficulties within these areas (the lack of precision in interview data and the number of people involved in an investigatory process) have led to much research (and speculation) having to do with the reliability and accuracy of memory, the suggestibility of memory, and the related but important area having to do with checking the credibility of an interviewee's assertions. Another complexity in the technical area has to do with the lack of test instruments standardized to detect sexual abuse.

Still another problem has to do with the need to depend upon group-generated data when trying to decide an important issue in an individual case. This, of course, spills over into the preceding category as well, since any standardized psychological instrument will depend upon some type of data base, and it is unlikely that anything is going to achieve an accuracy rate of 100 percent. And should one discover a test that yields very few, maybe even no false positives, one typically then has a test that probably yields many false negatives. That is, I happen to believe the PORT yields some signs that occur only when the child has suffered some sexually related trauma; however, these signs do not appear frequently. Thus, it is likely that when these signs appear, a sexual trauma occurred. However, it is difficult to assess the number of false negatives that would be yielded by the PORT since the absence of these signs in no way can rule out sexual abuse. (Research projects that could establish such values are difficult to carry out, since there is no trustworthy way to establish the actual incidence of abuse in any group.) Further, since trauma is in large part "in the eyes of the beholder," these test-based signs cannot tell the law what it most wants to know, that is, what actually happened. What is a trauma for one child is not necessarily what would be traumatic to another child. (So far, we have tracked data on 600 cases where abuse was alleged. We have seen about 60 cases where abuse could be proven either by physical evidence or confession. In all 60 cases, there were indications of abuse on the PORT. However, there is no real way to know in how many cases abuse really occurred, since the methods of so-called "validation" would involve determinations by a children-and-youth service organization, the members of which use methods of variable and/or unknown accuracy.)

The difficulties with using group data on individual cases applies whether one is talking about techniques designed to pick up potential abusers or talking about so called "victim profiles," that is, techniques designed to show whether or not a child has the signs that are typical of those who have suffered known sexual abuse.

We would like to present a list of items to assist the custody evaluator to gather and organize information relevant to an allegation of sexual abuse. This list is offered *solely* for the personal use of the evaluator, since it is one thing to generate information and/or come to conclusions in the privacy of one's head and quite another to decide what to do with such data.

There is a good bit of disagreement not only among respected authors but also in case laws regarding the proper role of a mental health professional in offering testimony about sexual abuse allegations. What actually happens in various courtrooms around the country when this issue comes up amidst a custody trial seems to me to reflect an even more chaotic character.

These strategies have been culled from a variety of sources, which will be listed later. One of the most promising (but controversial) avenues of approach is that which is called "criterion based content analysis," and the larger type of investigation of which this is a specific subtype, "statement validity analysis." The latter uses a variety of sources to check the likelihood that a particular "story" is credible.

It should be noted that the particular concern of a mental health professional in an investigation of potential sexual abuse is often the credibility of a witness. To paraphrase Raskin and Esplin (1991, p. 153), the great difficulty in a sexual abuse investigation is not to tell whether or not a child is necessarily able to provide a completely accurate account. A more important matter is the child's underlying motivation in providing an account at all, as well as the credibility of that account.

All of the following strategies are offered as ways to check either the credibility of an allegation or the likelihood that an abusive event occurred. They are offered as investigatory tools only. All of the aforementioned caveats would have to be observed in regard to arriving at conclusions on their bases. Some practical suggestions will be offered later.

- Have the child describe either a typical day or a recent school trip or outing. Credibility is enhanced to the degree that the account matches in several important variables the account of the abuse. Some of these variables would include the amount of detail offered, the logical structure of the narrative, etc.
- The evaluator must make sure the child can tell the difference between the truth and a lie, and also have an ability to differentiate "I do not know" from "I do not want to tell" from "I am confused by the question you are asking."
- The following strategies are thought to enhance memory; hence, the reasoning goes that when these enhancement techniques are used they should result in an expansion of the story. It is commonly assumed that when a person makes up a lie, he or she usually makes up just enough to constitute the lie. A person who is fabricating an account rarely bothers to figure out how the lie will dovetail, especially if the liar is a child, with

all of the other events with which it would be contextually embedded. The enhancement techniques would include asking the child what was going on just before each episode happened, having the child recount the story with the instructions to "not leave anything out at all," and having the event recalled from a different perspective, e.g., as if the child were standing outside of the room looking in when the events took place. As mentioned, credibility is increased if these techniques lead to the addition of further details.

- There are a whole host of factors that relate to discovering a possible motivation to lie or to misrepresent the truth. Hence, an investigation would always include interviewing all persons involved to discover what they have to gain or lose by disclosure. This would involve finding out how the initial revelation was made and to whom, and who had to gain or lose by this revelation. Generally speaking, credibility increases when a parent supporting disclosure is ambivalent about this, knowing that it is going to be painful for the child no matter what happens subsequently. This parent may also show remorse for not having provided greater protection in the past.

- In line with the above, there are a whole host of factors that are thought to influence whether or not a respondent has the *desire* to tell the truth. False charges could stem from any of the following: visitation and custody disputes (see Cooke & Cooke, 1991); an adolescent desire to rebel; hatred for the alleged perpetrator for a variety of reasons; revenge for perceived psychological abuse by the alleged perpetrator; desire to remove the latter from circulation; an attempt to protect someone else; a misinterpretation of good-touch versus bad-touch lectures; contagion via overdramatized media presentations; a child's need to protect a parent from serious physical abuse by the alleged perpetrator; a need to draw attention away from the child himself or herself, especially if there is a need to do so. Here, the evaluator would need to know what else is going on in the child's life—e.g., failing school or possible sexual involvement with someone other than the alleged perpetrator.

- It is always important to check if the child's language used during the "charges" is appropriate to the child's age. It is commonly thought that if the child is using language inappropriate to his or her own age, there is a chance that the wording has been suggested by someone else. This would not be the case if the child is reporting a conversation that took place during the alleged abuse. As a matter of fact, if a child reports a conversation that took place during the abuse, it should *not* be in the child's own language; it would be in the language of the person with whom the conversation took place.

- In young children, special attention must be paid to the way sensory experiences are detailed, such as smells, sounds, tastes, etc. The more vividly a child describes the sensory experiences of abuse, the more likely it is that it actually took place. Of course, children frequently get things confused here as when a child uses the word pee-pee or urine to refer to semen.

- It is important to check whether the child's affect seems congruent with the events being reported. However, it is important to remember that trauma sometimes leads to flattened affect. Also, and I think this is a point that is frequently ignored, the child has typically told his or her story so many times that the affect may have been wrung out of it by the time the evaluator gets to see the child.

- The child's behavior should show a change from before the alleged abuse. When there has been such a change, credibility is increased.

- To the extent that the child shows himself or herself able to describe things accurately and precisely (as opposed to in vague and distorted ways), credibility is increased.

- Here is a list of some of the signs that have been noted as important changes when some form of abuse has taken place: signs of post traumatic stress disorder (tension, irritability, distractibility, reliving of the event during day or night "dreams," etc.), depression, regressive behavior, seductive behavior, social withdrawal, somatic complaints, tarnished self-esteem. In very young children one might observe thumbsucking, eating disorders, sleep disruption, enuresis, tics, excessive fears and/or self-mutilation, hints about sexual activity, distrust of persons previously trusted, inappropriate sex play.

- Recantations are the order of the day with children. Actually, in contradistinction to what one might think from a commonsense perspective, our experience is that recantations occur almost as often in true abuse cases as in cases where nothing can be proven; thus, they probably do not have great discriminating potential. Children are bombarded by such a host of loyalty conflicts that this makes perfect sense.

- If the alleged perpetrator made a threat or offered a reward for secrecy, and this is in the child's account, credibility is enhanced.

- If the alleged perpetrator gave the child an explanation to explain what he or she "is doing," credibility is enhanced, e.g., "This is a tickle-game."

- If the child shows a fairly invariant sequencing of the critical items, credibility is enhanced. Also important is the degree to which the child provides interlocking links between the events that took place during the abuse and other things going on in the child's environment. For example, if a child is telling a story in which something happened and the father was wearing a certain item of clothes, credibility would be enhanced if the child comments that: "Daddy usually wears this when he goes to bed." In this same vein, the story should be such that enough time is allowed so that the things portrayed could have really happened. In other words, the timing of the events have to correspond with reality capabilities.

- If the story is fine-tuned and added to with retelling, credibility is increased. This goes along with the fact, mentioned earlier, that when people make up a lie they typically make up just enough to constitute the lie. Even adults, and especially children, do not often take the time to provide all of the ways the events in the lie would link up with other aspects of the ongoing life of a given individual. However, and this is a big however, questions that elicit additional information cannot be leading questions; liars and children will often go along with whatever is proposed. For example, if a questioner says to a child (or older fabricators), "He was wearing his green pants, wasn't he," the response will more often than not be affirmative. In this same regard, one must be careful regarding a child's denying something previously said. I have observed children change their assertions merely on the basis of my saying, "What did you say?" This honest-on-my-part request to hear a response again meant to the child I was displeased with the first answer, leading to the child's desiring to do a "better job" the second time around.
- Credibility is enhanced if an older child shows signs of embarrassment and hesitation in telling the story.
- Needless details that are added, such as "Someone came to the door" enhances credibility. This again goes along with the fact that when children make up lies, they make up usually just enough to constitute the lie.
- Credibility is enhanced to the degree that the interviewer remembers to frequently ask the child questions that are mildly challenging but not suggestive. This would be a question such as: "Who told you to say this?" In general, much has been written about interviewing technique. To the extent that all of the interviewers in a given chain who may have seen the child remember to observe the first and foremost rule, that is, to start with very general questions before becoming specific and to ask no leading questions at all, then credibility is increased. In my own experience, this is never the case. And once *anyone* in the chain has asked blatantly leading questions, the whole enterprise is in trouble. However, both Myers (1992) and Hoorwitz (1992) present extensive discussion on the legitimacy of and need to use "mildly encouraging" questions. Their arguments are convincing.
- Giving whole portions of a conversation, especially in the language that the alleged perpetrator may have used, increases credibility quite a bit.
- The evaluator should be on the lookout for adult cover-up phrases, such as, "That's how Daddy shows he loves me."
- The subsequent history after the alleged abuse might show a gradual progression toward more overt sexual activity.

- All of the above fall under what might be called "statement validity analysis." This is where all of the data are used to gauge the likelihood that the truth is being told and/or revealed.

The evaluator should have a fairly good idea about what constitutes "normal" sexual behavior in children. (Note, however, that it is dangerous to assume in an individual case that some behavior is "okay" because it is frequent. Any investigated behavior must be understood in its individual circumstances.)

All of the following (many of which have been claimed as serious "red flags") are frequent behaviors in nonabused young children: extreme shyness, walking around nude, kissing strangers, excessive masturbation. (For a brief but far-ranging consideration of this area, see the Virginia Child Protection Newsletter, 1993, Volume 40 (Fall), pp. 8–10. Write to the Commonwealth of Virginia, Dept. of Social Services via Joann Grayson, Ph.D., Dept. of Psychology, James Madison University, Harrisonburg, VA 22807, or phone (703) 568–6482. This newsletter is an excellent resource in general.)

To me, the clearest and best account of criterion based content analysis is offered by Steller and Boychuk (1992). Another important article on this method is given by Raskin and Esplin (1991). A cautionary note and an essentially dissenting opinion are offered by Wells and Loftus (1991).

Criterion-based content analysis is the most important research that has taken place in this entire area in recent decades. In spite of the caveats offered by Wells and Loftus, this area deserves serious research attention; the data reported so far are quite impressive. While I have such limited faith in the interview to begin with, I see these as the first serious efforts to bring interview-derived data into the scientific world (in this area).

This approach was pioneered (so far as I can tell) by Undeutsch in 1967. It essentially applies 19 separate criteria to the "story" told by the alleged victim. These would have to do with the logical structure of the story, the quantity of details offered, the degree to which the story is contextually embedded in other events, the nature of the descriptions of the interactions, and various peculiarities of content that lend credibility to the story, as well as motivation-related aspects that could be measured by such things as spontaneous corrections, admitting to a lack of memory, raising doubts about one's own testimony, self-deprecation, pardoning the perpetrator, etc.

I personally have greatest faith in a test based approach to the investigation of sexual abuse charges, which does not require asking the child *any* questions whatsoever.

There are several cautionary notes worth keeping in mind. First of all, when one uses psychological tests, *one is never actually measuring what has happened*. One is measuring the *possible psychological sequelae of what happened*, and if the event left no sequelae there would be nothing to measure. With the PORT, for example, one is essentially measuring the extent to which a child has been traumatized. It is *never* prudent to offer ultimate issue testimony in such instances, since trauma is indeed in the eyes of the beholder. A very major event may have very minor impact on one child, and the reverse can be true for another. Further, an abuser frequently sells what he or she is doing to the child under a benign label. For an excellent description of all of these possibilities, one should consult a book called *The Clinical Detective* (Hoorwitz, 1992, Chapter 10).

Another difficulty in this area has to do with the fact that when we deal with a situation where the consequences for the alleged perpetrator can be so severe, one should develop only test procedures that yield very few or no false positives. This is easier said than done, and typically would involve accumulating an enormous array of test items that can distinguish true abuse from nonabuse cases; only with a huge net of highly accurate items can one end up with a tolerable proportion of true versus false positives, along with few false negatives. Of course, the greatest difficulty in validation has already been mentioned: The only absolutely valid ways one can tell if abuse has taken place is in the face of meaningful confession or overwhelming physical evidence. It is rare that one can attain either of these conditions.

When all is said and done, what can an evaluator make of the data whose interpretation more often than not depends on statistical probabilities? And in the case of data arising from tests, one has also to deal with the fact that at best all such data can reveal is the presence of psychological trauma (defined operationally) associated with sexual themes. There is often no reliable way to ascertain the exact physical acts that caused the trauma.

What, then, is one to do about possible testimony based on the types of data that have been described? Regarding these data, we deal with two general classes. One involves "... expert testimony offered as direct evidence of abuse (e.g., an opinion that a child was abused)" (Myers, 1992, p. 122), while the other category has to do with the more limited area of "... rehabilitating a child's credibility" when some defense attorney has made the child's credibility an issue by attacking it (Myers, 1992, pp. 122, 133–142). (A prosecutor can shore up via expert testimony the credibility of his or her witness only if it has first been challenged.)

Myers (1992) believes the Melton and Limber position (1989, p. 1230) that a court should not admit testimony from a mental health professional about whether or not a particular child has been abused to be a "minority position" (Myers, p. 123). This is obviously a highly controversial issue with merit on both sides, as is the one dealing with witness credibility. In this latter area, the expert can do no more than offer information that *indirectly* supports a given witness' credibility (e.g., present data about the frequency of recantations, or the "normalcy" of delays in reporting, etc.). The expert may *not* offer a direct opinion on whether or not a given individual is telling the truth. (This prohibition stems, at least in part, from the assumption that experts are no better at detecting truth-telling than are lay persons, and hence can render no useful assistance to the trier-of-fact. If, however, statement validity analysis proves over time to do consistently better than lay people in discriminating between truth-telling and lying, this prohibition may change.)

What, then, is the mental health professional to do if in the midst of an evaluation, he or she believes a sufficient number of red flags have been raised?

First, the evaluator must cope with the mandate to report suspected abuse, often with little faith that the forces thereby set in motion will do much to help. (Thus, the typical children-and-youth service organizations often can do little to bring scientific clarity to the process.) In my experience, the range of scientific and/or clinical sophistication one encounters in "child and youth agency" investigations is quite extensive.

One big concern is to protect the child from current and future harm.

Another is to pull the negative self-fulfilling prophecy aspect of the situation out of the scenario, by making sure that a parent who may truly believe a child is being exposed to toxic behavior has his or her fears alleviated.

The only solution I can think of (where nothing can be proven definitely —a negative finding by a children-and-youth agency is not very reassuring to a truly worried parent) is to request that a judge order co-counseling. The fearful parent can hopefully realize that if the child has a neutral and continuing forum for expression, and the adults have a way to at least have some communication with one another, the chances that toxic behavior could continue to happen are at least greatly lessened.

While such a recommendation may not meet current "Daubert" criteria as "good science," I still believe it is a solid one (if one says that in any event therapy may help and is unlikely to cause harm, i.e., would be good whether abuse occurred or not, one is essentially coming to a "conclusion" that is not "falsifiable").

However, I can live with this, given some of the payoffs associated with the involved probabilities. If abuse that cannot be proven has occurred or is occurring, what is the "harm potential" in having such a forum ordered? (Note that in co-counseling it is not necessary that both parents attend the sessions at the same time.)

As far as the legal aspect of this area is concerned, once a mental health professional has decided whether suspected or alleged abuse meets the requirement for mandated reporting, the next task is possible testimony on, or a written report of, one's findings. The only path I see in either case is for the evaluator to present pertinent data from the instant case, along with appropriate research data in terms of which the instant data can be understood, so the decision-maker can judge for himself or herself the legitimacy, relevance, and accuracy of the proffered information. Thus, on a case-by-case basis, the ultimate decision-maker would have to decide if the offered information is admissible and helpful.

I believe a truly "soft-sell" is in order here. It must be explained that statistical probabilities are just that, probabilities, but indeed there may be legitimate cause for concern. A shared-cost co-counseling situation has no apparent downside, and could be effective not only in lessening the chances that a child could be further hurt, but also in ameliorating the toxic self-fulfilling prophecy aspect of the situation by reducing the fears of a worried parent. It would be up to the trier-of-fact to decide if further action is required.

Much remains to be done. We still do not even know exactly where the harm or damage in sexual abuse comes from, that is to say, the proportional (negative) contribution of the sexual act itself, as against society's *reaction* to such a sex act. In this latter category, we would place a child's subsequent need (following the act) to keep secrets, aroused loyalty conflicts, etc. One could make a case that such "damage" variables do not follow from a sexual act itself, but from our collective societal reaction to the act. On the other side of the fence would be those who insist the act itself, by virtue of the passions, jealousies, and emotions stirred up within an ego too immature to moderate them, is sufficient to explain any resulting harm. (Where there is actual physical damage, this question would not arise.)

For a brief but important discussion of these issues, as well as a consideration of the continua along which the negative effects of sexual abuse can be understood, see Hoorwitz (1992, pp. 205–228).

The list of items to be considered as either increasing or decreasing the credibility of an informant, was put together from the following sources. I am listing the sources this way rather than giving individual references for individual items because in many instances I have regrouped information from several different sources, along with information gathered by our own research teams, into one category. As mentioned, the best source of actual statistical data is in the reported works on criterion based content analysis (Call, 1992; Goodman & Bottoms, 1993; Hoorwitz, 1992; Hoppe, 1992; McGraw & Smith, 1992; Raskin & Esplin, 1991; Steller & Boychuk, 1992.) For information on the effects of training in the use of criterion-based content analysis, see Landry and Brigham, 1992. For information on the reliability of the latter, see Anson, Golding and Gully, 1993. For some interesting thoughts and data on what "truth" means to a child, see Haugaard, 1993. For data on the use of anatomically detailed dolls, see Skinner and Berry, 1993.

THE SELF-FULFILLING PROPHECY NIGHTMARE

A very troublesome problem is when the evaluator firmly believes all three of the following statements to be true:

1. Parent A believes something terrible to be true about parent B;
2. Parent A is acting on that belief;
3. Parent A believes, heart and soul, that the facts upon which he or she is acting are absolutely true and therefore necessary for the protection of the child.

The parent alienation syndrome is, of course, a prime example of this scenario (although it is commonly assumed that at least some alienators do *not* necessarily believe the target parent is as evil as is being represented to an involved child). Many things are in the "mix" of causes of the syndrome, but the self-fulfilling prophecy is right in there in most cases. Thus, A *really believes* B is a dirty rat, and is acting on this premise, which not only creates a more polarized situation, but eventually forces B to become the very thing A is claiming to be true.

The self-fulfilling prophecy shows up in "softer" ways, as when parent A believes any or all of the following to be true of parent B:

B does not put the children to bed on time and that is why they are always tired;

B does not give the children medicine in a timely fashion;

B lets the children do pretty much whatever they want and this undermines discipline when the children are at A's home;

B lets the children stay out in the sun too long, without sunscreen;

B lets the children go to sleep dirty.

Some of the parent A types are well-meaning and actually understand the parent alienation syndrome very well. Such "informed" parents do not want to start trouble and, therefore, do not say anything out loud or make negative claims about B. Sadly, it is virtually impossible for a person *not* to ultimately manifest some deeply held belief, even though these manifestations may be quite subtle indeed (tightening of facial muscles, irregular breathing patterns, etc.). Such reactions will be picked up unconsciously, if not consciously, by the involved children.

We often see the damage of the self-fulfilling prophecy when there is a clash between a very conservative parental style and a proportionately to-the-left-of-center liberal style. As parent A becomes more and more nervous about the style of parent B, this nervousness is conveyed to the children. Since children more typically prefer a liberal parent style (later hours, greater tolerance for risk-taking on the part of the children, less adherence to bath and school demands, etc.), they become more and more distanced from A, and will often complain about A's behavior to B.

If at this point B chooses to use these complaints about A's "fussiness" as ammunition, he or she can (subtly or blatantly) strengthen the children's growing disenchantment with parent A.

The alienation will be strengthened even by supposedly innocuous remarks ("Yeah, Mom/Dad is really the nervous type"), as well as by more obviously negative ones ("Mom/Dad just doesn't like it when you're having fun").

Rare among custody disputants would be a healing response to a child's complaints: "We're both very different—that's probably why we decided not to remain together—and both of our approaches have good and bad points."

To solve such scenarios, the evaluator must address all the concerns of parent A, whether they are of the more abrasive accusatory types found in relation to the parent alienation syndrome or the "softer" kind mentioned above. This is a controversial point. First of all, it could be claimed this is a job for a therapist, not an evaluator. (I would disagree; an evaluator can legitimately offer creative solutions that are decidedly "in the best interests" of the children, especially when done in a way that makes no one "wrong," following the principles of nonadversarial communication.) Further, one could argue that there is no reason why parent B, who does not believe parent A's fears or beliefs are warranted, should have to put up with some plan of solution. We refer here to situations where B realizes that A really harbors fears and worries, but they are not justified; B does *not* doubt A's concerns are genuine, but *does* doubt A's wisdom. The proposed solutions are even more controversial if B does not believe in A's sincerity.

My answer is that the interests of the children must come first. If a parent is worried and frightened, he or she will act on this. Often, there is no way for an evaluator to discern the validity of a claimed fear.

The evaluator should seek a way to fashion a monitoring process that is not intrusive. Co-counseling along with appropriate testing at specified intervals may help.

AFTER THE EVALUATION: MONITORING PLANS AND RESOURCE FACILITATIONS

Once the evaluation is completed and some supposedly binding agreement is reached—whether this be via a court or some other route—there then exists the problem of ironing out the details and getting the plan to work.

The custody evaluator should keep in mind that he or she is dealing with a select group here. Melton et al. (1987, p. 329) estimate that most custody plans are arrived at by negotiations between the divorcing spouses. This figure is estimated at about 90 percent Hence, only about 10 percent require outside intervention to reach a custody arrangement. Hoppe (1993) puts this figure (for Los Angeles County) at about two percent.

Hoppe (1993) describes those people who become custody-visitation litigants as suffering from "relationship disorders." Some of the attributes he finds in greater-than-usual statistical abundance among such individuals is narcissism, along with a good bit of self-righteous indignation and rage (and with it the capacity to be very blaming); an inability to "suffer emotions" (as one of his subjects put it: "I don't get ulcers, I give them"); the conscious endorsement of notions that are deeply contrary to their unconscious deeper feelings; a good bit of unrecognized dependency; and a propensity for projection.

As seen from a different but overlapping perspective, we find in this group a good many people who are suffering from subtle learning disabilities and impairments in information-processing strategies that lead to a *deficiency in the resources required for smooth and effective interpersonal relationships*. Thus, I believe that many of the people who would end up having the kind of diagnostic classifications noted by Hoppe are those people who have blatant or subtle deficiencies in the way they process information, and therefore lack the skills to negotiate the normal ups and downs of intrapersonal as well as interpersonal relationships.

When I conduct and then write up an evaluation, unless I am dealing with a highly cooperative set of parents—which is almost never the case—I like to suggest a monitoring plan. In severe cases, other forms of psychological help will be suggested.

The monitoring set-up should be seen by all participants as taking place in very "neutral territory." It may be important to have the person serving in the monitor's role pledge that he or she will not take part in any subsequent legal proceedings, so that all people can be maximally honest. (However, the legal system can compel involvement if something serious arises. This must be specified. Further, custody disputants are rarely totally honest, no matter what.)

It is helpful and cost-effective to turn this role over to a trusted colleague. It facilitates things for this "monitoring" person to be a colleague, since the evaluator will already have in his or her hands a good bit of information that can be valuable to the monitoring process.

Here is the ideal forum for the "monitor" to model the nonadversarial form of communication outlined in Chapter Eleven. As mentioned in the previous section, tests such as the PORT can gauge the ongoing impact each parent is having on the child.

When the parent alienation syndrome is part of the picture, Ward and Harvey (1993, pp. 8–10) suggest a range of interventions that go from "mild" to quite stringent and invasive. At the mild end, they would insist that the family be engaged in a "family systems" therapy that concentrates on moderating all of the behavior of the parties in relation to the child. They insist that all therapists engaged with the family understand family dynamics and the parent alienation syndrome, have a systems approach, and clearly support the fact that the child would be better off, in the huge majority of instances, by having comfortable access to both parents.

They see the process as requiring the involvement of all attorneys, the judge, and, of course, the mental health professionals. There must be court-ordered "divorce impasse therapy" that has the full force of the court behind it; this order should be forceful and explicit. There should be a mechanism for enforcement of the order—a guardian *ad litem* who would have the authority, *independent of further court order*, to require whatever is needed to move these kinds of interventions along to successful resolution.

At the more stringent end of the continuum, they actually advocate a process modeled after the IEP (individual educational planning) approach. This should be very specific: "The child will see target parent A *x* times per week without parental conflict at times of transition"; "The child will telephone target parent A x times per week and talk about positive things for a minute or two..." (p. 10). Ward and Harvey's article should be read in its entirety for the number of forceful and creative solutions suggested.

WHEN ARE DATA STALE?

I am frequently asked how I handle the problem of evaluation information that may be out of date. This usually comes up when a mental health professional is going to testify and is afraid the test data and other information may have been obtained too long ago such that it may be challenged (with justification) by a hostile attorney.

There is no clear way to answer a question such as this precisely even if one has test-retest reliability data, since (subjectively evaluated) new information could at any moment alter a child's parental perceptions.

When using traditional tests, conduct reexaminations in accordance with the test manuals or if there is a known event in the child's life that could cause this child to change his or her perception of either parent. If one is relying on interview or observation data, data should always be exceedingly timely.

DOES CHILD-DERIVED DATA CHANGE ACCORDING TO WHO BRINGS THE CHILD TO THE EVALUATION?

A frequently asked question has to do with whether or not test data are likely to change in accordance with who brings the child for the evaluation. The reasoning goes that a child is always going to be more interested in pleasing the parent he or she happens to be with, so that if the mother brings the child for the evaluation, the child is likely to respond in ways that favor the mother, while the reverse will be true if the father brings the child.

The best way to handle this, at least in regard to *initial* tests and interviews, is to have *both* parents bring the child (and leave the office area while the child is tested). If this is not possible, have the parents agree on a neutral adult whom they both trust from every angle (physical safety as well as psychologically). It would be the job of this person to bring the child to the evaluator's office.

The critical thing to do if this is not possible (the parents are unable to agree on a trusted, neutral party) is to watch carefully what the unconscious indicators on the PORT (or similar test) have to say. These indicators will always give the most likely reflection of what a child's actual interactions have been like with a given parent. In our experiences, it would take years and years of a child's being programmed (alienated) by a given parent for this to affect the unconscious indicators.

The BPS is probably more prone to such an influence than more "disguised" tests like the PORT. Several BPS users have told me that they have given half of the BPS to the child when brought by the father, and the other half when the child was brought by the mother. There were changes in the proportion of items given to each under the two sets of circumstances, but the test-based POC was similar in all instances.

Keep in mind that the closer the scores on the BPS or *any* test for Mom and Dad items, the more important it is to use all of the tests one can think of. But remember also that "close calls" are frequent in typical custody evaluation cases; the parents are often fairly evenly matched.

In both the Speth data (1992) and in my own, when there *was* a change in the designated BPS POC on retesting, this almost always occurred where the scores were very close. That is, whoever was the POC on the initial testing gained that position by a very tiny magnitude; the new POC, on retesting, gained the new POC position similarly by a small magnitude.

The evaluator should note that there are several reasons a child's perceptions of his or her parents may shift in what seems to be an abrupt manner wherein the shift is *not* due to who brought the child to the evaluator's office, e.g., developmental change, new incident, or change in child's needs (Bricklin, 1995).

My guess is that with *any* assessment method (observations, interviews, etc.), consciously derived child responses are far more likely to be influenced by who brings that child to the evaluator's office than responses stemming from less conscious sources. (For interesting information on the valid recognition of truth telling from nonverbal rather than verbal sources, see Ekman and O'Sullivan, 1991.)

WHO HAS THE RIGHT TO SEEK AN EVALUATION, HOW MUCH DATA DOES ONE NEED, AND WHAT KIND OF PROOF OF ACCURACY DOES ONE NEED IN A COURTROOM?

These issues are of great importance to the evaluator, and the answers have to be considered from several overlapping (but not necessarily coincident) perspectives: the legal, the ethical (including what one should do to avoid ethical or malpractice charges), the scientific, and the "how-will-it-sell-in-court."

At least one author states: "In some states a noncustodial parent may not legally seek services from a psychologist for a child without permission from the custodial parent or by court order" (Boyer, 1990, p. 13).

However, consultation with several other attorneys has resulted in a different answer. The most frequent answer I have gotten to the question about who can seek an evaluation is that regardless of who has custody, whether a primary custodial parent or a noncustodial parent—and even in situations where joint legal custody prevails and parents are supposed to share jointly in all important decisions—the parent in whose care the child is at some given moment has the legal right to seek the services of a mental health professional.

Remember, the above is strictly from a legal perspective; the latter interpretation probably follows from two perspectives: One is that a noncustodial parent's rights are the same as a custodial parent's just so long as the latter's rights are not interfered with (or a court order contradicted), and the other is from a "medical emergency" model, in which it is presumed that if a child needs "care," the parent who happens to be taking care of the child at that moment must make this decision. Under this model it is further assumed that the consent of the other parent is not needed. However, it is *never* wise, in my opinion, to make this assumption without two pieces of information. First, members of mental health professions should consult with their state licensing boards (or, if unlicensed, with their national organizations) to learn about all relevant "consent" regulations. Second (and especially if the evaluator is approached by one parent and not both), it would be prudent to seek information on the pertinent divorce and/or custody order to see if it permits one parent independently of the other to seek an evaluation. (I require that an attorney involved in the case send me a copy of the existing custody order, with the relevant parts underlined, along with a letter stating that the underlined parts show that his or her client has the legal right to request an evaluation in the absence of the other parent's consent. If the wording is vague, the evaluator should consult his or her own attorney.)

If there is any doubt whatsoever about a consent issue, the evaluator would be wise to steer a conservative course and additionally seek a court order for whatever he or she proposes to do.

An area related to "consent" is "notification." While it may prove true that one can see a child without the consent of a particular parent, the question might arise as to whether this parent should be *notified* about what the evaluator intends to do. I would argue for great case-by-case discretion here, since I can think of some scenarios in which a get-in, get-out quiet approach would be far better for an involved child than one that leads to (more) open warfare. Consider this example. A mother phones to complain that the back-and-forth activity of a joint physical custody arrangement seems to be greatly upsetting her four-year-old. Her attorney claims she *can* seek an evaluation without the consent of her ex-husband. If the evaluator has tools to assess the child's status *that do not depend upon input from the mother*, should he or she proceed with the evaluation *without* notifying the father? If the father *is* notified, the usual "programming" and manipulating are sure to begin (the father likes the prevailing arrangement), and the child is put in the middle of a battle. If the evaluator proceeds, he or she may find the child is in fine shape and the issue could then disappear. The child has been spared tension and loyalty conflicts. If the evaluator finds the child *is* hurting from the back-and-forth confusion, the father can *now* be notified and invited to participate, or, if he chooses, seek his own evaluation. What is the right thing to do here? I am not sure; the issue merits debate.

Speaking now just from a *scientific* perspective, there is certainly nothing wrong with a mental health professional's seeing whomever he or she pleases, so long as any eventual conclusions and/or testimony follow from one's data. Ideally, proffered testimony is based on a relevant data base that can be articulated, i.e., the approach yields information on the degree to which the presented materials can be safely generalized to given contexts.

However, having said all this—from both the legal and scientific perspectives—I do not mean to imply these remarks can be safely extended to include ethical issues and the issue of how well a given procedure would sell in a courtroom. I merely state them because I think they are intellectually and legally defensible positions. They are my way of saying I do not always agree with the *mea culpa* types who seem to assume that as soon as a complaint of any type is brought against a mental health professional (for example, where the professional has seen only "one side" in a custody issue), the bringer of the complaint is automatically right and the mental health professional is automatically wrong. (See also Shein, 1993, pp. 59–60.) The critical legal and scientific point is that one's testimony must be carefully matched to the scope of one's evaluation. (See also Saunders, 1993a, for a concise but information-packed discussion of many of these issues.)

The caveat that no comparative statements can be made on the basis of a LIM-CPE (based on the correct notion that one should not make statements about people who have not been directly evaluated) must be interpreted carefully. For example, when one uses the PORT or BPS (or any similar device), and one seems to be making comparative statements about the mother and/or father, one is making comparisons *among a child's perceptions*. Statements made on the bases of such tests have nothing directly to do either with the parents or even with parental behavior. One is making statements about a child's nonverbal perceptions and what the available research data suggest these mean.

Also, an attorney's use of a so called "hypothetical question" might (legitimately) seek a response from an expert witness based only on assertions the witness is to assume are true. Such an inquiry could very well be about someone the expert has not seen.

A related issue of how much data one has to have in order to make a legitimate contribution in a court room is related to the above points. Conceptually, I am dealing here with the issue of whether the mental health professions have any single test, tool, or procedure with enough predictive strength to stand on its own. Prevailing wisdom is that in the mental health professions, unless lots of sources all tell the same story, one is on thin ice in accepting the particular story from any single source. This is, of course, *good* wisdom, and actually the prevailing wisdom in *all* fields, not just the mental health fields. But the key question remains as to whether each and every participant, even so called experts, must come in with the "whole story." My belief, stated in Chapter One, is that this is not the case, that single pieces of information, though not usually sufficient (in *any* field) to establish the truth of some matter, can nevertheless be important. Keep in mind that many who would *not* object to a radiologist's bringing a single piece of evidence to a courtroom *would* object to a mental health professional doing the same thing. But when it is remembered that the utility in a courtroom of an X-ray typically depends on an accumulated database (indicating how whatever is revealed in the X-ray will affect the involved person over his or her lifetime), then we realize that the more critical factor is not the *number* of items one brings, but the *quality and scope of the databases* involved.

A related conceptual issue having to do with how much data one must bring to court to be a useful contributor has to do with a situation in which one individual uses, say, a projective test to reach a conclusion, and cannot universally demonstrate or "prove" the basis upon which this was done. Controversies over such an issue usually become "public" over the work of individuals who are seen as "particularly gifted" with projective tests, but in which it is claimed that it is not the test that is "good" or "valid," but the interpreter. We have probably all met people like this, so-called wizards in the use of psychological tests, especially projective tests, and it is commonly said that these people are "artists" and not "scientists." Sometimes their skills are labeled "intuitive." I bring up this issue because I wish to draw a distinction between two different notions about intuition and, by extension, proof. One, I believe is legitimate in a scientific sense, while the other is not.

This issue is a variant of the universal demonstrability problem: the assumption that if only some people can do something, and not everyone, it "ain't science."

Robert Waelder (1960), in a brilliant and far ranging analysis, considers the problems of universal demonstrability (pp. 27–31). While it would take us too far afield to cover his whole series of arguments, he essentially concludes: "The notion that the . . . physical sciences are universally demonstrable (while the psychological sciences seem not to be) boils down to the fact that they have gained a vast prestige . . . because of the demonstrability and usefulness of their technical applications . . ." In other words, many of the *principles underlying* successes in the physical sciences are not *universally* demonstrable. (This would certainly be clear to anyone who has attempted to understand all the different interpretations of quantum theory. The theory has been wonderfully successful as a practical and applied branch of physics, resulting in the laser, the transistor, and the superconductor, among other contributions. Nevertheless, it is not necessarily demonstrable to all or even most people. As Niels Bohr said: "Anyone who is not shocked by quantum theory has not understood it" [Davies, 1983, p. 100]).

Piotrowski (1957) says that some people are better able to see regularity and order in test data than others because they are using a more finely differentiated or useful or subtle set of empirical referents; the facts they are looking at are "better" facts than those observed by others. In his characteristically polite way, he opines that some "subtle empirical referents" may be "beyond the reach" of some. His conclusion: "This makes these referents no more subjective than differential calculus is made more subjective by the fact that fewer people can master it than the multiplication table" (p. 23).

Because a Piotrowski can learn far more from a *Rorschach* than most others can, does not make such endeavors invalid or not scientific. Here are some useful distinctions to keep in mind. It is one thing to say "I cannot demonstrate the decision rules upon which I interpret the *Rorschach* to *everyone's* satisfaction, but I will submit my *predictions* to appropriate testing." Whether the resulting database is in terms of so-called "blind analyses" or in the accuracy of predictions compared to independent criteria, a database accumulates in what I think of as "good" intuitive science.

One may legitimately say, "I intuitively think the mother/father is a better bet for PCP but I cannot demonstrate to everyone's satisfaction why I say this" *so long as one can offer data about how accurate are predictions made in this way*. If one cannot offer such evidence, I do not think one should make such "intuitive" predictions.

I have heard some experienced custody evaluators claim human beings are particularly good at using an "intuitive" sense to look at loads of information in a custody evaluation and "choose" a PCP.

This, to me, is legitimate if he or she is able to back up the "intuitions" with an impressive predictive scorecard.

CUTTING COSTS IN CUSTODY EVALUATIONS

Custody evaluations can be expensive. I frequently hear of cases in which $7000 or more has been charged. (An average fee in large urban areas is somewhere around $2000. This would be for a family of two parents, two children, and a sprinkling of significant others.)

High fees are understandable, given the tremendous number of hours that must be committed to the task. Many hours of testing and interviewing, followed by a significant number of hours in reading court records and other documents, can easily lead to a situation in which the custody evaluator will spend up to 50 hours on a given case. One leading custody evaluator told me that in one case alone he spent more than 50 hours *merely administering psychological tests*.

At one time, I tried to meet this challenge by working in concert with a county-run agency in a midwestern state to develop a "streamlined" battery of tests and tools. This would have involved somehow paring down or shortening some of our tests and tools. At the same time as I was working on this project, I attended an excellent seminar with David Faust on forensic issues. I was reminded that it is not a good idea to take a test that has good validity figures and shorten it. Needless to say, I put this streamline-the-battery project on hold following this seminar. (It is interesting to note that even in the public agency with which we attempted this project, the typical evaluator had to spend up to four full days of time in trying to put together a decent evaluation. Thus, it was not uncommon, when we broke the evaluation load down into time per unit and task, to see a total of upwards of 32 hours spent on a given case.)

In spite of the high costs of custody evaluations, I frequently feel I have been able to make a useful contribution toward the resolution of a dispute for as little as several hundred dollars.

This strategy essentially consists in trying to reduce the "need to know" areas to the minimum required for the types of decisions each side sees as having to be made. This would typically come up in two different ways. One is when it turns out that there is only one, or at the most, two, critical issues involved. A scenario here would be where parent A believes everything went downhill following parent B's involvement with person X. From the moment of X's involvement in the situation, negative incidents seemed to escalate. Upon careful discussion with all critical participants, it turns out that parent A would be satisfied with more information about the impact of X in the child's life. I am, of course, aware that, from a systems approach, the intrusion of one element into a system can certainly change more than just one aspect of that system. However, given the fact that this *is* a legitimate way to approach decision-making, and assuming that one can get cooperation from all involved, one can often delimit the area of what needs to be evaluated. Keep in mind also that this approach places no constraints upon future options. If anyone is dissatisfied, that person can always request a full-fledged, comprehensive evaluation.

Another scenario is where parent A is concerned about some limited aspect of a child's involvement with parent B. This may pertain to the on-time taking of medications, etc. Sometimes, a monitoring plan is a lot more cost-effective than a comprehensive evaluation.

Still another scenario arises when there is a question of optimal educational placement for a child. The typical situation is for the mother to be upset that the father will not spend the necessary amount of money to provide the children with the education she thinks they ought to have. Here, the thrust of the evaluation is to determine the exact educational needs of the child and create information relevant to this aspect. Of course, within this scenario, one can run into all of the complexities mentioned in connection with "ultimate issue testimony." For example, if it is the mothers' position that the children should not have just an education that addresses certain problems, but the *best* education available, it is unlikely that such a question will be answered by the introduction of data in any event, since one is arguing about value systems. Even if one could show that the involved children have exceptionally high intelligence quotients, this would not necessarily provide a compelling argument that they should have absolutely the best education money can buy. Things are more clear-cut if a child has some special need that is not being met in his or her current school placement.

WALKING THE LINE WITH ATTORNEYS

It seems to me that consultations with attorneys is a more complex issue in the area of custody evaluations than in other forensic areas. For example, Melton et al. (1987) state: "Ideally, the ground work for a forensic evaluation, report, or testimony is laid through a series of consultations between the clinician and the attorney (or court) responsible for the referral" (p. 348).

Well, there is nothing wrong with that, so far. A comprehensive custody evaluation involves speaking to all critical participants to clarify legal as well as psychological issues, and the mental health professional's clarifying his or her own exact roles in the process. If there are legal, rather than psychological, criteria that must be applied in the resolution of some aspect of a given dispute, it is important that the evaluator understand such criteria.

The advantage of such a consultation is in finding out what all of the critical issues happen to be, including some of the more subtle ones. It also could serve as a springboard for the evaluator to discern that there are fewer critical issues involved than might initially have been suspected.

The danger is that this also exposes the mental health evaluator to subtle influences including tainted data, selected facts, the great charm that most attorneys have in being oh-so-sincere and convincing people that they are interested only in what's best for the children, etc., all of which may be true or untrue to varying degrees.

The difficulty comes in with any postevaluation, pretrial conference. Again, to quote Melton et al. (1987): "Although it may not always be feasible, we recommend that whenever possible the mental health professional and the attorney confer with each other prior to trial" (p. 354).

This can be a delicate issue in a comprehensive custody evaluation.

The complexity sets in if the evaluator has entered the case via a close relationship with one of the involved attorneys. Under these conditions, the evaluator might choose to meet with this attorney only. In my experience, this happens more frequently than one might wish. It also happens (the evaluator meeting with one attorney only) when word gets out whom the evaluation favors. The other side simply drops out of the consultation process. This may come after the report has been read, but before any trial.

I, myself, after conducting an ALL-CPE, never meet with a single attorney prior to a custody trial except under special and rare circumstances. If I cannot meet with both of them—and this I do under special circumstances—I will not meet with just one. Whether I deal with an ALL-CPE or a LIM-CPE, I always refuse to be *coached* by an attorney, even in situations where I might consent to a meeting.

There are some who would say this is foolhardy, that it is senseless to walk into a courtroom and expose oneself to cross-examination without such coaching. Some might even say it is wrong to take this approach within an adversarial system. They may argue that the evaluator owes it to his or her own data to represent them in the most powerful way or that one owes it to one's client to represent him or her in the most persuasive way possible. But herein lies the problem. Who is the evaluator's "client" in a custody evaluation? The common answer is "the children." While this is probably closest to the mark, it might be more accurate to say "everyone" or the "children within a certain dynamic system." That is, although it is clear that the "best interest of the child" takes precedence over the wishes of the parents (or parental convenience factors), it is also clear that everyone's interests should receive fair and neutral, albeit proportional, consideration. (It never made psychodynamic sense to me that a procedure could hurt a parent yet somehow spare an involved child who has even a moderately close relation with that parent.)

Further, I believe there is a big difference between clarifying issues, on the one hand, and being coached on the other, especially when one is serving as an expert witness. I also believe there are enough good things written these days about the special skills or resources one needs to be an expert witness such that coaching by an attorney is not needed. A mental health professional who has not taken the time to make use of these materials probably has no business serving in any kind of forensic setting anyway.

Things are, of course, tougher for the mental health professional serving (or called upon to serve) as a fact witness. This individual should never present himself or herself as an expert witness, and meeting with an attorney under such circumstances is different than for the expert witness. This is absolutely *not* to say, however, that an evaluator providing a LIM-CPE is automatically a fact rather than expert witness. This is a complex issue, and would depend on exactly what was done in a given case. I believe it is wrong to assume that an evaluator who does not seek to provide the "big picture" need necessarily be something less than an expert who, to me, *is inherently neutral in stance* when testifying. It may be that those who truly believe 100 percent in what due process implies (each participant is entitled to make his or her strongest case) believe it is wrong in a LIM-CPE *not* to be prepared by the appropriate attorney (see Schutz et al., 1989, p. 100). Many evaluators believe that once an evaluation is done and a PCP favored, the evaluator should automatically "side-up" with the attorney representing this PCP. I disagree. Further comments on this issue are offered in the "Testifying in Court" section of this chapter.

My own procedure is to issue a written report and then call for a conference with the two involved attorneys. If things seem friendly enough and I do not expect bitter fights, I invite the parents to this conference. However, this is rarely the situation and one might be better off meeting with the attorneys only. It is my intention to have an opportunity, in a more relaxed environment than that of a courtroom, to explain the concepts and measurement tools employed in generating the information in the report. These sessions often become an opportunity for the two attorneys to attempt to come to agreements among themselves, or for one to attempt to influence the other. I stay out of these discussions when they occur, since they are not within the province of the evaluator.

Note that some authors see potential dangers in a pretrial conference with attorneys, and insist it be conducted as a formal deposition. "Without the protection of that structure, the impartial evaluator caught between the two (or more) attorneys will quickly feel like the guest of honor at the Texas Chainsaw Massacre" (Schutz et al., 1989, p. 100).

WHY NOT JUST ASK THE CHILDREN?

It is widely known that judges do this all the time, that is, simply ask involved children with whom they would prefer to live. Indeed the UMDA, Section 402, asserts the importance of "a child's wishes." The degree of interviewing sophistication shown by judges with whom I have had personal contact varies wildly from exceedingly competent and sensitive to downright goofy. Because judges are often treated with such ultra-respect by the people with whom they have contact, it is my belief that too many judges begin to believe in their own omnipotence. They really think that when they speak, or ask questions, the answers or responses they get are more truthful than would be obtained by mere mortals. I have heard so many judges pompously lecture people in court like this: "Now you will just have to stop all this fighting" and then go on to act as though this will actually happen. I also believe the same syndrome shows up when a judge asks a child a question. They typically try to put on sweet and loving faces and dredge up mellow tones of voice when dealing with children, and then go on to assume they are getting honest or "true" answers.

Nevertheless, there is merit to the question about "just asking the children."

And since it is one of my major theses that a child should in fact take a very important part (via test data) in a custody evaluation, it is a valid point to wonder why one does not simply ask them about their preferences.

Judging from our data, which compared responses emanating from extremely conscious sources to those emanating from less conscious sources, my belief is that if children were asked with whom they would prefer to live, their judgments would agree with those of genuine experts in about 35 to 65 percent of instances.

As to whether or not it does harm to the children to ask them, we go back to the same kind of evidence cited before in the considerations of mediated versus nonmediated settlements as well as the effect of adversarial versus nonadversarial processes. Although I have not been able to find any direct research on this assumption, that is, what would happen psychologically if one simply asked the children, my own feeling is that it would be exceedingly helpful in some cases and injurious in others. Melton et al. (1987) tilt toward the beneficial effects of asking children, quoting again the research which states that to the degree one feels some control over one's fate, and to the degree that one can reduce ambiguity in a strange situation through a direct discussion of it, one is helped. (See the discussion in Melton et al., 1987, p. 341.) This is an interesting issue and, I suspect, a controversial one.

TESTIFYING IN COURT

The best way to be relaxed in a court proceeding is to take very seriously the notion as to just what one is in the courtroom, an expert witness. An expert witness is neutral regarding "sides," and is there solely to offer information to the trier of fact.

It is good preparation to rid your mind of any notions of being a defender-of-the-truth, no matter how appealing or righteous such a position seems to be. You are there to present information, not "truths," which are really something different and typically involve ultimate issues.

The other secret of relaxing in the courtroom—to whatever degree one is capable of achieving this—is preparation. I am often reminded of the controlling maxim in real estate, that the three basic rules pertaining to a good piece of real estate are: number one, location; number two, location; and number three, location. For courtroom appearances, the three most important secrets of success are preparation, preparation, and preparation.

This does not mean necessarily (in a custody evaluation context) via an attorney, as would be the case in almost all other forensic settings. To my way of thinking, a mental health professional who has been "prepared" by an attorney is stepping out of the expert witness role. I know this is a controversial issue, and there are those who would point out that "preparation" in a custody case is not designed to tilt the balance in the favor of either disputant, but merely to acquaint the mental health professional with the fact that the rules of the game are different in a court of law than they are in the clinician's office. They would further point to the need for the mental health professional to understand these different ground rules and to thoroughly understand what the issues are that must be addressed and any possible legal, not psychological or clinical, standards of resolution. There is also the mental health professional's desire to be sure he or she will be asked questions that optimize the clarity of proffered testimony. This last issue can be handled in a two-second pretrial conference with an attorney, i.e., "Ask me what I did." (By using this question, I get to describe the evaluation *my* way, so that *I* decide how to sequence the information. I do not like the procrustean beds created by an attorney's questions, even the attorney on "my side.")

I believe the huge majority of testimony issues should all be clarified in advance, not at a pretrial conference with one attorney. Further, if some legally complex issue arises during the course of the evaluation, there is ample time for the evaluator to seek clarification prior to the trial.

At some point, prior to the evaluation, the mental health professional who will serve as an expert witness should clarify with all critical parties whether he or she is willing to testify about an ultimate issue.

Returning to the issue of preparation, if you have read (and agree with) what is written in Chapter Ten about aggregation, you will know that the two keys to what you will be presenting have to do with the credibility of each piece of evidence and the relevance of each piece of evidence, as well as the credibility and relevance of any overall conclusions that are offered. (Credibility assessment is a job for the trier-of-fact; the term should not be used directly by an expert witness.) Relevance is essentially related to validity, because something is relevant to the degree that it accurately differentiates between different possibilities.

I believe that an expert witness without a database does not belong in court, although I have been disputed on this point by many people I respect, who argue that humans are particularly "good" at intuitive thinking and, indeed, that from a decision-making point of view, such thinking is legitimate. (Schutz et al., 1989, make the point repeatedly that they are *not* in the business of making predictions, that their system "... is descriptive, not predictive..." [p. 111]. This, to me, is a [very clever] but at least somewhat artificial distinction, much like the one between concurrent and predictive validity. *Logically* these are similar concepts. In each instance, one is making assertions that are calibrated against an articulated independent criterion. A special difficulty in custody evaluations is the instability of the systems we aim to predict; from the child's perspective alone we might deal with a new stepparent, a new school, etc.)

Many cross-examination ploys are variations on the following theme: a subtle shift of emphasis away from what the expert considers a critical conceptual issue, to the conceptual ballpark in which the attorney wants the game played out. Once this shift is made, once the attorney can get you to play in the ballpark in which he or she wants you to play, the expert is in a difficult position.

Here is an example of what I mean. I was testifying in one case about a child who, when asked to "draw a secret," drew a picture that portrayed, among other important things, his daddy hugging him while he, the child, was pushed up against the father's genital area. I felt the drawing (along with other supporting data) had probative value in this particular case.

The attorney brought in a newspaper photo of an adult person hugging a child in a roughly similar manner. It was his intention, I suppose, to prove that this was a typical way adults hug children, or at least that what was drawn was not as unique as I was implying.

Never mind that the child in the photo was much older than the child in the involved case. Never mind, also, that we were told nothing of the special conditions that could have surrounded the taking of this picture, e.g., people being pushed together in a crowded airport, perhaps seeing each other for the first time after a long absence. And never mind that a particular picture does not prove something is ordinary or typical or "normal."

The critical question was not, after all, about how adults hug children, *but why the child chose to draw this out of the infinite variety of things he may have spontaneously chosen to draw in response to the question.* This is what I mean by a subtle shift in conceptual ballparks.

Cross-examination goals are to get information out of you to support the person your data do not favor and to impeach your credibility. Most strategies will aim to prove one or more of the following points: You're biased *in favor of* the person your data favor, you're biased *against* the other participant, you've made inconsistent statements, your methods are flawed, your testimony is implausible (Bergman & Berman-Barrett, 1993, Chapter 10).

One interesting expert witness ploy (in response to cross-examination questions) suggested by Hambacher (1994) is for the mental health professional to refuse to answer any question whatsoever about a single test, test finding, or any other individual piece of evidence. The expert is instead to claim that the data are used interactively at all times, and no particular conclusion follows from any specific piece of evidence. This would imply that there is no "meaning" to be discovered about any particular datum. A cross-examining attorney is likely to challenge such a strategy quite vigorously.

I chose not to offer many details in this section because there are already a number of excellent sources available to the mental health professional about testifying in court, including Brodsky (1991), Chapter 14 of Melton et al. (1987), and Chapter 9 of Schutz et al. (1989).

Another article I consider must reading for a mental health professional who would serve as an expert witness is the article, mentioned in Chapter One, by Saks (1990).

For the individual really serious about wanting to do a good job serving in a forensic field, the complete reading of the Melton et al. (1987) book would be an excellent idea. The major criticism of this book I have encountered (e.g., Friedrich, 1993) is that it is too conservative. I consider this its strength, since one never has to wonder about where the authors are coming from. This predictability of position allows the forensic expert to more accurately position his or her own view.

Before leaving this section I would like to share a personal method I use to increase my comfort in a courtroom by accessing just the specific attitude I want for some particular situation. It makes use of the SOA concepts covered in Chapter Eight.

Your initial task is to identify the ingredients you would want in an attitude "mix" when you are in a courtroom.

Let me illustrate how these ingredients might vary from court situation to situation.

When I anticipate a situation where a lot of "teaching" is going to be involved, I would like, in addition to wide-awake alertness, a lot of warmth and affection in the mix. Without this, without feeling something "positive" for my audience, I am not particularly inclined to be patient, to take the time to supply the background details and associated facts and theories in terms of which a listener can gain a better and richer understanding of the topic under discussion. My "mind" tends to race ahead (often in a very "linear" way), and one of the few things that slows it down is a mind-set in which I remember to put myself in the position of my listener. I am most likely to do this when I *care about* whoever is listening to me

If, on the other hand, I anticipate interacting with an overly rude and needlessly aggressive attorney, I might want to access patience some other way, i.e., *not* via love (when we describe how to use these ideas, we will suggest how to access various psychological states). Also in the mix, one might want whatever attitude would help one to deal with an aggressive cross-examination. Here, one could use as a resource situation the feelings and attitudes one gets while playing a competitive game with a brilliant opponent who shouts a lot (but where one realizes it's just a game). Or, you may want to use humor, e.g., attending a zoo where one watches with great attention a bunch of chattering monkeys—noisy, but not threatening.

Hence, before using the technique to be described, spend a good bit of time thinking about all the major ingredients (attitudes) you would wish to access in some particular situation. In the present case, this would be a courtroom. Along with this, think of the things that might trigger these attitudes (vivid memories of specific situations and/or key words and/or key images, etc.).

Each time you use this technique, choose your ingredients to dovetail with the demands of a particular situation, basing the latter on all of the information available to you. Next, think of situations where you already have these ingredients or resources available. I can get to a patient attitude many different ways: caring about someone I'm with, doing my exercise workout routine (I never "cheat" or rush or leave parts out; here is a much more emotionally neutral access-code for patience than love would be), dealing with elderly or sick people, and so on. I am patient in all of these situations, but some are more powerful "accessors" than others, and each has its own unique features. As you think about situations or memories of situations that will access in you the psychological states you want, pay careful attention to such distinctions.

Here is how to fashion a technique from these ideas. (There are in actuality countless ways to use them. Readers will recognize the influence of Milton Erickson, Ernest Rossi, Richard Bandler, John Grinder, and others.)

Imagine you are a movie director on a set in which you are directing

yourself as an actor or actress. In this fantasy or inner visualization, participate first as the director, imagining all things from the perspective of the director. From this perspective, you would *not* see the director, because it would
be as if you were looking out at things through the eyes of the director. You
would see the "you" that is the actor or actress, the rest of the set, etc. You
would hear things also from the director's perspective.

From this perspective, imagine a courtroom set, built to your specifica-
tions. Bring in other players as needed (judge, attorney, etc.)

Your purpose is to run a scene, say two to three minutes (or more) in
length, and have it go as you would wish, e.g., to have the "actor" run through
a scene looking and acting and speaking, say, alertly, calmly, collegially, com-
petently, patiently, etc.

Now here is the crucial part. As a director, you can control only certain
"external" aspects of the actor or actress: posture and other muscular-skeletal aspects (very, very important!), words spoken, tone of voice, pacing and
clarity of speech patterns. You cannot, however, direct a person to "feel comfortable." What you *could* do, in the latter case, is to control all of the external (basically muscular-skeletal) responses by means of which an individual
conveys the impression of comfort. Hence, the director can address all of such
"external" variables in the actor or actress to create the desired scene: sit up
a bit straighter, let your facial muscles be more neutral, speak a bit more
slowly, etc.

But before you do this, before you direct and fine-tune the scene as many
times as necessary to achieve the mini-movie you want, relive as a full participant the prior situations in which you already had available the resources you
are calling on the actor or actress to portray.

In other words, as you are directing the acting individual to use every aspect of his or her muscular-skeletal, including the vocal, "output" motor system to represent some desired state, *you as the director should first pause to relive
some prior situation in which this attitude was present.* Let the actor's or actress's
responses then become the outward manifestations of this attitude.

Run the scene as many times as needed, adding all desired ingredients to
the mix. Sometimes, the addition of a new ingredient will cause a slight shift
in what you ask the actor or actress to do at a given moment, and sometimes
not.

When the entire scene has been run so that it looks and sounds and feels
right to the director, there is one final step: Run the entire scene once more,
now from the inner perspective of the actor or actress. At this point, you are,
say, sitting in the witness stand. The directing-you is off to the side and out of
sight. Run the sequence as though it is actually happening. Remember, from
this perspective you would *not* see the you that is the actor or actress. It is
rather as if that "you" is now fully participating in the scene, and would see
and hear and feel whatever would occur from this particular perspective.

If you are not content with the results as run from this perspective, return to the director perspective and make adjustments. You either did not sufficiently correlate the director-actor variables (the inner feelings as generated from prior situations with the actor's or actress's manifestations of these feelings in their actions) or did not choose a proper mix of ingredients to begin with, i.e., you misjudged the attitudes that would be helpful to you in the target situation.

TEST SECURITY VERSUS DUE PROCESS

Although I am frequently asked what I bring into the courtroom, I'm not certain the typical mental health professional who asks this question thinks about *test security* aspects of this question as frequently as do those of us who have spent years developing databases that could possibly be compromised by the wrong kinds of exposure. A related issue follows from the armchair, out-loud, psychological speculations that can happen in courtrooms crowded with participants and onlookers when raw test data are there to be picked apart.

At this point, let us take a closer look at the test security aspect only of the broader what-does-one-bring-to-a-trial question. (The "what-do-you-bring-to-court" issue is covered later.)

Just as the law itself harbors individually legitimate goals that are inherently in conflict with one another (to punish versus to rehabilitate, free speech versus protecting moralities, etc.), so, too, do we encounter this complexity with the issue of test security versus a participant's access to important data.

The physical sciences themselves are not immune to the intrusion of a need for such decision balance points or value-laden compromises.

The testing of most scientific hypotheses depends on some notion of probability (an hypothesis is accepted or rejected based on the probability that a given finding could have occurred by chance). And achieving any given degree of certainty *always* (*theoretically*, not just practically) involves cost factors (which may be time factors, human exertion, etc., as well as plain money). Hence, the degree of certainty one desires depends on what one is willing to spend (in some form of resource) to achieve that level of certainty. This issue may tilt toward the "practical" side, for example, when an auto manufacturer has to decide how much resource to expend to achieve a given degree of certainty regarding an automobile's safety. But the issue is theoretical as well, since the amount of expendable resource in any given example, is *conceptually limitless*.

As a result, the very heart of what we think of as "hard-nosed physical sciences" involves decisions about optimal cut-off points in which one gains along some dimension according to what one is willing to pay along some other dimension.

As Waelder points out in his thoughtful book, *Progress and Revolution* (1967, pp. 50–52), even the cherished ideals of personal liberty and equality-of-station are at odds with one another. When humans are left alone, with no outside force to watch over them, a natural pecking order emerges (within some particular context). Those with more physical strength, or wealth, or control over moral judgment, or with a greater army, or more intelligence, or more diligence, or more cunning, find themselves in the top, desirable "command" positions. We see this in schools, governments, and children's playgrounds. If a group of children is left unattended, fairly soon the stronger, more aggressive children will have access to all the best swings, slides, and toys. The only way to prevent this is to have some adult interfere and put in place some different decision process as to who has access to what. The only way to ensure equality is to have some coercive police-like force in operation so as to prevent these natural forces from asserting themselves (or to re-arrange the contexts in which top dogs are chosen, e.g., intelligence becomes rewarded rather than brute physical strength).

What all this means is that equality is purchased at the expense of liberty: the more of the former that is desired, the less we have of the latter.

What is needed in all such instances is some flexible form of compromise—*balance points which seek to give proportional due to all legitimate goals and aspirations.*

A mental health professional's duty to protect the security of the tests he or she uses (in which the data bases may have taken dozens of years to gather) and a participant's right to have access to important data are two such competing "rights." A solution to this dilemma must serve each of these rights. It is important that raw test data (i.e., data whose exposure would compromise the future objectivity of the test) should not be shown in public arenas, where it would be possible for persons with access to this raw data to memorize or photocopy it and then coach future takers of the tests. At the same time, there must be some mechanism by means of which participants could gain access to the data in whose name decisions vital to this participant's rights are being made.

Illinois is the first state I know of to address this question forcefully. Many states, in their licensing regulations, mention the importance of "preserving test security," but none that I know about do so as forcefully as does Illinois.

A new confidentiality act was worked out. In the course of addressing these issues, the important notion of test security came up. Actually, much more was involved than behavior on the part of a mental health professional or anyone else that could compromise the future objectivity of a test. They were also concerned with very private data being bandied about in an open forum in a way that could be detrimental to some participant in the process. One frequently hears mental health professionals and attorneys arguing over whether or not a participant in a legal process has or had, for example, paranoid schizophrenia or is "latently homosexual." The issue would come up because the diagnostic term would have been in some data that a mental health professional was forced to disclose or appeared in some record that was made public. There is also the concern that laypeople might assume they understand what raw test data mean from the data alone.

While the law makes the distinction between "work product" materials (personal conjectures, memoranda, etc.) on the one hand and discoverable materials on the other, this distinction is only roughly followed by mental health professionals. In Illinois, the distinction had been made that there were two separate aspects to a mental health professional's records. One aspect had to do with his or her personal notes. These might include hunches and other materials that the professional wants to write down as future hypotheses to be checked out. For example, a mental health professional might write: "Check out whether the individual has sadistic fantasies." It is easy to see how such materials could be extremely damaging to the individual if they were admitted into a public record merely because they happened to be in the professional's records as a conjecture.

The other aspect of the documents in a file corresponds to what we can call the client's "actual" records. Once something is entered in a record and it is not clearly "work product," this item is not necessarily assured of confidentiality.

It was first assumed that the public airing of data that would compromise the future objectivity of an involved test could be protected by entering pertinent materials into the work product category. It was later felt this was not a strong enough protection, and so the act went on to spell out in much finer detail exactly what it is that may not be brought into a public arena. The act further delimits the persons to whom this rule applies, "the recipient of mental health services."

The Illinois law, signed in September of 1991, is a provision in a confidentiality act. It asserts that "Psychological test material whose disclosure would compromise the objectivity or fairness of the testing process may not be disclosed to anyone including the subject of the test and is not subject to disclosure in any administrative, judicial or legislative proceeding." This issue arose when lawyers in custody disputes demanded access to raw data regarding their client's psychological evaluations. (Bruce Bennett, personal communication).

While the keeping of raw materials out of the public parts of a custody dispute process handles test security issues, what about concerns regarding due process? The solution to this dilemma is suggested in the wording of the Illinois law. It states: "(A)ny recipient who has been the subject of a psychological test shall have the right to have all records relating to that test disclosed to any psychologist designated by the recipient." This means that only psychologists appropriately trained can have access to the raw test materials. This would include the test itself, the scoring sheet, and the person's responses. Neither the person who took the test nor that person's attorney can see the material directly, but he or she can have a psychologist review it. In a court case, if the opposing lawyer wants another analysis of the test, a psychologist can be chosen to review the material and advise the lawyer, or testify as an expert witness about the test or conclusions based on the test.

It seems to me that this is a fair way to balance both of these legitimate interests, test security and due process.

I do not advance these thoughts with the implication that it is always easy to reconcile the two competing rights. As a matter of fact, when an involved issue is quite serious, as in an allegation of sexual abuse the consideration of which could deprive an individual of important privileges and freedoms, the system should err on the side of increasing the risks of compromising test security and decreasing the risks of any infringement of due process. It is helpful in such situations to request that all relevant documents be sealed following the trial, so that they could be accessed only through court order. Judges will often grant this condition when asked.

I often bring a copy of my state's (Pennsylvania) licensing law and regulations to court. It expressly warns that test security must be maintained. Check in your own jurisdiction, and if this *really* becomes an issue in some particular case, read and cite the important article by Tranel (1994).

SPLITTING UP SIBLINGS

Although almost all mental health professionals assume one should not split up siblings, I can find no convincing evidence either in the research literature or elsewhere that this assumption has been proven. We are speaking specifically of separating siblings in the aftermath of a divorce. It is widely assumed that in the crisis atmosphere surrounding the period after a divorce such splitting would be particularly unwise.

Based on my own clinical experience, this does seem, in the main, a solid assumption. However, I am also convinced there are more exceptions to this rule than others might agree to be the case.

Several *Custody Newsletter* polls have recently yielded some interesting opinions by mental health professionals, from almost all fifty states.

When asked to speak about the reasons for splitting up siblings and/or conditions that would have to prevail in order to consider this possibility, these professionals offered some of the information that follows.

The most frequently mentioned reason for splitting siblings was when, in the evaluator's judgment, the good to be achieved in doing this (by creating a better parent-child matchup) was superior to what would be achieved in an arrangement where this action was not taken. The other main reason had to do with situations in which a particular child was being abused by a parent, or by another sibling.

These issues can become especially troublesome when one parent is clearly superior to the other, and the split-up involves moving a particular child from the better set-up to the less desirable parental set-up. These cases are more troubling than those in which a child would be moved from one parent to another parent where this second parent is seen as a better matchup for both parent and child. Here one deals only with the possibly negative effects due to removing the child from his or her siblings; this can be more than offset by a better parental placement for that child.

One *Custody Newsletter* respondent expressed my view; this person wrote: "In my opinion, the importance of a good parent-child relationship takes precedence over the importance of sibling attachment."

Another point was expressed by a good number of respondents. Where the sheer number of children involved is large and the task of taking care of all of these youngsters is overwhelming to a single parent, splitting up the siblings was seen as a "least detrimental" alternative. In the tumult and crisis that follows a divorce, parental stability and patience are in short supply. It may be that we mental health professionals place more emphasis on keeping the children together than is warranted in such circumstances. However, this line of reasoning may *not* apply if some of the children are old enough to assume household responsibilities. Stolberg and Bush (1985, p. 53) found some data to suggest that a mother's having many custody children may create a "tangible support network" that leads to a greater sharing of household responsibilities, and hence serve to reduce maternal stress. Indeed they found a *positive* relation between the number of children and maternal postdivorce adjustment.

Another point of view frequently expressed was the conviction that very young children, presumably preschool children, should probably be placed with the more available parent, regardless of other factors. By this I take it they mean they would be willing to split up siblings if they saw, for example, the father as an equally adequate choice as the mother, but would opt for the latter by virtue of her greater availability (for very young children).

Here are a variety of other (paraphrased) comments made on this important topic.

- I would only think of separating children from one another once they have outgrown whatever stability they each could gain by being together. (Although this comment certainly makes sense, I am not sure how one would operationally determine when this condition has been met, i.e., that the involved children have gained whatever stability they are going to gain by virtue of being together.)
- I think an important reason to separate siblings is when some important

problem develops among them. (This was most frequently mentioned in cases where one child physically or sexually abused one of his or her siblings.)

- I would consider separating them if we are dealing with large age gaps and the splitting would result in better matchups.
- I would consider splitting them up if we were dealing with extremely dysfunctional families. (I would imagine this is a variation on the theme of the parenting job being too overwhelming for one solo parent.)
- This would be less of a problem if the children are already living apart.
- Physical conditions may play an important role here, for example, one would have to consider how much space is available in the new residences.
- I would consider this only with teenagers.
- If the children are older, I would consider it, providing the children had clear preferences.
- I would consider it only under conditions where a given parent is specifically rejecting a particular child.
- I would do this only if the children could be together on the weekends.
- I would do this if the prevailing primary caretaking parent could not handle adolescent behavior, and it was best to make a change.

Many respondents expressed the thought that the younger the children are, the more important it is for them to stay together.

Interestingly, none of the respondents mentioned the importance of placing a child with a parent of the same sex as the child. Since there is at least *some* research evidence that same sex match-ups are optimal (Santrock & Warshak, 1979; Camara & Resnick, 1989) it is interesting how few experienced evaluators find this information compelling.

In my clinical experience, I do note that, other things being equal, older children, from about 12 years of age and up, seem to do better in single-parent families when they reside with a same-sex parent. However, there are such a host of factors that can mitigate against this as to make it difficult to use this clinically based intuition in actual cases. Older children who acted out when living with their mothers seemed to do better for longer periods of time when they were moved so as to live with their fathers, but these good effects did not seem to last over extended time periods (anything more than seven or eight months).

The more an evaluation indicates that a given parent's personality is uniquely constituted so as to interact favorably with that of a given child, the greater the potential for that relationship to help *each* overcome other life adversities. A child placed with a parent whose fit for himself or herself is more nearly "ideal," would tolerate a lot of external stressors much better than would a child living with a parent where the fit is less than this. I would thereby assume an evaluator could feel more secure about splitting up siblings (if such is indicated via clinical and/or life-history data) if the resulting match-ups found very *strong* confirmation in BPS (and PORT) or similar data. Also, PORT-like data can be used to gauge the degree of bonding between selected siblings.

SAVING TIME AND AGGRAVATION

Many hours can be saved in a custody evaluation since much of the information needed does not have to be gathered by the evaluator in face-to-face situations. The use of good printed forms can be enormously helpful.

There is one important exception to where one would use such forms, and that involves consultation with participating attorneys.

Two competing motives are aroused in the evaluator in dealing with attorneys. One is the desire *not* to get drawn into the adversarial aspects of the case. The other is to allow one's humanitarian and friendly impulses (which run high in mental health professionals) to cause one to fall under the influence of one particular attorney's version of what is "true" about the involved case. This bias might be based either on an acceptance of a particular attorney's selected data or charm or on a better matchup between a given attorney's symbol systems and information-processing strategies and those of the evaluator. Note that compatibility (and thereby, trust) are strengthened between *any* set of communicators by the factors described in Chapter Three, as well as by congruences in many usual demographic variables, such as age or race.

Hence, it might be imagined that printed forms would be an ideal way to interact with attorneys (their use would lessen the impact of the aforementioned variables).

My problem is that I am not sure what I need to ask the involved attorneys until I talk to them. It is exceedingly important for a mental health professional who practices forensics to understand the legal issues involved in a case. It is not enough to understand the psychological issues. It very well may be there is a legal issue involved that involves standards for resolution that are derived from legal statutes or regulations. The mental health professional must understand such factors. Without this information, one could not make informed choices as to the tests and tools to be employed in a given case.

In dealing with parents, we pursue our basically nonadversarial orientation even in the ways that our forms are printed. All of them are labeled "Child's Access to Parental Strength." We want, as much as possible, to help the parents move away from a win versus lose scenario into one whose purpose is to make the best of what each parent can offer available to the involved children.

Among the items covered in one of the questionnaires I mail out to the participants are those covering the following points: the full names of the children involved, their dates of birth, current age, and current school grades; the current living/custody arrangements for each child; a description of all previous marriages, what led to their break ups, and the children resulting from each; the current amount of time spent with each child; a complete listing of every person with whom a child would have contact under the competing arrangements and who would be responsible for each involved child for each hour of the day; a listing of self-described parental strengths and weaknesses; a good bit of information on the instant parent's view of the other parent; much information on the involved child's physical and mental development; information about religion, income, and contact with previous psychotherapists; information on limit-setting, and on helping a child with homework. One important question asks: "If a decision-maker decided the involved children should be divided up between you (the respondent) and the other parent, what should the arrangement be?"

We always leave room for the respondent to tell us anything else he or she thinks is important for us to know.

Another form, called "Self-Report Data" asks more personal questions, including items about: current occupation, the extended family, physical and sexual abuse, alcohol and drug habits, occupational and educational history, what the respondent feels must be done to build a more positive relationship with the other parent.

I have frequently been asked about materials sent out that would be roughly equivalent to a contract, the agreement that exists between myself and the involved participants.

Dr. Kenneth Byrne, a colleague who now practices in Australia, suggests the following areas should be covered in a contract mailed out ahead of time to the major adult participants in a comprehensive custody evaluation.

1. It should be made clear as to the role (ALL-CPE, LIM-CPE, etc.) the evaluator is willing to assume and the conditions under which a modification in this role would be feasible. All participants in the evaluation should be listed. The evaluator might wish to clarify his or her position on ultimate issue testimony, especially if one is dealing with a LIM-CPE. Make sure, via a copy of any existing divorce or custody decree as well as direct question, that the individual seeking the evaluation has a legal right to do so, in the possible absence of agreement from the other parent.

2. The evaluator might wish to insist that he or she be allowed to interview (and/or observe) whoever is deemed an important source of information (as many times as may be necessary) and have access to all relevant living quarters.

3. The evaluator should insist on access to any documents deemed important. There might be reference to having access to "*any* information con-

sidered important whatsoever." Signed release forms must be obtained. Attorneys should be requested to clarify all relevant legal issues involved.

4. Each participant must agree to take any tests deemed relevant by the evaluator.

5. It must be spelled out that the usual rules of confidentiality cannot apply in a custody evaluation, e.g., the evaluator may have to tell parent B what parent A said about some issue, to get B's reactions. Further, if something truly serious and negative emerges (such as abuse), the evaluator may find that his or her report and/or raw data are discoverable in some future or collateral legal action. Detail that consent is being solicited to: evaluate the involved children, conduct interviews and procure documents, make observations, and administer and interpret tests. Note that you are also seeking consent to *share* information (see above). (Schutz et al., 1989, p. 60, label one of their "consent" forms a "Consent for *Exchange* of Information," italics added.)

6. Fees and conditions for payment should be covered.

7. Any possible deadlines should be discussed (and either agreed to or alternate arrangements specified).

8. The "output" end of the evaluation should be discussed. Will there be a conference? Who will attend? Who is entitled to a written report?

9. Specify the possibility of delays and/or continuances, which may necessitate follow-up testing and/or interviewing.

10. It should be made clear that the evaluation and any testimony given in its name will be totally unbiased. There is the distinct possibility that a major participant may not agree with the evaluation data and/or report, and his/her signature on the form acknowledges awareness of this possibility.

11. Conditions for courtroom testimony should be spelled out. This may involve payment of fees, as well as the mention that the evaluator may end up testifying about things "negative" to one of the participants.

12. The evaluator may seek permission to consult with another professional regarding any aspect of the ongoing evaluation.

The forms should be dated and signed by all major participants. It should be made clear that the signatures signify consent regarding "all of the above."

HOMOSEXUALITY IN CUSTODY DISPUTE RESOLUTION

One encounters wild variability in the way courts react to this issue. In some states, homosexuals are automatically denied primary custody regardless of any other things that may be said in their favor. In other states, the issue is addressed by requiring proof that a given parent's homosexuality will not have any adverse effects on the child.

Some custody disputes arise not following a divorce, but following the death of a biological (homosexual) parent who has maintained a relationship with a person of the same sex who might have become a "psychological parent" to an involved child. In such instances, the court must decide whether custody of the child will remain with this nonbiological "parent" or be transferred to some third party, usually a relative of the biological parent. In these cases, as in others, one encounters great variability from court to court. When a nonbiological parent gains custody of a child, it is usually on the basis of the fact that this individual has in the past indeed served as a "psychological parent" to the child.

I can find no long-term follow-up research that can be helpful in contributing to a resolution of such disputes. No one has demonstrated, one way or the other, what the results will be of a child being brought up by either a homosexual alone or by a homosexual living with or married to another homosexual.

There are some short-term studies that strongly suggest the custody evaluator should approach a homosexual person exactly the same as he or she would approach any other person. Flaks (1993) performed a study in which he compared 15 lesbian-mother families formed through donor insemination with 15 matched heterosexual-parent control families. The families in both groups consisted of two parents and at least one child between the ages of three and nine. A wide variety of assessment tools were used to study the children's mental health, the parents' dyadic adjustment and parenting skills, and the families' relationships and interactions. Overall, the findings supported the conclusion that lesbian mothers and their children are similar to (or slightly better than) heterosexual parents and their children in almost all respects. (See also Cramer, 1986.)

The only sensible way for a custody evaluator to approach this situation is on a highly individual basis. In other words, the controlling factor must always involve a specified relationship between any known or observed or measured parental disposition and the effects of the latter on the child.

THE NITTY-GRITTY DETAILS OF A CUSTODY PLAN

One reason evaluators should avoid assuming the role of mediator is the tremendous number of details that must be worked out between two parents following a divorce. This requires expertise in areas that the average custody evaluator is unlikely to have.

The details of a time-sharing arrangement make up one such area. While the custody evaluator can offer recommendations couched in the language of the best possible matchups between a given parent and a given child in *certain contexts*, such as during the school week and getting involved in working out birthdays, holidays, and vacations, may require special skills and patience and *cannot* be done scientifically. Details need to be worked out for religious holidays, summer vacations, weekends, etc.

Day-to-day responsibilities involve not only baby-sitters, but getting back and forth to school or to day-care centers, and also after-school activities and religious classes. Special arrangements have to be made if either parent is going to travel and wants to take the child along. Relocation issues constitute a real Pandora's box. Courts vary wildly in this area, not only among themselves, but even in how a given jurisdiction interprets its own standards. Some lean toward allowing a primary custodial parent great leeway in doing what would be "best" for himself or herself, with the assumption that anything that makes life better for a PCP makes things better for the child. Other courts are much more restrictive in this matter. (The so-called "McGinniss ruling" in California, which attempted to spell out a procedure to follow in relocation cases, does little to help. See Halon, 1994. Of great help is Weissman, 1994.)

All of these issues must be resolved following a divorce, along with a tremendous number of financial issues, including who will pay for special clothing or equipment the child needs for after-school or play activities. Agreements must be forged about: who will take the child to a pediatrician or other physicians and who will pay for same, whether or not the child needs and who will pay for psychotherapy, and who will provide insurance coverage for the child.

It is often wise to build into your custody evaluation recommendations a plan for what the parents should do to resolve these troublesome disputes. In strongly adversarial dyads, it might be part of the recommendations that such a resource be mandatorily consulted. Not only are the items above likely to lead endless arguments, but so might such things as the child's bedtime, how rigorously medication schedules should be followed, the qualifications for baby-sitters, the quality of schools attended, the quality of day-care centers, as well as the qualities of significant others with whom the child would come into contact under the competing arrangements.

Remember, the people with whom you, the custody evaluator, are typically dealing are not good at dispute resolution. In the conceptual bases developed here, it is highly likely the two parents in a custody dispute have dissimilar symbol systems and are very different in how they take in and use information. They probably lack an adequate capacity for multiple-perspective-taking, as well.

While it is decidedly advantageous to forge an eventual plan that has ironclad rules regarding just about everything likely to come up (these are not flexible people; the less a given set of parents have to argue about, the better for everyone concerned), it will often not be possible to have such agreements come out of the evaluation proper. I strongly recommend that adversarial couples work with a communication specialist, who can assist in dispute resolution for all these many issues, and also (even more important) have an opportunity to model for each parent the science and art of nonadversarial communication.

WHAT SHOULD THE CUSTODY EVALUATOR BRING
TO THE COURTROOM?

Many years ago, before I knew the difference between what was legitimately discoverable and what was not, I had an aggressive attorney grab a case folder out of my hand, wander back to his table, and look through it, trying to find materials to help him formulate questions that I would not be able to answer. He was also looking for materials favorable to the client he represented, and unfavorable to the client whose position my information favored.

After this incident, I took to planting what I thought of as time bombs throughout the folder, should this ever happen again. Here, I refer to statements the implications of which would be decidedly unhelpful to any attorney "against" me. These would consist of true statements that I had deleted from any final report, feeling that their mention would hurt someone's feelings beyond what was necessary and/or exacerbate the adversarial bitterness between the already beleaguered participants.

For example, in one case I wrote prominently in a memo to myself: "There were many, many more strongly negative things discovered about the mother in this case than I included in the report. I did not want to hurt her feelings in court, or make the adversarial nature of the case even worse." I followed this with an appropriate list of items.

When an attorney (known for his aggressiveness) representing the mother grabbed this folder, wandered back to his table, and discovered this and similar notes, he simply returned my folder without comment. The message I wanted to get across was: "I don't think you're going to like what you find if you rummage through this folder."

I no longer do this. Attorney rudeness elicits only about a 3 on my internal Richter scale, rather than the 7's and 8's of yesteryear. (I use the techniques described earlier in this chapter.)

Nowadays my folders are exceedingly organized, and contain only legitimately discoverable materials. I bring many printed handouts to court, four copies of each, for distribution to the judge, each attorney, and myself. Back in the old adversarial days of the sixties, before there were any good tests for custody use, my rule of thumb was to say as little as possible in court. I would follow to a "t" the maxim that one should simply answer each question asked in the most concise way possible.

This is not possible when one is introducing concepts with which a court may not be familiar, such as the importance of the utilization model in custody decision-making.

The handouts are positioned as the materials I use when lecturing at continuing education workshops, or in teaching at colleges or universities. They are the things one would put on a blackboard, show with an overhead or standard slide projector, or use with a video demonstration.

In other words, these must be positioned as educational aids. If they are seen as part of a report proper, they perhaps would have been included with the discoverable materials and made available to the attorneys prior to the trial. Hence, these materials should never deal directly with the participants in the present case.

Remember to arrange everything in the folder in the same order as one will need them in a courtroom. All papers belonging to the same subject should be carefully fastened together with a clip, so things pertaining to a given category remain together. Under the rigors of zealous cross examination, it is unhelpful to have to root through one's folder looking for something.

It is important to adequately reference all materials offered in the court as information.

The topic of whether or not to bring raw test data has been covered elsewhere.

An evaluator will have to decide on a case-by-case basis what is "work product" material and what is part of a participant's "record." Some authors have a wonderfully clear and helpful credo about what to bring to court; for example, Schutz et al. suggest that "A copy of the report should be sufficient" (1989, p. 102).

WHAT ABOUT HOSTILE JUDGES?

I have been quite surprised by the range of attitudes I have encountered among judges who try custody-related cases. Some seem very warm and friendly. Others can be very cold. Others are actually hostile, and make little secret of their contempt for expert witnesses. I have encountered this even in situations where I was the neutral evaluator agreed upon by both sides in the dispute. Some are exceedingly interested in the data and information I present, and ask many questions on their own. Others are polite, but totally devoid of interest in what is being offered. Even realizing that many of these people intend to read printed transcripts of the hearings (and hence do not always pay very careful attention while they are actually happening), it was obvious that some were unmoved by expert testimony now and would be unmoved by it later.

A Custody Newsletter survey (in press) asked the respondents about their own experiences in court. One question sought information about how judges reacted to expert witness testimony, and offered the following response options: very much welcomed the input; seemed neutral to the input; seemed hostile, resistant, and/or not interested.

On the average, 75 percent of the judges encountered by this sample of respondents welcomed expert witness input. Twenty-five percent of the judges seemed neutral, and three percent were hostile.

Another question sought to discern where the judge's interest centered in a given case. That is, I was trying to find what component of an expert witness' testimony seemed most compelling to a judge. One category focused on the judge seeming mainly persuaded by clinical and life-history data as reported from interviews and documents. Another category asked about the degree to which judges seem persuaded by data coming from office or home visit observations, while the third category asked about the attention paid to data emanating from psychological tests.

In our sample, 37 percent of the judges were mainly persuaded by clinical and life-history data as elicited from interviews and documents, 20 percent from observations made in the home or in the office, and 42 percent by data emanating from psychological tests. The latter figure, although personally pleasing, seems rather high to me, and may be somewhat a function of our particular sample. Note, again, that the respondents to this poll were spread out through all 50 states, but the poll was probably biased toward those who favored a test-based approach.

Another question was worded as follows: "Even though you may not be in a courtroom while persons other than yourself offer testimony in all instances, what is your estimate of how judges are persuaded by the following?"

One choice was that the judges seem mainly persuaded by the testimony of the two main litigants (usually the two parents). Another category was that the judges seem mainly persuaded by testimony from each of the main litigant's friends and character witnesses, while the third category had to do with judges who were mainly persuaded by testimony from expert witnesses.

The numbers, respectively, here were: 35 percent, nine percent, 55 percent. I was heartened by the relative lack of influence, as observed by these seasoned veterans, of the friends and cohorts of the main litigants.

Note: the main way to win over a hostile judge is to remain calm, friendly, and neutral. Easier said than done.

HOW DOES ONE MATCH UP PARENTS AND CHILDREN WITHOUT TESTS?

Although the BPS and PORT were designed explicitly to offer information helpful in the creation of good match-ups between parents and their children, once in awhile I get a request for help in this task from mental health professionals who do not use tests.

Things are not easy here, since it would take, to my mind, a lot of money and a fairly big staff of assistants to gather the kinds of observations one would need in the absence of test data.

I favor the kind of arrangement described in Chapter Five, where we reviewed (structured) observations made to collect data for the development of the PORT.

I first began to think about compatibility in communication in the late 1950's, when I was intrigued by a research finding by Zygmunt A. Piotrowski. In 1956, he and Stephanie Dudek showed that marital mates who remain together in spite of conflict had similar numbers of human movement or M responses on their respective *Rorschach* records, while mates who separated under the same conditions had dissimilar numbers of such responses. Along with Sophie Gottlieb, I expanded on these ideas in 1961, and fashioned a *Rorschach* marital compatibility index. It was my hypothesis, confirmed in the investigation, that not only would the number of M responses be predictive of heightened compatibility as communication increased, but so too would be *shared types* of M responses. In other words, under conditions of increased communication (which was the only way it made sense to me to think about testing compatibility; mates who rarely speak with one another can hardly be said to be compatible *or* not compatible), those mates who had similar types, as well as numbers, of M would grow closer together (as measured by an independent criterion) as communication increased, and those mates who had dissimilar numbers and types would grow farther apart. (In fact, several couples with highly dissimilar M types eventually divorced—the only ones in the 36-couple sample to do so—even though this had not been contemplated by them when the study began. It covered a two-year time span.)

In a very important article for all of us who are interested in the development of projective tests as an aid to understanding and predicting personality, DeCato (1993) pulls together much of the important things Piotrowski has had to say about the human movement response. Stated succinctly, these responses represent an individual's deep-seated tendencies to assume certain attitudes in dealing with others who are considered important. Such attitudes may be, for example, assertive, compliant, passive, etc. (One would have to consider an *individual* M response to extract all of its ideographic information.)

All of my own research in congruent communication showed basically that key similarities are most predictive of compatible or congruent communication. People with roughly the same numbers of human movement responses in their *Rorschachs* tend to have personalities of equal complexity. They would be approximately similar in the amount of conscious and unconscious mental activity expended in working out ways to relate to others, and the levels of sophistication utilized in arriving at such crystallized patterns. This would mean they would tend to view the world in at least roughly similar ways, in that they could appreciate all of the multiple levels involved in considering any given situation.

Thus, I knew from the outset that certain key similarities were important in congruent or compatible communication. My investigation with Gottlieb (1961) showed very definitely that when mates with dissimilar M responses increased communication, they grew more and more frustrated with each other. (This was one of the first research demonstrations that "talking things over" does not invariably lead to better situations. In fact, this study showed the opposite is more likely true: When people who are dissimilar in certain key ways talk things over, matters go steadily downhill).

The old maxim that "opposites attract" is true in limited circumstances. Our clinical research in 1961 suggested that if there are key similarities in the personalities of a husband and wife (or any two companions), the presence of opposite qualities can be an asset. This "oppositeness" will, so to speak, add more resources to the mix of skills and capabilities possessed by both as a team. However, in the absence of the key similarities, the oppositeness factor only helps to make things worse.

My current conception is that shared numbers and types of M responses reflect, at least in part, similar complexity in information-processing strategies. In fact, it is quite likely that an individual's "complexity," reflected by the number of M responses, is in largest part a result of the *complexity of that individual's information-processing strategies*. It is further likely that the way a person psychologically builds or fashions the way he or she will relate to others is much more a product of *the complexity with which his or her brain handles or aggregates information* than a product of the *content* of this information, i.e., complexity of personality, as well as compatibility between people, is more the product of "structural" aspects of the organism than "content" aspects. This was certainly borne out in our original *Hand Test* data (Bricklin, Piotrowski, & Wagner, 1962). Most violent criminals were not characterized by complex personalities, as were our "normals." Among the latter, the "normals," balance was achieved by high amounts of forces pushing toward "acting out," competing with forces of human warmth and human need pushing in the opposite direction. In most (but not all—there were important exceptions) acting-out criminals, there were very few aggressive forces and *little or no* human warmth and human need forces. My hunch is that these persons would also have few M responses—reflecting personalities of little complexity. I expected to find raging wars inside the acting-out criminal heads. Instead, I found little of anything.

All of these data strengthen my belief that the more people share similar M responses, the more similar they are in information processing strategies, and in what we can call "complexity" of personality. Hence, they are more likely to approach any given area with similar degrees of multiple-perspective-taking, and in this fact would lie their potential for congruent communication.

What all of this boils down to is that for those people who do not wish to use tests, but who still wish to create good match-ups between parents and children, a way would have to be found to observe the operation of variables like those described in Chapter Three, in some controlled setting.

MIXED MESSAGES FROM THE UNCONSCIOUS MIND

The NBOAIs or not-based-on-actual-interaction scenarios (of which the parent alienation syndrome is a subset) are identified by situations in which the conscious (C) and unconscious (U) indicators tell a different story. The "classic" NBOAI situation is where the C indicators for the "target" parent are negative, and the U indicators positive (i.e., the child's actual interactions with the target parent are much more positive than the child is representing consciously). However, it is also conceivable (although relatively rare) to get a mixed message from unconscious sources as well.

This simply (and sadly) means the child *is indeed getting* mixed messages from a particular parent. If some of the unconscious test signs are good and some are bad, it would mean this is likely the kinds of interactions the child is having with the portrayed parent: some are good and some are bad. Note: we speak here of extreme variation. A child's experience with *any* parent, even a fabulous one, will never be a continuous bowl of cherries.

One could also get this scenario (mixed unconscious messages) where the child has been consistently alienated from a target parent over many years, *especially in situations where the child has not been able to consistently see the target parent and experience "corrective" information.* This is, however, a rare situation; it takes a long time to "wear down" or manipulate unconscious sources.

With all such mixed situations, the custody evaluator would simply have to take all available information into account in fashioning a suggested arrangement.

CUSTODY EVALUATIONS: A PEEK INTO THE FUTURE

There has always been a tension between those who see advances coming to a field through the discovery of new "facts" and those who see new "concepts" as providing the important beginning points. Piotrowski (1957) believes each endeavor attracts very different kinds of people: "The scientist who is ... concerned with introducing new concepts... is a different type of person from the scientist whose chief interest lies in checking and verifying principles or propositions" (p. 22).

I can't help believing, however, that the next big advance in custody evaluations will come when someone asks a radically new and different question. (Mediation proponents probably believe they have already done this.)

There are always forces at work that lower the likelihood of new concepts appearing. Currently, these forces are the product of a political-legal system aimed more at political correctness than at solutions. While it is certainly the case that scientists and philosophers of yesteryear had even more to fear than do their modern counterparts by the introduction of a new concept (Galileo is one example), it is also true that the scientists of today are in the same boat. Although the current cost in terms of threat to life and limb are diminished as compared to what was true in Galileo's time, the obstructions are similar. And here we speak of even mundane, let alone radically new, concepts.

Is anyone allowed these days to propose the hypothesis that the only way to remediate some of the societal problems we face would involve *radical* intervention in certain family systems almost from the point of birth?

Would I be able these days to seek funds for a virtual reality research project to measure a child's reactions to standardized photos and videos of each parent in everyday situations by using a sophisticated type of polygraph measurement that would have to be placed and calibrated against a child's body, even though such an approach may constitute a truly superior way of measuring a "gut level" whole-organism reaction? (The charge that this would be "intrusive" could be made. I believe that such an interpretation would be a self-fulfilling prophecy, that someone would tell a child he is being intruded upon, following which the child would behave in accordance with this belief.)

Can we admit that an evaluation often uses standards for resolution that may demand more parental "perfection" than applies in ordinary families in which no divorce or parent contest took place?

Are the two parents who fight a custody battle both so off-center (see Hoppe, 1993) that what the state should mandate instead of an evaluation is continuous therapy for each of them?

I am, of course, aware that such issues cannot be answered empirically, just as every "scientific" approach is not wholly scientific since it involves disguised value-laden assumptions.

A careful reading of Chapter Two does suggest, albeit with exceptions, that the more contact a child has with each parent the better. However, it might be that what we are really measuring here is a degree of psychological health in a parent dyad above a certain point, i.e., the "health" may belong to either parent alone, or the absence of particular types of parental conflict, such that the apparent benefit that flows to the child does not really stem from having contact with both parents.

However, if it is true that contact with each parent is truly desirable, perhaps this should be implemented in ways other than through evaluations. It may be that each parent should be forced to contribute money (or some suitable substitute) to make possible a specific psychotherapy *for the child*. The purpose would be to teach the child how to deal with each parent to learn how to utilize the best of what each has to offer. The child could be taught how to convert or transform inputs from each parent into offerings that are useful and nurturant. Without using the big words of Chapter Three, the child could be taught to elicit information and behavior packaged to be maximally useful *from each parent*. In other words, the child would be taught to use a series of questions to call forth information matched to his or her style of using it. This is *truly* making use of a utilization principle. If you will recall, this Ericksonian principle states that whatever comes your way, good, bad or indifferent, you can learn to transform it to something useful. This is certainly in line with the findings of Mazur, Wolchik, and Sandler (1992), who essentially are telling us that what a child *expects* to result from a divorce is often more predictive of outcomes than actual divorce events.

Most important, children could be taught how to decline the role of "pawn" in an alienation scenario. If a child can learn a child's version of the "gentle-deflection" principles of nonadversarial communication, the child can be part of a mechanism that disallows a dispute, or at least one in which the child is forced to play a key role. If a child can be taught how to stay on the track of actively eliciting the best of what each parent can offer, and off the track of responding in *any* way whatsoever to entrapping behaviors, we are moving in the right direction.

A tall order? Maybe, but given the facility with which children learn, by no means impossible.

It might be appropriate to end this book here.

We began with the premise that if we want to find out who is the better parent for a child, the child is really in the best position to provide us with an answer.

It may also be that the child is in the best position to be a fulcrum point for creating solutions to the problems that happen after divorce. Children are far more open to, and better users of, information than are adults.

References

Abarbanel, A. (1979). Shared parenting after separation and divorce: A study of joint custody. *American Journal of Orthopsychiatry, 49* (2), 320–329.

Abelsohn, D., & Saayman, G.S. (1991). Adolescent adjustment to parental divorce: An investigation from the perspective of basic dimensions of structural family therapy theory. *Family Process, 30,* 177–191.

Abidin, R.R. (1990). *Parenting Stress Index.* Charlottesville, VA: Pediatric Psychology Press.

Achenbach, T.M., & Edelbrock, C.S. (1986). *Child Behavior Checklist and Youth Self-Report,* Burlington VT: Author.

Ackerman, M.J., & Kane, A.W. (1993). *Psychological experts in divorce, personal injury, and other civil actions.* (2nd ed.). Colorado Springs, CO: Wiley Law Publications.

Ackerman, M.J., & Schoendorf, K. (1992). *Ackerman-Schoendorf scales for parent evaluation of custody.* Los Angeles: Western Psychological Services.

Ahrons, C. (1981). Joint custody arrangements in the postdivorce family. *Journal of Divorce, 3,* 189–205.

Allison, P.D., & Furstenberg, F.F. (1989). How marital dissolution affects children: Variations by age and sex. *Developmental Psychology, 25,* 540–549.

Amato, P.R., & Keith, B. (1991). Parental divorce and the well-being of children: A meta-analysis. *Psychological Bulletin, 110* (1), 26–46.

Anson, D.A., Golding, S.L., & Gully, K.J. (1993). Child sexual abuse allegations: Reliability of criteria-based content analysis. *Law and Human Behavior, 17* (3), 331–341.

Bandler, R., & Grinder, J. (1979). *Frogs into princes.* Moab, UT: Real People Press.

Barton, S. (1994). Chaos, self organization, and psychology. *American Psychologist, 49* (1), 5–14.

Beck, A.T. (1967). *Depression: Clinical, experimental, and theoretical aspects.* New York: Harper & Row.

Beck, A.T. (1976). *Cognitive therapy and the emotional disorders.* New York: International Universities Press.

Beck, A.T., & Steer, R.A. (1987). *Beck Depression Inventory manual*. San Antonio: The Psychological Corporation.

Beck, A.T., & Steer, R.A. (1990). *Beck Anxiety Inventory manual*. San Antonio: The Psychological Corporation.

Bergman, P., & Berman-Barrett, S. J. (1993). *Represent yourself in court*. Berkeley, CA: Nolo Press.

Berkowitz, L. (1993). *Aggression: Its causes, consequences and control*. New York: McGraw-Hill.

Bisbing, S.B., & Faust, D. (1992, August). *Effective expert psychological evaluations, testimony and practice: A guide*. American Psychological Association 100th Annual Convention, Washington D.C.

Block, J.H., Block, J., & Gjerde, P.F. (1986). The personality of children prior to divorce: A prospective study. *Child Development, 57*, 827–840.

Block, J., Block, J.H., & Gjerde, P.F. (1988). Parental functioning and the home environment in families of divorce: Prospective and concurrent analyses. *Journal of the American Academy of Child and Adolescent Psychiatry, 27* (2), 207–213.

Borrine, M.L., Handal, P.J., Brown, N.Y., & Searight, H.R. (1991). Family conflict and adolescent adjustment in intact, divorced, and blended families. *Journal of Consulting and Clinical Psychology, 59* (5), 753–755.

Boyer, J.L. (1990). Assuming risk in child custody evaluations. In *Psychological practice: Marketing, legal, ethical and current professional issues* (pp. 13–14). Washington DC: The National Register of Health Service Providers in Psychology.

Braun, B. (1983). Psychophysiological phenomena in multiple personality. *The American Journal of Clinical Hypnosis, 26* (2), 124–137.

Bray, J.H. (1991). Psychosocial factors affecting custodial and visitation agreements. *Behavioral Sciences and the Law, 9* (4), 419–437.

Bricklin, B. (1962, 1989). *The Perception-of-Relationships Test*. Doylestown, PA: Village Publishing, Inc.

Bricklin, B. (1984). *The Bricklin Perceptual Scales: Child-Perception-of-Parents Series*. Doylestown, PA: Village Publishing, Inc.

Bricklin, B. (1985). My Parent Would . . . Questionnaire. Doylestown, PA: Village Publishing, Inc.

Bricklin, B. (1990a). *The custody evaluation report*. Doylestown, PA: Village Publishing, Inc.

Bricklin, B. (1990b). *The Parent Awareness Skills Survey*. Doylestown, PA: Village Publishing, Inc.

Bricklin, B. (1995). Getting optimum performance from a mental health professional. *Family Law Quarterly, 29* (1), 7-17.

Bricklin, B., & Bricklin, P.M. (1967). *Bright child-poor grades: The psychology of underachievement*. New York: Delacorte Press.

Bricklin, B., & Elliot, G. (1991). *The Parent Perception of Child Profile*. Doylestown, PA: Village Publishing, Inc.

Bricklin, B., & Elliot, G. (1995). *ACCESS: A Comprehensive Custody Evaluation Standard System*. Doylestown, PA: Village Publishing, Inc.

Bricklin, B., & Gottlieb, S.G. (1961). The prediction of some aspects of marital compatibility by means of the Rorschach test. *Psychiatric Quarterly Supplement, 35* (2), 281–303.

Bricklin, B., Piotrowski, Z.A., & Wagner, E.E. (1962). *The hand test*. Springfield, IL: Charles C. Thomas.

Brodsky, S.L. (1991). *Testifying in court: Guidelines and maxims for the expert witness*. Washington, DC: American Psychological Association.

Brodzinsky, D. (1993). On the use and misuse of psychological testing in child custody evaluations. *Professional Psychology: Research and Practice, 24* (2), 213–219.

Brown, J.H., Eichenberger, S.A., Portes, P.R., & Christensen, D.N. (1991). Family functioning factors associated with the adjustment of children of divorce. *Journal of Divorce and Remarriage, 17* (1/2), 81–95.

Call, J.A. (1990). In re joint v. sole custody. *The Custody Newsletter*, Issue No. 1, 4–7.

Call, J.A. (1992). Sexual abuse in preschool children. *The Custody Newsletter*, Issue No. 5, 1–9.

Camara, K.A., & Resnick, G. (1989). Styles of conflict resolution and cooperation between divorced parents: Effects on child behavior and adjustment. *American Journal of Orthopsychiatry, 59*, 560–575.

Campbell, T.W. (1992). The "highest level of psychological certainty": Betraying standards of practice in forensic psychology. *American Journal of Forensic Psychology, 10* (2), 35–48.

Cherlin, A.J., Furstenberg, F.F., Chase-Lansdale, P.L., Kiernan, K.E., Robins, P.K., Morrison, D.R., & Teitler, J.O. (1991). Longitudinal studies of effects of divorce on children in Great Britain and the United States. *Science, 252*, 1386–1389.

Chess, S., & Thomas, A. (1984). *Origins and evolution of behavior disorders from infancy to early adult life*. New York: Brunner/Mazel.

Churchman, C.W. (1961). *Prediction and optimal decision*. Englewood Cliffs, NJ: Prentice Hall.

Clingempeel, W.G., & Reppucci, N.D. (1982). Joint custody after divorce: Major issues and goals for research. *Psychological Bulletin, 91* (1), 102–127.

Cooke, G., & Cooke, M. (1991). Dealing with sexual abuse allegations in the context of custody evaluations. *American Journal of Forensic Psychology, 9* (3), 55–67.

Cramer, D. (1986). Gay parents and their children: A review of research and practical implications. *Journal of Counseling and Development, 64*, 504–507.

Davenport, M. (1932). *Mozart*. New York: Charles Scribner's Sons.

Davies, P. (1983). *God and the new physics*. New York: Simon and Schuster.

De Cato, C.M. (1993). On the Rorschach M response and monotheism. *Journal of Personality Assessment, 60* (2), 362–378.

Derdeyn, A.P., & Scott, E. (1984). Joint custody: A critical analysis and appraisal. *American Journal of Orthopsychiatry, 54* (2), 199–209.

Dilts, R.B. (1983). *Applications of neuro-linguistic programming*. Cupertino, CA: Meta Publications.

Einstein, A. (1936, March). Physics and reality. *The Journal of the Franklin Institute*.

Ekman, P., & O'Sullivan, M. (1991). Who can catch a liar? *American Psychologist, 46* (9), 913–920.

Emery, R.E. (1982). Interparental conflict and the children of discord and divorce. *Psychological Bulletin, 92* (2), 310–330.

Emery, R.E. (1988). Children in the divorce process. *Journal of Family Psychology, 2* (2), 141–144.

Erickson, M., & Rossi, E. (1979). *Hypnotherapy: An exploratory casebook*. New York: Irvington.

Esplin, P.W., Houed, T., & Raskin, D.C. (1988, June). *Application of statement validity assessment*. Paper presented at NATO Advanced Study Institute on Credibility Assessment, Maratea, Italy.

Fauber, R., Forehand, R., Thomas, A.M., & Wierson, M. (1990). A mediational model of the impact of marital conflict on adolescent adjustment in intact and divorced families: The role of disrupted parenting. *Child Development, 61,* 1112–1123.

Faust, D., & Ziskin, J. (1988). The expert witness in psychology and psychiatry. *Science, 241,* 31–35.

Faust, D., & Ziskin, J. (1989). Computer-assisted psychological evaluation as legal evidence: Some day my prints will come. *Computers in Human Behavior, 5,* 23–26.

Federal Rules of Evidence. (1984). St. Paul, MN: West Publishing.

Fischer, R. (1971). A cartography of ecstatic and meditative states. *Science, 174,* 897–904.

Flaks, D.K. (1993). *Lesbian couples and their children: Psychological and legal implications.* Unpublished doctoral dissertation, The Institute for Graduate Clinical Psychology, Widener University, Chester, PA.

Forehand, R., Neighbors, B., & Wierson, M. (1991). The transition to adolescence: the role of gender and stress in problem behavior and competence. *Journal of Child Psychology and Psychiatry, 32* (6), 929–937.

Forehand, R., Thomas, A.M., Wierson, M., Brody, G., & Fauber, R. (1990). Role of maternal functioning following parental divorce. *Journal of Abnormal Psychology, 99* (3), 278–283.

Forehand, R., Wierson, M., Thomas, A.M., Armistead, L., Kempton, T., & Fauber, R. (1990). Interparental conflict and paternal visitation following divorce: The interactive effect on adolescent competence. *Child Study Journal, 20* (3), 193–202.

Forehand, R., Wierson, M., Thomas, A.M., Fauber, R., Armistead, L., Kempton, T., & Long, N. (1991). A short-term longitudinal examination of young adolescent functioning following divorce: The role of family factors. *Journal of Abnormal Child Psychology, 19* (1), 97–111.

Freedman, M.R., Rosenberg, S.J., Gettman-Felzien, D., & Van Scoyk, S. (1993). Evaluator countertransference in child custody evaluations. *American Journal of Forensic Psychology, 11* (3), 61–73.

Friedrich, W.N. (1993). The law and child abuse. *Contemporary Psychology, 38* (12), 1319–1320.

Garb, H.N. (1992a). The *trained* psychologist as expert witness. *Clinical Psychology Review, 12,* 451–467.

Garb, H.N. (1992b). The debate over the use of computer-based test reports. *The Clinical Psychologist, 45* (2), 95–99.

Gardner, R.A. (1987). *Parental alienation syndrome and the differentiation between fabricated and genuine child sex abuse.* Cresskill, NJ: Creative Therapeutics.

Garmezy, N., & Rutter, M. (Eds.) (1983). *Stress, coping, and development in children.* New York: McGraw-Hill.

Gately, D.W., & Schwebel, A.I. (1991). The Challenge Model of children's adjustment to parental divorce: Explaining favorable postdivorce outcomes in children. *Journal of Family Psychology, 5* (1), 60–81.

Gately, D.W., & Schwebel, A.I. (1992). Favorable outcomes in children after parental divorces. *Journal of Divorce and Remarriage, 18* (3/4), 57–78.

Golding, S.L., Roesch, R., & Schreiber, J. (1984). Assessment and conceptualization of competency to stand trial: Preliminary data on the Interdisciplinary Fitness Interview. *Law and Human Behavior, 9*, 321–334.

Goodman, G.S., & Bottoms, B.L. (Eds.) (1993). *Child victims, child witnesses: Understanding and improving testimony.* New York: Guilford.

Gordon, R., & Peek, L.A. (1988). *The custody quotient.* Dallas, TX: The Wilmington Institute.

Greif, J. (1979). Fathers, children, and joint custody. *American Journal of Orthopsychiatry, 49* (2), 311–319.

Grisso, T. (1986). *Evaluating competencies: Forensic assessments and instruments.* New York: Plenum.

Grisso, T., & Saks, M. (1991). Psychology's influence on constitutional interpretation. *Law and Human Behavior, 15* (2), 205–211.

Guidubaldi, J., Cleminshaw, H., Perry, J., & McLaughlin, C. (1983). The impact of parental divorce on children: Report of the nationwide NASP study. *School Psychology Review, 12*, 300–323.

Guidubaldi, J., & Perry, J.D. (1984). Divorce, socioeconomic status, and children's cognitive-social competence at school entry. *American Journal of Orthopsychiatry, 54*, 459–468.

Guidubaldi, J., & Perry, J.D. (1985). Divorce and mental health sequelae for children: A two-year follow-up of a nationwide sample. *Journal of the American Academy of Child Psychiatry, 24*, 531–537.

Hahn, M., & Hilton, W. (1990). What to do when one parent will not cooperate. *The Custody Newsletter*, Issue No. 1, 3–4.

Halon, R.L. (1990). The comprehensive child custody evaluation. *American Journal of Forensic Psychology, 8* (3), 19–46.

Halon, R.L. (1994). Child custody "move away" cases: McGinniss and psychology. *American Journal of Forensic Psychology, 12* (1), 43–54.

Hambacher, W. (1994, November). *The expert witness role in child custody evaluations.* Pittsburgh, PA: Pennsylvania Psychological Association.

Hammer, E.F., & Piotrowski, Z.A. (1953). Hostility as a factor in the clinician's personality as it affects his interpretation of projective drawings. *Journal of Projective Techniques, 17* (2), 210–216.

Hathaway, S.R. & McKinley, J.C. (1989). *Minnesota Multiphasic Personality Inventory*-2. Minneapolis, MN: Nation Computer Systems.

Haugaard, J.L. (1993). Young children's classification of the corroboration of a false statement as the truth or a lie. *Law and Human Behavior, 17* (6), 645–659.

Healy, J.M., Malley, J.E., & Stewart, A.J. (1990). Children and their fathers after parental separation. *American Journal of Orthopsychiatry, 60* (4), 531–543.

Heilbrun, K. (1992). The role of psychological testing in forensic assessment. *Law and Human Behavior, 16* (3), 257–272.

Hetherington, E.M. (1979). Divorce: A child's perspective. *American Psychologist, 34* (10), 851–858.

Hetherington, E.M. (1989). Coping with family transitions: Winners, losers, and survivors. *Child Development, 60*, 1–14.

Hetherington, E.M., Cox, M., & Cox, R. (1982). Effects of divorce on parents and children. In M. Lamb (Ed.), *Non-traditional families* (pp. 233–288). Hillsdale, NJ: Lawrence Erlbaum.

Hetherington, E.M., Stanley-Hagan, M., & Anderson, E.R. (1989). Marital transitions: A child's perspective. *American Psychologist, 44,* 303–311.

Hodges, W.F., Landis, T., Day, E., & Oderberg, N. (1991). Infant and toddlers and postdivorce parental access: An initial exploration. *Journal of Divorce and Remarriage, 16* (3/4), 239–252.

Honor, S. (1994). Custody Evaluation: Is something missing? *The Custody Newsletter,* Issue No. 10, 2–7.

Hoorwitz, A.N. (1992). *The clinical detective: Techniques in the evaluations of sexual abuse.* New York: Norton.

Hoppe, C. (1992). A seven year retrospective of the pedophilic index. *The Custody Newsletter,* Issue No. 7, 1–10.

Hoppe, C. (1993, August). *A data based description of relationship disorders.* Paper presented at the American Psychological Association, Toronto, Canada.

Ilfeld, F.W., Ilfeld, H.Z., & Alexander, J.R. (1982). Does joint custody work? A first look at outcome data of relitigation. *American Journal of Orthopsychiatry, 139* (1), 62–66.

Jenkins, J.M., & Smith, M.A. (1993). A Prospective study of behavioral disturbance in children who subsequently experience parental divorce: A research note. *Journal of Divorce and Remarriage, 19* (1/2), 143–160.

Johnston, J.R., Kline, M., & Tschann, J.M. (1989). Ongoing postdivorce conflict: Effects on children of joint custody and frequent access. *American Journal of Orthopsychiatry, 59* (4), 576–592.

Kalter, N., & Rembar, J. (1981). The significance of a child's age at the time of parental divorce. *American Journal of Orthopsychiatry, 51* (1), 85–100.

Kalter, N., Kloner, A., Schreier, S., & Okla, K. (1989). Predictors of children's postdivorce adjustment. *American Journal of Orthopsychiatry, 59* (4), 605–618.

Kelly, J.B. (1988). Longer-term adjustment in children of divorce: Converging findings and implications for practice. *Journal of Family Psychology, 2* (2), 119–140.

Kelly, J.B., & Wallerstein, J.S. (1976). The effects of parental divorce: Experiences of the child in early latency. *American Journal of Orthopsychiatry, 46* (1), 20–32.

Kline, M., Tschann, J.M., Johnston, J.R., & Wallerstein, J.S. (1989). Children's adjustment in joint and sole physical custody families. *Developmental Psychology, 25* (3), 430–438.

Koppitz, E.M. (1968). *Psychological evaluations of children's human figure drawings.* New York: Grune & Stratton.

Kressel, K. (1988). Parental conflict and the adjustment of children in divorce: Clinical and research implications. *Journal of Family Psychology, 2* (2), 145–149.

Kurdek, L.A. (1988). Issues in the study of children and divorce. *Journal of Family Psychology, 2* (2), 150–153.

Kurdek, L.A., & Berg, B. (1983). Correlates of children's adjustment to their parents' divorce. In L.A. Kurdek (Ed.), *Children and divorce.* San Francisco: Jossey-Bass.

Kurdek, L.A., Blisk, D., & Siesky, A.E. (1981). Correlates of children's long-term adjustment to their parents' divorce. *Developmental Psychology, 17* (5), 565–579.

Landry, K.L., & Brigham, J.C. (1992). The effect of training in criteria-based content analysis on the ability to detect deception in adults. *Law and Human Behavior, 16* (6), 663–676.

Leonard, R.D., & Elias, S. (1990). *Family law dictionary.* Berkeley, CA: Nolo Press.

Lind, E.A., & Tyler, T.R. (1988). *The social psychology of procedural justice.* New York: Plenum.

Lindley, D.V. (1975). Probabilities and the law. In D. Wendt & C. Vlek (Eds.), *Utility, probability, and human decision making*. Dordrecht: Reidel.

Matarazzo, J.D. (1990). Psychological assessment versus psychological testing: Validation from Binet to the school, clinic, and courtroom. *American Psychologist, 45*, 999–1017.

Matarazzo, J.D., & Fowler, R.D. (1988). Psychologists and psychiatrists as expert witnesses. *Science, 241*, 8.

Mazur, E., Wolchik, S.A., & Sandler, I.N. (1992). Negative cognitive errors and positive illusions for negative divorce events: Predictors of children's psychological adjustment. *Journal of Abnormal Child Psychology, 20* (6), 523–542.

McDermott, J.F., Tseng, W., Char, W., & Fukunaga, C.S. (1978). Child custody decision making: The search for improvement. *Journal of the American Academy of Child Psychiatry, 17*, 104–116.

McGraw, J.M., & Smith, H.A. (1992). Child sexual abuse allegations amidst divorce and custody proceedings: Refining the validation process. *Journal of Child Sexual Abuse, 1* (1), 49–62.

McKenry, P.C., & Fine, M.A. (1993). Parenting following divorce: A comparison of black and white single mothers. *Journal of Comparative Family Studies, 24* (1), 99–111.

McMaster, M., & Grinder, J. (1980). *Precision: A new approach to communication*. Beverly Hills, CA: Precision Models.

Mednick, B.R., Baker, R.L., Reznick, C., & Hocevar, D. (1990). Long-term effects of divorce on adolescent academic achievement. *Journal of Divorce, 13* (4), 69–88.

Meloy, R. (1992). *Violent attachments*. Northvale, NJ: Jason Aronson.

Meloy, R. (1993, December). *Assessment of violence potential*. Seminar for Specialized Training Services, Cherry Hill, N.J.

Melton, G.B. (1994). Expert opinions: not for "cosmic understanding." In B.D. Sales & G.R. VandenBos (Eds.) *Psychology in litigation and legislation* (pp. 59-99). Washington DC: American Psychological Association.

Melton, G.B., & Limber, S. (1989). Psychologists' involvement in cases of child maltreatment: Limits of role and expertise. *American Psychologist, 44* (9), 1225–1233.

Melton, G.B., Petrila, J., Poythress, N.G., & Slobogin, C. (1987). *Psychological evaluations for the courts*. New York: Guilford.

Meyers, M. (1991). When custody collides with addiction. *Family Advocate, 14* (1), 36–39.

Monahan, S.C., Buchanan, C.M., Maccoby, E.E., & Dornbusch, S.M. (1993). Sibling differences in divorced families. *Child Development, 64*, 152–168.

Morey, L.C. (1991). *Personality Assessment Inventory*. Odessa, FL: Psychological Assessment Resources.

Munsinger, H.L., & Karlson, K.W. (1994) *Uniform child custody evaluation system*. Odessa, FL: Psychological Assessment Resources.

Murray, H. A. (1943). *Thematic Apperception Test*. Cambridge, MA: Harvard University Press.

Mutchler, T.E., Hunt, E.J., Koopman, E.J., & Mutchler, R.D. (1991). Single-parent mother/daughter empathy, relationship adjustment, and functioning of the adolescent child of divorce. *Journal of Divorce and Remarriage, 17* (1/2), 115–129.

Myers, J.E.B. (1992). *Legal issues in child abuse and neglect*. Newbury Park, CA: Sage.

Neighbors, B., Forehand, R., & Armistead, L. (1992). Is parental divorce a critical stressor for young adolescents? Grade point average as a case in point. *Adolescence, 27* (107), 639–646.

O'Hanlon, B., & Wilk, J. (1987). *Shifting contexts: The generation of effective psychotherapy*. New York: Guilford.

Ornstein, R. (1991). *The evolution of consciousness: Of Darwin, Freud, and cranial fire: The origins of the way we think*. Englewood Cliffs, NJ: Prentice Hall.

Pearson, J., & Thoennes, N. (1990). Custody after divorce: Demographic and attitudinal patterns. *American Journal of Orthopsychiatry, 60* (2), 233–249.

Piotrowski, Z.A. (1950). A new evaluation of the Thematic Apperception Test. *Psychoanalytic Review, 37*, 101–127

Piotrowski, Z.A. (1957). *Perceptanalysis*. New York: Macmillan.

Piotrowski, Z.A., & Dudek, S. (1956). Research on human movement response in the *Rorschach* examinations of marital partners. In V. Eisenstein (Ed.), *Neurotic interaction in marriage* (pp. 192-207) New York: Basic Books.

Poythress, N.G. (1978). Psychiatric expertise in civil commitment: Training attorneys to cope with expert testimony. *Law and Human Behavior, 2* (1).

Pruitt, D.G., Peirce, R.S., McGillicuddy, N.B., Welton, G.L., & Castrianno, L.M. (1993). Long-term sucess in mediation. *Law and Human Behavior, 17* (3), 313–330.

Raskin, D.C., & Esplin, P.W. (1991). Assessment of children's statements of sexual abuse. In J. Doris (Ed.), *The suggestibility of children's recollections* (pp. 153–164). Washington, DC: American Psychological Association.

Reber, A. (1985). *The Penguin dictionary of psychology*. London: Penguin Books.

Rogers, R., Bagby, M., Crouch, M., & Cutler, B. (1990). Effects of ultimate opinions on juror perceptions of insanity. *International Journal of Law and Psychiatry, 13*, 225–232.

Rohman, L.W., Sales, B.D., and Lou, M. (1987). In L. Weithorn (Ed.), Psychology and child custody determinations: Knowledge, roles and expertise (pp. 59–105). Lincoln, NE: University of Nebraska Press.

Rossi, E.L. (1986). *The psychobiology of mind-body healing: New concepts in therapeutic hypnosis*. New York: Norton.

Rossi, E.L. (1993). *The psychobiology of mind-body healing: New concepts in therapeutic hypnosis*. (Rev. ed.). New York: Norton.

Rossi, E.L., & Cheek, D.B. (1988). *Mind-body therapy: Ideodynamic healing in hypnosis*. New York: Norton.

Saks, M.J. (1990). Expert witnesses, nonexpert witnesses, and nonwitness experts. *Law and Human Behavior, 14* (4), 291–313.

Sales, B., Manber, R., & Rohman, L. (1992). Social science research and child-custody decision making. *Applied and Preventive Psychology, 1*, 23–40.

Santrock, J.W. (1977). Effects of father absence on sex-typed behaviors in male children: Reason for the absence and age of onset of the absence. *The Journal of Genetic Psychology, 130*, 3–10.

Santrock, J., & Warshak, R. (1979). Father custody and social development in boys and girls. *Journal of Social Issues, 35*, 122–125.

Saunders, T.R. (1993a). Some ethical and legal features of child custody disputes: A case illustration and applications. *Psychotherapy, 30* (1), 49–58.

Saunders, T.R. (1993b). From bauhaus to bowhouse: The story of the COPPS position papers on child abuse and child custody. *Division 42 of the American Psychological Association: The Independent Practitioner, 13* (6), 249–250.

Schum, D.A., & Martin, A.W. (1982). Formal and empirical research on cascaded inference in jurisprudence. *Law and Society Review, 17* (1), 105–151.

Schutz, B.M., Dixon, E.B., Lindenberger, J.C., & Ruther, N.J. (1989). *Solomon's sword: A practical guide to conducting child custody evaluations.* San Francisco, CA: Jossey-Bass.

Schwartz, L.L. (1987). Joint custody: Is it right for all children? *Journal of Family Psychology, 1* (1), 120–134.

Shaw, D.S., Emery, R.E., & Tuer, M.D. (1993). Parental functioning and children's adjustment in families of divorce: A prospective study. *Journal of Abnormal Child Psychology, 21* (1), 119–134.

Shedler, J., Mayman, M., & Manis, M. (1993). The illusion of mental health. *American Psychologist, 48* (11), 1117–1131.

Shein, S. (1993). Little known facts about ethics codes and procedures for psychologists: The dangers they pose and some possible remedies. *The Independent Practitioner, 13* (1), 59–60.

Shiller, V.M. (1986). Joint versus maternal custody for families with latency age boys: Parent characteristics and child adjustment. *American Journal of Orthopsychiatry, 56* (3), 486–489.

Skinner, L.J., & Berry, K.B. (1993). Anatomically detailed dolls and the evaluation of child sexual abuse allegations. *Law and Human Behavior, 17* (4), 399–421.

Slobogin, C. (1989). The ultimate issue issue. *Behavioral Sciences and the Law, 7,* 259–268.

Sorenson, E.D., & Goldman, J. (1990). Custody determinations and child development: A review of the current literature. *Journal of Divorce, 13* (4), 53–67.

Speth, E. (1992). Test-retest reliability of the Bricklin Perceptual Scales. Unpublished doctoral dissertation. Hahnemann University and Villanova School of Law.

Stahl, P.M. (1994). *Conducting child custody evaluations: A Comprehensive guide.* Thousand Oaks, CA: Sage.

Steinman, S. (1981). The experience of children in a joint-custody arrangement: A report of a study. *American Journal of Orthopsychiatry, 51* (3), 403–414.

Steller, M., & Boychuk, T. (1992). Children as witnesses in sexual abuse cases: Investigative interview and assessment techniques. In H. Dent & R. Flin (Eds.), *Children as witnesses* (pp. 47–71). New York: Wiley.

Stolberg, A.L., & Bush, J.P. (1985). A path analysis of factors predicting children's divorce adjustment. *Journal of Clinical Child Psychology, 14* (1), 49–54.

Stolberg, A.L., Camplair, C., Currier, K., & Wells, M.J. (1987). Individual, familial and environmental determinants of children's post-divorce adjustment and maladjustment. *Journal of Divorce, 11* (1), 51–70.

Strochak, R.D. (1991). A court-related custody evaluation/conciliation service. *The Custody Newsletter,* Issue No. 4, 1–4.

Stromberg, C.D., Haggarty, D.J., Leibenluft, R.F., McMillian, M.H., Mishkin, B., Rubin, B.L., & Trilling, H.R. (1988). *The psychologist's legal handbook.* Washington, DC: The Council for the National Register of Health Service Providers in Psychology.

Thibault, J., & Walker, L. (1975). *Procedural justice: A psychological analysis.* Hillsdale, NJ: Erlbaum.

Thomas, A., & Chess, S. (1977). *Temperament and development.* New York: Brunner/Mazel.

Thomas, A., Chess, S., & Birch, H.G. (1968). *Temperament and behavior disorders in children.* New York: New York University Press.

Thomas, A.M., & Forehand, R. (1993). The role of paternal variables in divorced and married families: Predictability of adolescent adjustment. *American Journal of Orthopsychiatry, 63* (1), 126–135.

Thompson, R.A., Tinsley, B.R., Scalora, M.J., & Parke, R.D. (1989). Grandparents' visitation rights: Legalizing the ties that bind. *American Psychologist, 44* (9), 1217–1222.

Tribe, L.A. (1971), Trial by mathematics: Precision and ritual in the legal process. *Harvard Law Review, 84,* 1329-1393.

Tranel, D. (1994). The release of psychological data to nonexperts: Ethical and legal considerations. *Professional Psychology: Research and Practice, 25* (1), 33-38.

Tschann, J.M., Johnston, J.R., Kline, M., & Wallerstein, J.S. (1990). Conflict, loss, change and parent-child relationships: Predicting children's adjustment during divorce. *Journal of Divorce, 13* (4), 1–22.

Underweger, R., & Wakefield, H. (1993). A paradigm shift for expert witnesses. *Issues in Child Abuse Accusations, 5* (3), 156–167.

Undeutsch, U. (1967). Beurteilung der Glaubhaftigkeit von Aussagen. In U. Undeutsch (Ed.), *Handbach der Psychologie, Band ll: Forensische Psychologie* (pp. 26–181). Goettingen: Hogrefe.

Uniform Marriage and Divorce Act. (1979). *Uniform Laws Annotated.* (Previous versions: 1970, 1971 and 1973).

Waelder, R. (1960). *Basic theory of psychoanalysis.* New York: International Universities Press.

Waelder, R. (1967). *Progress and revolution: A study of the issues of our age.* New York: International Universities Press.

Wagenaar, W.A. (1988). The proper seat: A Bayesian discussion of the position of expert witnesses. *Law and Human Behavior, 12* (4), 499–510.

Wallerstein, J.S. (1984). Children of divorce: Preliminary report of a ten-year follow-up of young children. *American Journal of Orthopsychiatry, 54* (3), 444–458.

Wallerstein, J.S. (1991). The long-term effects of divorce on children: A review. *Journal of the American Academy of Child and Adolescent Psychiatry, 30* (3), 349–360.

Wallerstein, J.S., & Corbin, S.B. (1989). Daughters of divorce: Report from a ten-year follow-up. *American Journal of Orthopsychiatry, 59* (4), 593–604.

Wallerstein, J.S., & Kelly, J.B. (1976). The effects of parental divorce: Experiences of the child in later latency. *American Journal of Orthopsychiatry, 46* (2), 256–269.

Wallerstein, J.S., & Kelly, J.B. (1980). *Surviving the breakup: How children and parents cope with divorce.* New York: Basic Books.

Walsh, P.E., & Stolberg, A.L. (1989). Parental and environmental determinants of children's behavioral, affective and cognitive adjustment to divorce. *Journal of Divorce, 12,* 265–282.

Ward, P., & Harvey, C. (1993). Family wars: the alienation of children. *The Custody Newsletter,* Issue No. 9, 2–14.

Warren, J. (1991). Roles and dilemmas of mental health professionals in child custody evaluations. *The Custody Newsletter*, Issue No. 2, 2–4.

Wedding, D., & Faust, D. (1989). Clinical judgement and decision making in neuropsychology. *Archives of Clinical Neuropsychology, 4* (3), 233–265.

Weissman, H.N. (1994). Psychotherapeutic and psycholegal considerations: When a custodial parent seeks to move away. *American Journal of Family Therapy, 22* (2), 176–181.

Wells, G.L., & Loftus, E.F. (1991). Commentary: Is this child fabricating? Reactions to a new assessment technique. In J. Doris (Ed.), *The suggestibility of children's recollections* (pp. 168–171). Washington, DC: American Psychological Association.

West, D.J., & Farrington, D.P. (1973). *The delinquent way of life*. London: Heinemann Educational Books.

Wierson, M., Forehand, R., Fauber, R., & McCombs, A. (1989). Buffering young male adolescents against negative parental divorce influences: The role of good parent-adolescent relations. *Child Study Journal, 19* (2), 101–115.

Williams, A.D. (1992). Bias and debiasing techniques in forensic psychology. *American Journal of Forensic Psychology, 10* (3), 19–26.

Wirt, R.D., Lachar, D., Klinedinst, J.K., & Seat, P.D. (1977). *Multidimensional description of child personality": A manual for the Personality Inventory for Children*. Los Angeles: Western Psychological Services.

Wolchik, S.A., Ramirez, R., Sandler, I.N., Fisher, J.L., Organista, P.B., & Brown, C. (1993). Inner-city, poor children of divorce: Negative divorce-related events, problematic beliefs and adjustment problems. *Journal of Divorce and Remarriage, 19* (1/2), 1–20.

Wolman, R., & Taylor, K. (1991). Psychological effects of custody disputes on children. *Behavioral Sciences and the Law, 9* (4), 399–417.

Wood, J.I., & Lewis, G.J. (1990). The coparental relationship of divorced spouses: Its effect on children's school adjustment. *Journal of Divorce and Remarriage, 14* (1), 81–95.

Woody, R.H. (1977). Behavioral science criteria in child custody determinations. *Journal of Marriage and Family Counseling, 3* (1), 11–18.

Wyer, Jr., R.S. & Krull, T.K. (Eds.). (1993). *Perspective on anger and emotion*. Hillsdale, NJ: Erlbaum.

Zaslow, M.J. (1989). Sex differences in children's response to parental divorce: 2. Samples, variables, ages, and sources. *American Journal of Orthopsychiatry, 59* (1), 118–141.

Ziskin, J. (1981). *Coping with psychiatric and psychological testimony* (Vols. 1–3, 3rd ed.). Marina Del Rey, CA: Law and Psychology Press.

Ziskin, J. (1993). Ziskin can withstand his own criticisms: A response to Rogers, Bagby and Perera. *American Journal of Forensic Psychology, 11* (4), 17–34.

Ziskin, J., & Faust, D. (1988). *Coping with psychiatric and psychological testimony* (Vols. 1–3, 4th ed.). Marina Del Rey, CA: Law and Psychology Press.

Zornetzer, S. (1978). Neurotransmitter modulation and memory: A new neuropharmacological phrenology? In M. Lipton, A. DiMascio, & K. Killam (Eds.), *Psychopharmacology: A generation of progress*. New York: Raven Press.

Name Index

Subject Index